To Debbie + Tom,

with great respect + thanks for all
of your help –

Best wishes Always,

To Life!.

Serge

GOLF IN AMERICA

ILLINOIS HISTORY OF SPORTS

Series Editors

Benjamin G. Rader
Randy Roberts

A list of books in the series appears at the end of this book.

GOLF
IN AMERICA

GEORGE B. KIRSCH

University of Illinois Press
Urbana and Chicago

Frontispiece. First photo taken of golf in America.
Shows St. Andrews Golf Club's first course, North
Broadway, Yonkers, N.Y., in 1888, just before Judge
Fitch's home in the background was completed.
Left to right, Harry Holbrook, A. W. Kinnan,
John B. Upham, and John Reid. Caddies are Warren
and Fred Holbrook, sons of Harry Holbrook. Photo is
by Edwin Levick, N.Y. Copyright Unknown. Courtesy
USGA Archives.

© 2009 by the Board of Trustees
of the University of Illinois
All rights reserved
Manufactured in the United States of America
c 5 4 3 2 1
∞ This book is printed on acid-free paper.

Library of Congress Cataloging-in-Publication Data
Kirsch, George B.
Golf in America / George B. Kirsch.
p.   cm. — (Illinois history of sports)
Includes bibliographical references and index.
ISBN 978-0-252-03292-9 (cloth : alk. paper)
1. Golf—United States—History.
I. Title.
GV981.K57   2009
796.352—dc22   2008027209

FOR DANIEL E. KIRSCH
AND TO THE MEMORY OF
SUSAN L. KIRSCH

CONTENTS

PREFACE

In August 2005, Thomas L. Friedman, writing for *Golf Digest*, asked: "Hasn't golf really replaced baseball as America's national pastime?" Ignoring football, he answered simply: "Of course it has." To prove his case he pointed to the game's popularity among people of all ages, its spirit of individualism, its democratic and philanthropic qualities, and the challenges it presents to its players. He concluded that golf was the sport "that most deeply reflects the American character" and that "this is without question the greatest time ever to be an American golfer." Further proof of Friedman's thesis may be found in the billions of dollars spent by tens of millions of participants in the United States on country club dues and related expenses, fees on semiprivate and municipal courses, and the purchase of equipment, not to mention the vast media coverage of golf professionals competing in dozens of tournaments.

This volume does not present a comprehensive history of all aspects of golf in the United States. Rather, its more modest dual goal is to provide a concise narrative and social history of the sport in America from the 1880s to the present. First, in relating the story of American golf, this book pays special attention to the founders of the first private golf clubs and associations, the Americanization of the game's courses and equipment, and the men and women who achieved heroic status for their championship performances in amateur and professional tournaments. It chronicles the challenges the sport encountered during two world wars and one great depression, and it examines the forces behind a series of golf booms throughout the twentieth century. The role of television merits special attention in explaining the phenomenal growth of the game since the 1950s.

Second, this work explains how and why golf became popular among the masses of the American people—first among the privileged members of the country club set and later among the working and middle classes of all ethnic and racial groups. Suburbanization, the rise of a business culture that valued golf, boosterism by presidents and celebrities, thrilling performances by champions, and the motorized golf cart all played major roles in spreading the game among the American people. I highlight the history of public golf courses in the United States, including both municipal facilities and daily-fee semiprivate grounds—topics that have previously received little notice from the sport's historians. I also devote special attention to the experiences and contributions of women and African Americans and the central role they played in the democratization of golf in America.

A major theme of this book is the surprising growth of golf as a popular, mainstream sport in the United States. I contrast its image as a sport for rich people with the reality of widespread enthusiasm for the game by people of both sexes from a wide range of classes, ethnic backgrounds, and races in the United States—long before the rise of Tiger Woods. While it is true that golf still retains a strong association with upper-class, socially exclusive country clubs, it also boasts a dedicated following among less privileged Americans, including many of very modest means. In short, this work tells the story of golf in America through the experiences of all the participants—upscale members of country clubs, presidents, legendary professionals, patrons of municipal links, women, African Americans, Jews, Hispanics, Asians, film and television celebrities, handicapped and blind golfers, and others who have become so addicted to the Scottish pastime that it rivals baseball for the honor of being acclaimed "America's national pastime."

◎ ◎ ◎

My golfing life began at the age of fourteen on public courses in Bergen County, New Jersey, so my first thanks go to friends of my youth. Michael Weinstein taught me the fundamentals of the sport and helped me gain the last place on the golf team at Hackensack High School. Outside of school matches, I enjoyed countless rounds with Henry Cenicola, Barry Cohen, Kevin Clermont, Richard Prager, Barry Vasios, and Stephen Wexler. During my college and graduate school years golf outings with Martin Leeds provided welcome relief from study, research, and writing. At Manhattan College my colleague Mark Taylor became my regular golfing partner, first on the Van Cortlandt Park course in the Bronx, N.Y., and later at the Blue Hill grounds in Rockland County. I owe Mark a debt I can never repay, both for his friendship over the past thirty-six years and especially for his thoughtful critique and editing of a draft of this book. I also appreciate the kindness and encouragement of Joseph Castora, Juliana Gilheany, Jeff

Horn, Stephen Kaplan, Claire Nolte, Julie Leininger Pycior, and Frederick Schweitzer.

Among academics I am especially grateful to Steven Riess, who reviewed several versions of the proposal for this project; Steven Schlossman, who graciously read several chapters; and Kevin Clermont, who evaluated and edited my discussion of the desegregation of municipal golf courses. I also thank the staff at the golf library at the United States Golf Association, especially Patty Moran, Doug Stark, Nancy Stulack, and Ellie Kaiser. I must single out Patty for special praise for her constant good cheer and her vast knowledge of the resources at the USGA library. I also appreciate the help provided by the editors and production staff at the University of Illinois Press, especially Richard Wentworth, who provided early assistance, and Bill Regier, whose enthusiasm and support have been invaluable.

Once again I pay tribute to the memory of my parents, Anne Rizack Kirsch and Nathan S. Kirsch. They instilled in me a love of learning that enabled me to pursue an academic career. My son, Adam L. Kirsch, wisely never tried to play golf, but I treasure his computer assistance and especially his love and compassion during difficult times.

I dedicate this book to my brother, Daniel E. Kirsch, and to the memory of my wife, Susan L. Kirsch. Although Dan never took up golf, he distinguished himself as a sportsman as an All-American fencer, a medal-winning senior track and road racer, and a recreational kayaker and rock climber. I also thank his wife Laura and their daughters Jennifer, Gabrielle, and Elissa for all the good food and family bonding at festive meals and celebrations.

I honor Susan for her devotion to me over nearly forty years of marriage. She was brave and strong through her final days. She stood by me when I was most in need of help and I will love her forever.

THE RISE OF GOLF
IN THE UNITED STATES

In June 1902 William Garrot Brown, writing in the *Atlantic Monthly*, announced that "three new things have come into our American life in recent years." "Bring together anywhere a company of reasonably alert and reasonably well-to-do Americans," he explained, "and the chances are their talk will shortly concern itself with one of three subjects which ten years ago would have gone unmentioned. They will talk of money . . . as a social and economic force, money massed in billions and warring with other billions. . . . Or they will talk of things military and naval and diplomatic; of colonies and races, . . . and our own emergence as a world power. Or, they will talk of golf. Empire, trusts, and golf,—these are the new things in American life." Brown linked the recent passion for the Scottish game with the growth of big business and the expansion of American territory and interests overseas as he pondered the meaning of the sport at the dawn of the twentieth century. At first glance, business corporations, imperial adventures, and golf may seem totally unrelated, but upon closer examination there do seem to be some important connections between the three. American companies were naturally concerned with prospects of growing global markets provided by the expansion of trade facilitated by a more aggressive United States foreign policy. Golf soon became a popular diversion for American businessmen and a significant part of corporate culture in the United States. It was also a Scottish export that was part of a late nineteenth-century British sporting imperialism that included cricket, tennis, football, and other pastimes. During this era American baseball players were trying to promote their favorite pastime in England and around the world (with notable success only in Japan and in parts of the Caribbean), but they were also reacting to the incursions of Scottish and English golfers. And while golf was initially part of the British

Empire, in its North American form it evolved into an important game in the twentieth-century sporting imperialism of the United States.

Many factors shaped the development of golf in the United States between the 1880s and World War I. These included the nature of the game itself, Scottish ethnic communities, the culture of business, suburbanization, topographical features, the advent of summer communities and year-round resort hotels, technological innovations, social class structure, and the changing status of women. Golf flourished in America during that time because of a fortuitous combination of forces and because its enthusiasts adapted it to suit their needs. The result was the Americanization of a Scottish ethnic game, which quickly became part of the mainstream athletic culture of the United States.

The sporting traditions of Great Britain profoundly shaped the growth of sports in colonial America, and after the American Revolution the most popular recreations and games of England and Scotland gained substantial support in the United States. Elite sportsmen emulated English gentlemen and university students through horse racing and aquatics (rowing and yachting), and workers and lower-class men patronized animal and blood sports—especially bare-knuckle prizefights. English immigrants introduced cricket and recruited upper-class Americans (especially in Philadelphia) and middle-class artisans. England's national pastime became the first modern team sport in the United States, but then faded in popularity, to be replaced by baseball during the Civil War. Tennis crossed the Atlantic during the 1870s and became a fixture of club life for upper-class men and women. Beginning in the mid-1800s Scottish immigrants introduced curling and track and field. While curling on frozen ponds or ice rinks did not win many adherents outside of Scottish communities, their Caledonian clubs sponsored Highland Games (athletic festivals) that attracted great interest and increasing participation throughout the nineteenth century. Upper- and middle-class urban sportsmen in numerous American cities organized their own track and field clubs and eventually took control of the sport prior to 1900.

Although most sport historians credit Scotland as the birthplace of modern golf, there is considerable controversy over its origins. One theory holds that golf evolved from a Roman game called paganica, in which teams of men equipped with curved branches tried to bat a feather-stuffed ball against their rival's goalpost. Those who champion Holland as the cradle of golf point to a pastime known as *kolven*, citing a fifteenth-century ordinance banning it within church precincts and also illustrations from the *Book of*

Hours (1500–20). The Dutch amused themselves with a pastime called *kolf*, which was played both on frozen canals and indoors, in which contestants attempted to strike a ball against wooden posts placed at the end of the court. In its basic structure this game appears to be more an ancestor of hockey than of golf. In Scotland, the first reference to golf appears in a 1457 prohibition of the sport by the Scottish Parliament. But despite this and later official attempts to ban golf, the game gained in popularity in Scotland throughout the next few centuries. In 1744 the Honorable Company of Edinburgh golfers began play on the Leigh links, and on May 14, 1754, twenty-two noblemen and gentlemen launched the Royal and Ancient Golf Club of St. Andrews. They adopted thirteen articles as the first official rules of golf, perhaps using the laws of their Edinburgh counterparts as the basis for their code. As golf historian Herbert Warren Wind has noted, "the Scots were the first to play a game in which the player used an assortment of clubs to strike a ball into a hole dug in the earth. This is the essence of the game we know as golf."

Although there is considerable evidence that a few hardy sportsmen played golf in various towns and counties in colonial, revolutionary, and nineteenth-century America, the modern era of the game in the United States dates from the 1880s. English and Scottish immigrants and Scottish Americans pioneered the revival of the game in Oakhurst, West Virginia; Dorset, Vermont; Foxburg, Pennsylvania; Burlington, Iowa; Sarasota, Florida; Omaha, Nebraska; and Yonkers, New York. At Oakhurst, in Greenbrier County, George Grant, an Englishman, persuaded his neighbor Russell W. Montague to dedicate part of his estate for use as a golf course. Montague was a native New Englander and a Harvard graduate who was willing to try the new game. He recruited other neighbors, Alexander and Roderick McLeod, who were Scottish immigrants. Grant's cousin Lionel Torin was a golf enthusiast who assisted with the layout of the first holes at Oakhurst, possibly as early as 1882. George M. Donaldson, also a Scotsman, joined in the fun. There is more definite evidence that this group of friends regularly played on their course and organized themselves into a very small club in 1884. A few years later Donaldson had an unpleasant encounter with customs inspectors in New York who confiscated his imported golf clubs as suspicious "implements of murder." Despite his protests, he had to wait six weeks before officials at the Treasury Department in Washington permitted him to take possession of the clubs. These West Virginia sportsmen enjoyed playing on their rudimentary links at Oakhurst for about a decade, until the men scattered and the course gradually returned to a state of nature. In

1886 several Scotsmen from Troy, New York, laid out a rough nine-hole course across the Vermont border and founded the Dorset Field Club, with A. W. Harrington, Jr., as its first president. In 1908 it built a new nine-hole layout, which was superimposed on the original grounds. Joseph M. Fox was a member of Philadelphia's Merion Cricket Club who observed a golf exhibition in Scotland at the renowned St. Andrews course. After returning to his summer estate at Foxburg in western Pennsylvania, he laid out an eight-hole course in 1885. In 1887 he built a second course, which remains the oldest golf course in continuous use in the United States. Andrew Bell of Burlington, Iowa, was educated in Scotland, returned to his home state in 1881, and built a four-hole course on his father's property. J. Hamilton Gillespie was a Scotsman residing in Sarasota, Florida, who played golf informally there as early as 1883. A few years later another Scot, Alex Findlay, introduced the game in Omaha, Nebraska.

Although the St. Andrew's club launched in Yonkers in 1888 is generally recognized as the first modern golf club in the United States, both the Dorset and Foxburg clubs have challenged its claim to be the oldest golf club in continuous existence in the United States. John Reid (often called "the father of American golf") was a native of Dunfermline, Scotland, who had earned a small fortune in the iron industry in New York. In 1887 Robert Lockhart, his friend and fellow native of his home town, purchased a set of golf clubs and some balls from Old Tom Morris at St. Andrews on one of his regular business visits to Scotland. Although for many years a tale was told that Lockhart was arrested by a policeman for trying out his clubs and balls in Central Park, his son later recalled that his father first attempted to hit some shots along the Hudson River near Seventy-second Street, in what is now Riverside Drive. There was an officer of the law who witnessed the scene, but he rode away after trying a few swings himself. A few months later Lockhart brought his equipment to Reid's property in Yonkers, which Reid and a few of his friends tried out in his cow pasture on Washington's Birthday, 1888. On November 14th of that year these gentlemen founded the St. Andrew's Golf Club. Over the next nine years it moved several more times until it settled on its present site in Hastings-on-Hudson in 1897.

Another founding father of American golf was Charles B. Macdonald, a Chicagoan and second-generation Scottish American. The driving force behind the Chicago Golf Club, he distinguished himself as a prominent player, golf course architect, and critic of new trends in the game. In 1872, at the age of sixteen, he had journeyed to the land of his ancestors to stay with his grandfather at St. Andrews and attend college. There he took sufficient time away from his studies to become a proficient golfer, but upon his return to Chicago a few years later he devoted himself to business. He renewed his sporting career in the 1890s, when he was in his late thirties, just as the golfing craze was sweeping through the East. After a few frustrating defeats he finally won a major tournament when he captured the United States Amateur Championship in 1895. Three years later he expressed his satisfaction that the old Scottish style of play had not been lost on this side of the Atlantic. He wrote: "In the adoption of the game in this country it was feared the tradition and spirit would be Americanized out of it; happily innovations have been rare, and not half as much fault is found with American golf as one frequently hears [about] the 'Englished' golf. So far in America there has appeared no disposition to modify or accentuate any of the points of the game." But that would change significantly over the next decade.

To understand how native-born sportsmen adapted golf to suit American needs and conditions, one must begin with those resident Scots and Scottish immigrants who introduced their favorite pastime into the United States. As Reid, Macdonald, and other Scottish Americans pioneered golf in the United States, they welcomed professional players from their homeland and England who were eager to capitalize on the sudden boom in the demand for their sporting expertise in North America. In 1891 three prosperous Long Island gentlemen (W. K. Vanderbilt, Edward S. Mead, and Duncan Cryder) invited Willie Dunn to journey to Southampton to design a twelve-hole seaside links, which became Shinnecock Hills. Dunn employed 150 Indians from the nearby Shinnecock reservation and incorporated their ancestral burial mounds into his layout. In 1895 an English golf magazine reported that American entrepreneurs were offering experienced clubmakers passage to New York and fifteen dollars per week in wages. The following year John Dunn, a Scotsman, recounted that during a five-month stay in the United States he taught novices every day from morning until night. He especially enjoyed his three-month visit with Willie Dunn at the "Millionaires Golf Club" at Ardsley, with its private railway station, dock for yachts, stables, and swimming pool. He concluded his tour with six weeks under more spartan conditions in Buffalo, teaching even through a Scottish mist and with snow on the ground. Before returning home he enjoyed the hospitality and festivities sponsored by the Buffalo Gordon Highlanders and the New York Caledonian Club. By the end of the decade the trickle of Scottish professionals became a flood, as the number of new American clubs skyrocketed in the Northeast and the West. R. B. Wilson, James Foulis,

5

W. H. Way, the Smith family from Carnoustie, and others flocked to the New World to seek their fortunes as teachers and as prize winners in open competitions. Many of the newcomers stayed on as teachers, greenkeepers, and clubmakers.

A few more golf clubs appeared on the American sporting landscape during the early 1890s, but the real takeoff occurred in 1894 and 1895, when at least fifty more clubs laid out courses. In dozens of larger towns and smaller suburban communities, newspapers reported the latest rage. On November 24, 1894, a writer for the *Montclair Times* of New Jersey commented: "The victims of acute golf mania are to be avoided by all who are not in touch with the passing vogue, for they can talk of nothing but golf, dream of it, radiate it in fact, in spite of the mournful fact than an expert has said that it takes three years to become proficient in the game." Most of the fledgling country clubs were in the Northeast, but sportsmen across the land emulated the easterners, founding associations in California, Colorado, Washington State, Georgia, Oregon, South Carolina, Illinois, Missouri, Ohio, and Maine. By 1900 the roster had swelled to nearly a thousand as golf fever infected the nation. According to one early chronicler, New York boasted a total of 165 separate courses, followed by Massachusetts with 157, Pennsylvania with 75, and New Jersey with 63, with every state counting at least one course. On June 29, 1901, a contributor to *Harper's Weekly* estimated the total number of organizations at 1,200, with about 120,000 members, plus at least 30,000 more hacking away on public links, all together spending a grand total of about $15 million on the pastime. In 1905 the *Boston Globe* estimated that a million people in the United States played golf. In 1915 the *New York Times* reported that there were 112 courses within fifty miles of New York City, with at least 30,000 players. That year the *Times* also estimated that about 600 clubs were members of the United States Golf Association, with between 2.5 and 3.5 million golfers active on private and public links.

A related phenomenon in the United States was the advent of numerous golf courses at summer colonies and vacation resorts, patronized mostly by more affluent players. Shinnecock Hills at Southampton, Long Island, New York, was the premier example of a seasonable club founded by summer residents. The York Country Club in Maine provided a retreat for New Englanders. Hotel proprietors in the mountains and the seashores from New Hampshire to Florida were quick to see the value of constructing links at their resorts. By the late 1890s golfers were trying out new courses in the White Mountains, the Adirondacks, the Poconos, and the Berkshires in the North, while in the South, Hot Springs, Virginia; Pinehurst, North Carolina; and Palm Beach, Ormond, Belleair, and Tampa, Florida, all attracted well-heeled players during the winter months.

Overseeing this explosion of activity was the United States Golf Association (USGA), originally named the Amateur Golf Association and founded on December 22, 1894, by affluent gentlemen representing five elite clubs: St. Andrew's; Chicago; The Country Club of Brookline, Mass.; Newport, R.I.; and Shinnecock Hills of Southampton, N.Y. Its first president was Theodore Havemeyer, a captain of industry of the Gilded Age known as the "Sugar King." He became enraptured by the game while on vacation in Pau, France, and in 1890 he supervised the construction of a nine-hole course at Brenton's Point, near Newport, Rhode Island, where he introduced golf to high society at that fashionable resort. Inaugural vice presidents were Laurence Curtis of The Country Club of Brookline and Charles B. Macdonald of Chicago. Henry O. Tallmadge of St. Andrew's and Samuel L. Parrish of Shinnecock Hills filled the positions of secretary and treasurer, respectively. The goals of the association as stated in its constitution were to promote golf, establish and enforce uniform rules for the game, create a system of handicapping of players, and choose links for the annual amateur, open, and women's championships. Just one month after the USGA's founding, a prominent British golf journal praised the fledgling American organization. An editorial explained that the leaders of the game in the United States have "diagnosed the weak spot in the government of golf. They have seen that golf, unlike most other sports, is an unwieldy incohesive congeries of clubs, without any central controlling guidance, with no voice in the making of rules or in the arrangement and fixing of the amateur and open championships. Everything in the government of golf is haphazard and capricious." Within a few years this organization was exercising an enormous influence over the development of American golf, establishing rules of play and holding national tournaments for both men and women.

The precise definition of an amateur was a troubling question for the founding fathers of golf in the United States, and it would prove to be a vexing issue for many years to come. In its initial rules of 1895 the USGA described an amateur golfer as one "who has never made for sale golf clubs, balls or any other article connected with the game, who has never carried clubs for hire after attaining the age of 15 years and who has not carried clubs for hire at any time within six years, and who has never received any consideration for playing a match or for giving lessons in the game." In 1897 the Rules Committee narrowed the definition of an amateur by excluding those who had "laid out" or "taken charge of golf links for hire," or "who after January 1, 1897 had within the jurisdiction of this association played a match game against a professional for a money bet or stake," or "who played in a club competition for a money prize or sweepstakes." On February 27, 1897, *The Spirit of the Times* remarked (surprisingly) that this standard appeared to be simpler than the original rule, but conceded that "even in its present much improved form it is not deemed entirely satisfactory." That journal added that "time and experience only can show what changes are necessary," but the future would demonstrate the difficulty of excluding players from the amateur ranks who earned income through the increasing commercialization of the game of golf.

◎ ◎ ◎

The golf mania of the 1890s was a truly remarkable cultural phenomenon in the United States, comparable in some ways to the baseball craze of the late 1850s in its broad social class dimension, but even more widespread than the earlier baseball fever in that it enlisted numerous active female participants. While it is difficult to explain the particular timing of the "takeoff period" for any of the most popular sports in the United States, it is possible to suggest certain short- and longer-term factors that might explain the striking growth of American golf in the 1890s. The obvious explanation for the most important short-term influence is the role played by Scottish Americans and Scottish immigrants, who aggressively promoted and popularized the game. But their efforts would have had little impact without several crucial social and cultural trends that characterized late nineteenth-century American society. These included changing attitudes toward work and leisure, which made sports more acceptable and even desirable for middle- and upper-class men and women; an economic foundation that permitted people of moderate and greater means to have more discretionary leisure time for recreation; and the growth of suburbs, which provided the space needed for golf courses.

Although as early as the 1850s many newspaper and magazine editors and clergymen had criticized and modified the traditional Protestant aversion to recreation and sports, during the post–Civil War era considerable prejudice still persisted against athletics in America. In December 1894, Caspar Whitney wrote in *Harper's Magazine* that it used to be said that "Americans did not know how to live" and that "we did not know how to enjoy ourselves." He explained: "It must be admitted unhesitatingly that we are only just learning how to play; we have not been, nor are we yet, a nation of pleasure seekers.

8

We are a practical people; we build our living-house before undertaking landscape-gardening." On August 1, 1896, H. C. Chatfield-Taylor recalled in *Harper's Weekly* that ten or fifteen years earlier "the Chicagoan who indulged in out-of-doors sports was looked upon by his fellow-citizens as a person unfit for serious consideration." He remarked: "In those days there was but one occupation—business; but one god—Mammon. . . . Men were divided into two classes, the workers and the 'loafers.' The workers were thin, sallow-faced individuals, with the marks of premature old age upon their nervous faces; the 'loafers' were whiskey-drinking, fast-horse-driving debauchees, whose lives were given over to vice, and who were naturally without the pales of society. The man who was courageous enough to wear good clothes and to go in for sport in even so mild a form as tennis was looked upon as weak-minded." He added: "There are of course many of the old stagers left, who refuse to be converted to the new creed of health and happiness, but the younger generation and many of the older have certainly discovered that there is something more in life than mere business, some places more attractive than the counting-room. The only danger now is that the other extreme may be reached." Both writers believed that the advent of country clubs (initially for the elite classes and equestrian sports) followed soon thereafter by golf clubs had done wonders for the health and psyche of the middle and upper classes of society.

In October 1900, Price Collier addressed the issues of an economic base for golf and its timing in America in *The American Monthly Review of Reviews*. While he noted that some dismissed the golf mania as a "passing whim," he argued that the American people were ready for "this sudden and widespread love of out-of-door sport." He explained: "It could not have happened in 1860, or in 1870. . . . Sport follows the surplus. Money, in its last analysis, is merely leisure; leisure is choice, and choice is time. . . . We in the United States have reached a condition of prosperity when we can choose—when we are not forced to hammer and shovel and shoot to keep ourselves sheltered and fed. Golf, then, is not necessarily a fad at all. It is a very agreeable, wholesome, and suitable way of spending our surplus of time and energy."

A more positive view of the health and psychological benefits of sports supported the growth of golf in the United States during the 1890s, but the game could not have exploded in popularity without adequate space for courses. During the late nineteenth century the United States led the world in the suburbanization of its major metropolitan centers, as thousands of middle- and upper-class families purchased houses on the periphery of

9

major cities and towns. The key to this pattern of residential decentralization was electric trolleys and railroads, which made it possible for businessmen to commute to workplaces that were dozens of miles from their homes. Their desire for wholesome recreation and the availability of inexpensive land in the country made the golf mania possible. In 1899 the secretary of the United States Golf Association estimated that there was $50 million invested in golf in the country, with an annual expenditure of at least $10 million. He thought that the money was well spent: "Bicycles, trolley cars and golf have worked miracles in the direction of mitigating the monotony of American life, especially of country or suburban life, and making it attractive to persons who crave reasonable variety in their existences." He added: "They are all cheap, and not one of them is nasty." On June 1, 1901, writing in *Outlook*, Gustav Kobbé noted the attraction of golf for suburban business commuters, recalling that ten years earlier "the country resident was such in name only. Projected at half-past seven in the morning through twenty or thirty miles of space, more or less tunneled and odiferous, and back again in the evening, he was fit for nothing but to 'rest up' in order to stand the same experience the following day. To live in the country simply meant to sleep there." He continued: "But with the introduction of sport as a feature of country life—and especially of that sensible, democratic, and reasonably economic sport, golf—and the general adoption of the Saturday half-holiday, it is remarkable how much time the country resident finds he can give to healthful outdoor exercise and social recreation. The Nation is beginning to find as much fascination in driving a golf-ball as in driving a bargain." He believed that the year-round, suburban golf club "exists because the American who does business in a city, or lives there, has been seized with an uncontrollable and most commendable desire to be outdoors; and it promises to be the safety-valve of an overworked Nation." An example is the Hackensack (New Jersey) Golf Club, founded in 1899 by seventeen people, only three of whom had ever played the game. Two years later its rolls listed 350 members, including 100 ladies. Several railroads and a trolley provided access to its three-thousand-yard, nine-hole course on Hackensack Heights, only fourteen miles from New York City. In June 1901 *Golf* magazine commented: "City golfers appreciate the convenience of access, and already the 'out-of-towners' are crowding the town members. Forty-five minutes from the office to the first tee is a great temptation, and to an enthusiastic golfer hard to resist."

What was the appeal of golf to such a wide range of American men and women? A number of factors explain its initial and enduring popularity.

First, with the possible exception of croquet, there was no game like it on the American athletic scene. It was not a team sport and it did not compete directly against an indigenous rival, as was the case with cricket versus baseball or soccer versus American football. While it had a rival in another British import, tennis, which preceded it by a decade on the American sporting scene, golf did not feature the level of exertion or the personal confrontation with an opponent that characterized tennis.

Secondly, although many sport historians have stressed the early popularity of golf among the nation's most privileged classes, it also proved to be accessible to many people of more modest means. Two qualifications must be made to the traditional view that links the richest Americans to the newly imported Scottish game. Ironically, the initial golf mania coincided with the deep and disturbing business depression of the mid-1890s, which created much anxiety among businessmen and professionals. According to Price Collier, some of the more prosperous people turned to golf as an alternative to the more expensive sports of yachting, polo, hunting, racing, or shooting. He wrote: "We began playing golf at a time when business was dull, when money was dear, and when people were talking of hard times. . . . Men were glad to take up with some less extravagant form of amusement." In addition, while many rich people became avid golfers, it is also true that thousands of middle-class men and women became enthusiastic players before World War I. They could afford the initial outlay of funds for clubs and balls, and the construction of public courses in a few cities and towns gave them a place to play. There is also some scattered evidence that a few players from the ranks of the immigrants and racial minorities tried the sport during this period. In December 1898 in *Outing* H. L. Fitzpatrick conceded that golf was generally "restricted to the richer classes in this country," but he predicted (somewhat overoptimistically) that "the next progress of the game will be the general establishment of village links, virtually free, throughout the length and breadth of the land; and, once the pastime broadens from a class pursuit, on these lines, it will never die out." In 1901 Kobbé estimated the average annual expense for a typical golf club member at $135, including club dues of $25 and all equipment, caddie fees, special clothing, and "incidentals." That financial obligation was clearly beyond the means of most nonfarm employees in the United States, whose average annual earnings in 1901 were just under $500. In particular, the price was probably also too high for clerical workers, federal employees, and ministers, who had average annual incomes that year of $1009, $1033, and $731 respectively. In 1911 a writer for *The New York Times* listed membership in a major club at $100 per year, with balls averaging seventy-five cents and clubs two to three dollars each. But transportation, caddie fees, and other entertainment and incidental expenses could easily raise the annual tab to several thousand dollars. (That year the average annual earnings of clerical workers, federal employees, and ministers were $1,213, $1,116, and $856, respectively.) On the eve of World War I, U.S. Amateur champion Jerome Travers calculated the yearly cost at $182.50, with a club initiation fee and dues both set at $50.

For those who patronized public links, the cost was considerably less. H. B. Martin, an early chronicler of the sport, wrote that during golf's formative years a person could purchase a set of clubs for less than twenty dollars, with golf balls going for between fifty and sixty cents each. Prices actually went down before World War I because of mass production. In 1915, play on public grounds was clearly affordable for people with jobs in finance, insurance, and real estate (average annual earnings of $1,399), federal employees ($1,224), and even in wholesale and retail trade ($720) and public education ($608). The democratization of golf began early in the United States, although it proceeded at a relatively slow pace until after World War I.

More importantly, golf was a pastime that could be enjoyed by people of all ages and both sexes, even though it faced considerable resistance among many boys and young men who viewed it as a sissy sport for dudes and the effete. In his autobiography, Travers compared the nation's golf pioneers to the "sturdy Pilgrim Fathers." He doubted whether "their courage exceeded that of the heroes who introduced Uncle Sam to golf and tried to convince him it was a he-man affair." He recalled: "Uncle Sam couldn't see the he-manism of it; and he dismissed it as a sissy game and those who played it as dudes. So positive were the denizens of the Gas House District on this score that none was so bold as to venture into those quarters with a golf bag swung over his shoulders. Going over the top in France [in World War I] never held such terrors as this." He concluded that "when I look back at the stormy path of this game in its early days here, and all the fun that was poked at it, and the actual indignities its supporters sometimes had to endure, it seems to me that it is the only sport that has grown and flourished in the face of ridicule." In 1926 Robert Hunter, a social critic, wrote: "Less than thirty years ago the game was looked upon as something effeminate—an unmanly sport suited to the pink-coated fops and dandies who played it. And what moral courage was required in those days to walk the town streets or board a train dressed in knickers and carrying a bag of clubs! What a complete change has occurred in the view of the public since those days! For the moment, at least, golf has been taken to the heart of Demos. Pink coats are no more, but knickers are universal and the time seems not far distant when every man, woman, and child will have a set of clubs." Some of the social stigma attached to golf in its formative years no doubt derived from the sport's initial connection with the affluent class, but some of the resistance also resulted from its noncombative nature.

While most boys during this period preferred the competitive and more physical team sports of baseball, football, and basketball, a few devoted themselves to golf for enjoyment or even for its long-term benefits. 1913 U.S. Open champion Francis Ouimet recalled that as a boy at Brookline High School near Boston he had to decide between becoming captain of the school's golf team or second baseman on its baseball nine. When he chose golf, the coach and captain of the baseball team tried to persuade Ouimet to change his mind, calling golf "an old man's affair." But despite being "the butt of many uncomplimentary remarks" he stuck to his decision, believing that "once my school-days were over, baseball would be a thing of the past, whereas with golf I could continue to play that game long after I had set aside my books for a business career." Ouimet was fortunate to live across the street from The Country Club of Brookline and to learn the game as a caddie there. Many other youths became obsessed with the sport through their experiences as caddies.

For girls, women, and middle-aged or older men, golf did not demand an extreme expenditure of energy. As early as October 4, 1891, *The New York Times* remarked that "it requires less violent exertion and less in the way of special preparation, as in costume, implements, &c., and . . . it is especially commended by New-Yorkers who are familiar with it as a first-class substitute for the more violent sports, like baseball, tennis, cricket, football, lacrosse, and the like." On October 5, 1893, that journal added that although golf lacked the "vivid excitement, violent exercise, and breathless hurry and rush of baseball," it had an advantage over most outdoor games in that it was "suited equally to fat or middle-aged men and to lithe, active youths. Any one with two arms, two legs, and two eyes can play golf." On September 13, 1897, the *Times* noted golf's "fascination for athletes who have outlived the years in which they shone on the track or the ball field." On January 1, 1898, in the *Spirit of the Times*, T. W. Stevens stated that golf "offers opportunities for gaining athletic distinction to men who are no longer able to indulge in those forms of sport which require more violent exertion, and consequently stricter training and regimen." He continued: "It really gives a new lease to life to a man whose love of sport is deep seated, and who cannot give the necessary time and attention to the sports of his younger or college days." In 1899, Findlay S. Douglas, U.S. Amateur champion, asked "what is a man going to do after he is thirty years of age? If he wants to preserve good health he has to take exercise of some kind, and surely he is not going to play football and row in races all his life. Violent forms of open-air exercise are all right while a man is young, but when he commences to merge toward the sere and yellow leaf, only the gentlest sports should be indulged in." In April 1904, in *Golf,* Henry Wikel cited the lack of personal physical contact in golf as one its most important features for general adoption by all classes and conditions of men, women, and children.

The participation of women was another key factor in the golfing boom of the 1890s and early 1900s, and the game also played a critical role in this transitional era for females in American sports. As the Scottish game took root in American soil, it proved very attractive to middle- and upper-class ladies who were athletically inclined. Proponents of women's golf praised its health and social benefits, recommending it as a wholesome pastime for the new "athletic girl" of the twentieth century. Golf facilitated women's entry into country club life, and it was incorporated into the physical education curriculum of elite female colleges. It also helped to liberate women from the cumbersome clothes that so restricted their physical activity in the Victorian era. While a few newspaper features poked fun at females who were obviously overdressed for golf, before long women were demanding fashions that were both attractive and comfortable on the course. Pioneering female golfers of varied social strata struggled to improve their skills and gain respect from men. A few would earn championship honors and even compete in matches with males as their partners or opponents.

In late nineteenth-century America the Victorian ideal of womanhood stressed female physiological weakness compared to males, highlighting the ladies' supposed delicacy, fragility, piety, and spirituality. Women were viewed as domestic creatures, attractive to men but also submissive and obedient. While they might rule a separate sphere of home life, they were excluded from the masculine worlds of business and politics. These Victorian qualities were naturally antithetical to serious, vigorous sport for women; they shaped attitudes concerning which types of exercise and forms of athletics were most appropriate for females, especially the degree of competition and the proper costumes for ladies. As early as the 1830s health reformers had urged women to engage in light exercise to strengthen their bodies and especially to improve their capacity to bear children. But they had frowned upon the most strenuous and demanding sports, endorsing those requiring only moderate exertion and friendly competition and those that showcased feminine beauty and gracefulness—especially horseback riding, archery, croquet, swimming, and skating. But by the turn of the twentieth century a female athletic revolution was well underway, thanks in part to the rise of tennis and bicycling that preceded the advent of golf. The "athletic girl" had arrived—healthy, lively, energetic, at ease with new fashions and new sports, and more self-assured, even if she did not have the right to vote or access to the man's realm of business.

Golf became an attractive and popular sport for many upper-class American women in the 1890s and early 1900s because of its health and social attributes and especially because it was more appealing to them than the alternative pastimes favored by Victorian females. As early as December 1890 a writer for *Outing* proclaimed: "For those who object to the 'slowness' of archery or croquet, or the fatigue which a hard fought tennis battle entails, a splendid medium will be found in the grand old game of golf . . . the game is admirably adapted for a ladies' pastime . . . and it has the advantage of being an amusement in which the fair sex are not so heavily handicapped as in other games." The author praised "the pastime that proves an incentive to taking a brisk walk of a mile or two, over the fine breezy 'downs.'" Early essays on golf and American women frequently compared it to the preceding bicycling craze, which appeared to be diminishing by the late 1890s. Both pastimes provided healthy exercise and excitement for girls and women, and both liberated them from restrictive, uncomfortable clothing. In August 1896 Mrs. Reginald De Koven, writing in *Cosmopolitan*, praised both pastimes but highlighted the potential of golf for females of all classes. She proclaimed: "A game which will bring weak and idle women off their couches, and by its fascination carry them over miles of hills and meadows, among the sunbeams and breezes, should be considered in the light of a great blessing to humanity. Its rewards are for women as well as for men, for all ages and conditions, irrespective of rank or of wealth: a real game for America—democratic and free." On June 10, 1900, Lilian Brooks, an early leading player, wrote in the *New York Times* that "the bicycle has done more to emancipate us from the tyranny of clothes and conventionality than anything that has ever been given us." She happily recalled excursions along "the winding, blossoming country roads free as the air we breathed" but concluded that "we seem to be unfaithful to our first love." Her reason was "because still another sport has been given us, which needs less violent exertion than bicycling, yet requires nerve, skill, strength, endurance, and self-mastery." On May 30, 1897, the *New York Times* expressed no wonder about the popularity of golf, "if for no other reason than because the fair sex can add to it so much of dignity, elegance, and beauty." It added: "And what more healthful exercise could a young lady wish than a round or two on the golf links? Fresh, invigorating air, pleasant scenery, rich, green grass, and waving foliage, just enough excitement to keep the nerves strung at a proper pitch, a two or three mile walk over rolling meadows with a pleasant partner for company, the bodily exercise in sending the little white balls over the course, and the accuracy of judgment needed to use just the necessary force for strokes of various lengths, all these and many more combine to make the sport one of the most delightful pastimes ever invented for human enjoyment." On October 16, 1898, that paper affirmed: "The woman who wishes to be good and beautiful, which is to be healthy, must play golf. That will be good medicine for a great many women, and they can say truthfully that they are already taking it, and not in homeopathic doses."

Female golfers at the Midlothian Country Club, Midlothian, Ill., 1905. SDN-050868, *Chicago Daily News* negatives collection, Chicago History Museum.

The social aspects of golf proved to be critical in its adoption by American women, especially because of the willingness of men to encourage females to play and of country clubs to include them in their membership—even if they were not granted equal status with males. In her article in *Cosmopolitan*, De Koven described the benefits of sociability in golf, even as she expressed continuing deference to men: "The possibility of companionship with husband, brother or friend is an important and a luring reward for the practice of the game, even did not ample joy result from playing it. The name golf 'widow,' once a term of misfortune, need now be only that of reproach. But it behooves us always to be modest and self-effacing, if we wish to play upon the links which are allotted to the men and forsake the humble and unambitious course laid out for us." Golf also turned out to be well-suited for a courting ritual among the sexes. A June 1899 essay in *Outlook* pointed out that a man could use the mixed match as a perfect test of a woman's character. It was no longer necessary to take a six-week voyage with a prospective spouse: "He simply invites her to take part in a mixed foursome, and knows it all within the short space of two hours."

Golf also flourished during this era because its supporters believed that the game was beneficial to the players' health, spirit, and nerves. This was particularly important for businessmen who spent five and a half days a week in a highly competitive and stressful capitalist environment and who looked forward to their retreat to a country setting. A contributor to *Outing* in 1903 contrasted the pastoral scene of players on the St. Andrew's course with their everyday lives at work: "Lawyers and bankers and brokers and busy men generally, who, twenty-four hours before, had been hard at it in downtown New York, at downtown New York's cruel pace—fighting hard-headed battles in the realm of stock tickers and roaring exchanges and skyscrapers and trucks and trolley cars." Andrew Carnegie was bitten by the golf bug at the comparatively advanced age of sixty-three, and then he waxed poetic about the positive effects of the game he labeled "Dr. Golf." On June 1, 1911, he wrote in *The Independent*: "Every breath seems to drive away weakness and disease, securing for us longer terms of happy days here on earth, even bringing something of heaven here to us. No doctor like Doctor Golf—his cures as miraculous as those sometimes credited to Christian Science." In August 1920 Hawthorne Daniel noted in *World's Work* that "business recognizes the importance of keeping its highly paid office men in good physical condition. It sees the value of the time spent on the links." Using John D. Rockefeller as a role model for businessmen who played golf, he concluded that "the game has kept men in fit condition for hard, productive work when without it their business careers would have broken them down." On January 16, 1916, the *Times* reported a survey of physicians who weighed the medical merits of golf versus tennis. Most of the doctors viewed tennis as better exercise for men up to the age of thirty-five, with golf the preferred sport for older men.

During this period there were a few critics who warned about the potential dangers of golf for middle-aged men, but the defenders of the game impatiently brushed their arguments aside. In 1905 Lyman Glover warned about the ill effects of overstrenuous play by men over sixty who had not engaged in athletics earlier in their lives. He noted that "the danger of it is most insidious, for the reason that it seems easy, and theoretically may be taken easy, and without any excessive and sudden bursts of speed and exertion such as baseball, rowing or track athletics require." In January 1905 the editor of *Golf* magazine dismissed this argument by asking, "What sport can be named which can give the exercise, the keen enjoyment and the renewal of health which golf can? How many men have testified that golf has been their salvation, and their rejuvenation?" He continued: "Not rowing, not tennis, not bowling, not any sport which calls for exertion, can compare with golf as reviver—a revivifier—to the man who has passed the three score mark. Golf is an enemy of gout and of many other evils to which many clubmen and professional men would undoubtedly succumb, if they had no such exercise." On October 8, 1914, *The Nation* reacted with annoyance to an English report that declared that the sport was neither wholesome nor safe for those over the age of forty because of its tendency to cause neurasthenia and related nervous disorders, such as a "chronic condition of sub-acute melancholia—the idiosyncrasy of the week-end golfer." That magazine recommended that middle-age golfers should relax, enjoy their good shots, forget their high scores, and keep playing the game. While the public and the medical community continued to argue in favor of the health benefits of golf, there was lingering concern about the risks of the sport. During the years immediately preceding World War I, several journals and newspapers reported the deaths, nonfatal heart attacks, or paralysis of elderly men during or after rounds of golf. As a result, a few commentators conceded that there were some people who should not try the game.

Then, as now, a round of golf provided city people with a long walk of several hours' duration through a scenic piece of countryside. William Garrot Brown viewed the game as one method of returning to nature, a "means of awakening a sense of the beauty of wild flowers, and many another delicate loveliness in nature." He believed that golf "permits and induces moods scarcely conceivable in other athletic competitions," adding that "it permits one to be contemplative." For him it was the ideal pastime for businessmen, for "serenity and tranquillity are in truth the very moods which Americans of the classes who play golf need." In November 1901 in *Golf,* Arnold Haultain listed a few of its delights: "The great breeze that greets you on the hill, the whiffs of air—pungent, penetrating—that come through green things growing, the hot smell of pines at noon, the wet smell of fallen leaves in autumn, the damp and heavy air of the valleys at eve, the lungs full of oxygen, the sense of freedom on a great expanse, the exhilaration, the vastness, the buoyancy, the exaltation." Charles Blair Macdonald expressed similar sentiments in *Golf* in January 1898: "Wandering over the links, inhaling and enjoying the fresh air of the country, the senses are awakened, and all alert, one takes pleasure in the landscape, watching the varied shades of sunlight and shadow, which become features of the game, until with sunset, happily tired, he is primed to enjoy a good dinner and a restful evening."

It is ironic but not surprising that golf became a fixture of American athletics during a time when the team sports of baseball, college football, lacrosse, and basketball were enjoying great popularity. Unlike these games, golf was an individual sport that challenged its players to compete against themselves and the courses more than against their opponents. During an age when business corporations, labor unions, and civic, social, and religious groups were increasing their power as the dominant institutions in American culture, the Scottish pastime put the spotlight back on the lone human being, struggling to overcome obstacles encountered on his or her journey across the countryside. In Haultain's words, golf appealed to people because "there is no defensive play, no attacking an enemy's position, no subordination of oneself to the team, no captain to be obeyed, no relative positions of players. . . . Golf . . . is self-reliant, silent, sturdy. It leans less on its fellows. It loves best to overcome obstacles alone." Haultain explained: "In golf the contest is not with your fellow man. The foe in golf is not your opponent, but great Nature herself, and the game is to see who will overreach her better, you or your opponent. In almost all other games you pit yourself against a mortal foe; in golf it is yourself against the world: no human being stays your progress as you drive your ball over the face of the globe. It is very like life in this, is golf. Life is not an internecine strife. We are all here fighting, not against each other for our lives, but against Nature for our livelihoods."

Analysts admired golf because of its mental, psychological, and moral qualities, and especially because they believed that the game strengthened the players' minds and characters. For Brown: "From the variety of the situations it presents, there arises a constant demand upon the player's intelligence; from the unequaled importance of delicate adjustments, and the heavy penalties imposed upon very slight errors, there arises a constant demand upon his self-control; and it makes a quite peculiar demand upon his conscience by reason of the clearness with which its standard of excellence is defined." He elaborated on the last point: "No other game offers so constantly or so devilishly the temptation to be unfair. The rules are many and easy to misinterpret, and in ordinary matches, when there are no onlookers, the player is often at liberty to give himself the benefit of the doubt." Haultain argued that golf differed from other ball sports in that it required greater concentration. "In no other game," he wrote, "have you so to be master of yourself, . . . to steady yourself—your muscles, your nerves, your brain, nay, your mood and your temper, or to be master of yourself for so long a stretch." In December 1896 in *Outing*, Price Collier remarked on the value of golf for character development: "The only rational sanction for sport is, that it develops certain fine and needful qualities that are apt to be left in abeyance in a commercial country. To endure hardship, to control temper, to accept defeat cheerfully, never to take the smallest unfair advantage of your opponent, or to whine and excuse one's self, to be modest when successful, and not to boast or brag of past, probably, possible, or potential feats—all these are the possible teachings of honest sport." While he admitted that golf did not offer the same "test of physical endurance" as did many other sports, it still provided "a very peculiarly severe test of moral endurance and nerve." While some commentators conceded that the challenges of golf could frustrate players and occasionally provoke temper tantrums, its defenders countered with the assertion that these outbursts were uncommon and not very serious.

A final attraction of golf was the way it fostered sociability among partners and opponents alike. The Rev. Dr. W. S. Rainsford, a first-class player and rector of St. George's Episcopal Church in New York City, called it "the most companionable game I know of." Andrew Carnegie asked: "Does a game make opponents closer and dearer to each other, or does it arouse ill-feeling and jealousy and drive men apart as rivals, even foes, each grudging the success of the other?" In his view, golf differed from football and other sports because in the Scottish game "men become dearer friends than ever; the often they meet on the green, the fonder they become of each other and the greater the longing for their chum's society; in after years, if separated, each warms as the name of the other is mentioned, and ends his panegyric with the ever entrancing words murmured with emotion, 'Ah, we played golf together!'"

◎ ◎ ◎

During the 1890s and early 1900s one major cultural constraint threatened to retard the growth of the game that was fast becoming the premier pastime for tens of thousands of middle- and upper-class Americans. That force was the time-honored ban on Sabbath sports, which dated from the sixteenth century in England. Those who extolled the capacity of golf to elevate the mind, spirit, and soul of its enthusiasts faced a major problem raised by the issue of Sunday play. Most workers and businessmen had leisure time available only on Sundays (and sometimes also on Saturday afternoons), but flocking to the links on the Sabbath was either banned by blue laws or severely frowned upon in most communities. The controversy illustrated one aspect of the democratization of the sport, at first for upscale members of the country club set and later for players of more modest means on public courses. It also raised the troubling issue of Sunday play for country club children and especially for young boys of all social classes who sought employment as caddies. Carrying golf bags was an especially tempting alternative to attending church services and Sunday school for poor boys whose families benefited from the extra cash earned on the golf course.

For centuries the Puritan tradition in the United States had stifled or severely restricted recreation on the Sabbath, but by the 1890s the old code was weakening under the pressures of modern times. During this era many clergymen, concerned citizens, and women's groups such as the Women's Sabbath Alliance and the Women's Christian Temperance Union applied pressure to golf clubs to refrain from opening their courses on Sundays. Faced with the strenuous protests of clergymen, strict moralists, and crusading women, defenders of Sunday golf responded by contending that those who played on the Sabbath were not disturbing the peaceful observance of the Lord's day and could still be good Christians. On September 26, 1896, the *New York Herald* commented that "the moralities of golf playing on the Sabbath is one question, to be settled by individual conscience, but it is absurd to accuse those who play the game on that day of disturbing the peace, for there is no quieter or more orderly game in the list of outdoor sports, and the golf grounds are generally far removed from any locality where indulgence of the game would unduly desecrate the Sabbath." On

December 3, 1899, the *New York Times* summarized the justification for Sabbath golf: "Sunday offers one of the few possibilities to a business man for exercise, and a quiet game of golf is surely harmful to no one. The game itself is not noisy or boisterous, and as most of the clubs where Sunday playing is indulged in are well removed from residential localities there has been little cause for complaint." On June 10, 1900, a writer of a letter to the *Times* took issue with the Women's Sabbath Alliance's campaign against Sunday golf by asking: "Did it ever occur to these pious reformers that a hard-working man needed recreation on the Sabbath, in body as well as in spirit? And, that a man might still be a Christian though playing golf, and often find more evidence of God and His goodness in the fields than in the church?"

The question of Sunday play generated considerable tension in golf clubs in the Northeast and the Midwest prior to World War I. Most club members were devout Protestants who initially honored the traditional injunction against recreation or sport on the Sabbath, but by the early 1900s the balance had shifted in many associations toward allowing golf on Sunday afternoons. As clubs struggled to resolve the issue of Sunday golf, police departments and the courts adopted a variety of strategies concerning enforcement of local blue laws and prosecution of offenders. In some cases pressure by clergy or politicians led to criminal and legal action, but the outcomes depended on interpretation of the law by judges and juries. There were several arrests of Sunday golfers throughout the Northeast from the 1890s to 1919. Not surprisingly, New England held out the longest in the crusade to stop Sunday golf. In November 1915, in Newport, Rhode Island, the police chief shut down the local links, apparently because of a power struggle with the town's mayor. In 1919 in Massachusetts, two members of the Brae Burn Country Club agreed to be arrested while playing on a Sunday to create a test case for a state law that banned sport on the Sabbath. A district court held that although golf was not a sport, it was a game, and he fined the defendants five dollars each for violating the Sabbath law. In 1920 a district attorney decided not to take the golfers' appeal before the state's superior court because the legislature had recently adopted a new Sunday sports act. While these incidents provided amusement for those who considered them quaint relics of Puritan intolerance from bygone centuries, the authorities took them more seriously, and they did carry practical consequences for communities. As early as December 29, 1898, the *New York Times* responded to a Connecticut's court enforcement of the ban on Sunday golf by proclaiming that "if the game is forbidden on Sunday, there will presently be much real estate for sale in Connecticut towns at sacrifice prices, and butchers and bakers who are now prosperous will begin to call meetings of their creditors."

During the 1920s there were a few scattered examples of state legislators who tried to pass bills banning Sunday golf, but by then public opinion had become strongly supportive of Sabbath recreation. Clergymen increasingly tried to accommodate Sunday golfers. In April 1924, *Golf Illustrated* reported that in Kansas City, Dr. J. P. DeWolffe instituted a golf breakfast at 7:30 A.M. on Sundays for those who wished to play an early-morning round. That journal proclaimed: "Picture a congregation, two-thirds of them in golf clothes, listening to a pastor who can give par a battle on any course!" The long struggle over Sunday golf now became a matter of individual conscience, not state regulation. By the 1920s, good Christians could sanction the Scottish game that was rapidly becoming a fixture on the American sporting scene, even on Sundays. And while its enthusiasts were playing seven days a week, they were also initiating important changes in country clubs, course design, and equipment that would usher in a distinctive form of golf in the United States.

THE
AMERICANIZATION
OF GOLF

As golf conquered the United States in the decades preceding World War I, the British import took on new forms. Americans infatuated with golf established country and golf clubs, built ornate clubhouses, laid out inland park courses, experimented with new types of equipment, and even modified time-honored rules. Scottish and English officials resented the upstart Americans who dared to challenge the traditions and authority of the sportsmen of St. Andrews and other hallowed centers of British golf, but in the long run the British had little power to stop or even slow down the inexorable tide of change. Enthusiasts in the United States aggressively modified the sport to suit their needs.

The country clubs that spearheaded the golf revolution in the United States were products of several trends and forces among the nation's elite and middle classes during the late nineteenth and early twentieth centuries. These included the rise of gentlemen's city clubs and especially athletic associations, the growing popularity of summer resorts, the passion for outdoor sports, and increasing suburbanization. The first urban men's clubs in Boston, Philadelphia, and New York were dining and social organizations that restricted membership to local elites. The most exclusive were founded prior to the Civil War and generally did not sponsor sports, but the wealthiest gentlemen who were athletically inclined formed yacht and horse racing associations. Beginning in the mid-1800s, men of more modest means who sought more active recreation launched cricket, baseball, rowing, track and field, and lacrosse clubs. By the late 1800s affluent urbanites sought to escape from the heat and stench of their cities in the summer by traveling to seaside or rural resorts or health spas, especially Newport, Rhode Island; Saratoga Springs, New York; White Sulphur Springs, West Virginia; and the mountains of New York State and New England. They enjoyed simply being in fresh air in beautiful surroundings, and they also amused themselves with fishing, equestrianism (especially horseback riding), game and fox hunting, and other pastimes. The advent of commuter railroads enabled many to move to the suburbs, where middle- and upper-class families could pursue their favorite sports year round. New "borderland" communities featured private homes on landscaped spaces, modifications of the urban gridiron system of streets, park-like settings, and plenty of open land for recreational use, including golf courses.

The first country clubs naturally evolved from these developments. Two associations outside of Boston, the Myopia Club and The Country Club of Brookline, share the honor of being the first of their type in the nation. In 1878, Frederick O. Prince, a Boston lawyer, recruited 150 members for the Myopia Club on his estate eight miles north of Boston. His organization built a clubhouse and had grounds for tennis and baseball, but the featured activities were fox hunting and horse racing. A few years later several members sought a more convenient location for a retreat closer to their homes. In 1882 a group of Boston Brahmins led by J. Murray Forbes established The Country Club of Brookline. Their aim was "to have a comfortable clubhouse for the use of members with their families, a simple restaurant, bed-rooms, bowling-alley, lawn tennis grounds, etc; also to have race-meetings and occasionally, music in the afternoon." These two pioneer country clubs established the pattern that would be imitated by dozens and later hundreds of organizations over the next decade. Officials located their clubs near their members' residential neighborhoods and provided a comfortable clubhouse with dining facilities, a few bedrooms, indoor space for social events and games, and playing grounds for outdoor sports. Before long golf would replace equestrianism and hunting as the favorite pastimes. Significantly, these new associations differed from the earlier upper-class city and athletic organizations in that they welcomed women and children. They played a major role in promoting exercise and sporting participation among the wives and daughters of the American aristocracy. The example of upper-class females enjoying horseback riding, archery, croquet, tennis, golf, and other amusements also stimulated greater interest and acceptance of women's sports among the middle classes.

The country club movement of the late 1800s was in part a reaction by privileged urbanites against forces that were threatening the status of white, Anglo-Saxon Protestants. Increasing industrialization, urbanization, and the growing power of big business created a new class of corporate leaders and power brokers who were displacing the older elites. During these years, hordes of immigrant newcomers from eastern and southern Europe were struggling to achieve middle-class standing, thereby dramatically changing the cultural landscape for native-born citizens. Although the founding of these upscale associations and the golf boom they fostered had clear democratic implications, they also generated certain elitist, exclusionary, and antidemocratic tendencies. The founders and first members of these clubs sought to create small communities where members could find refuge from the modernizing forces of their times and socialize and play with friends and family. Historian Richard J. Moss views the founders of these first country clubs as local leaders who were striving to re-establish the vanishing village of nineteenth-century America, even as the federal government sought national solutions to social and political problems. In April 1902, Frank Arnett, writing for *Munsey's Magazine*, highlighted the communal appeal of country clubs: "It is really the love of home and the love of friends whom one would have about one's hearth that has brought about their organization. For the love of home involves also the neighborly idea, the love of one's fellows, of companionship, of something beyond 'highballs' and poker and the scandal or shop talk of the smoking room." In November 1905 Robert Dunn of *Outing* magazine expanded upon these themes by explaining the significance of the new country clubs for community, business, social class, and family across the country. He remarked:

> The country club seems almost destined to satisfy the somewhat communistic dream that in the middle of the last century, and sporadically ever since, brought about Brook Farm and such places; . . . Without the stress and tension of new-century town life, so generally condemned, country clubs could not have so multiplied. In states, as in individuals, vices encourage counterbalancing virtues. The amazing wholesomeness of country club life becomes the complement of the worst evils of the money struggle; our office faults are exaggerated into virtues, according to the paradox of tradition, after business hours and over Sunday at the club. . . . A club, by gathering under one roof persons of similar tastes and means, brings order to the chaos created by sudden prosperity. . . . It stratifies social development, and thus assures its permanence. Probably no two country clubs the land over are quite alike in ideals and manners, thus averting degeneration into rigid class distinctions, with inevitable vanity and adulation.

But early chroniclers of the country club phenomenon also recognized the contradictory trends they embodied. In their history of The Country Club of Brookline, Frederic H. Curtiss and John Heard explained: "In terms of psychology, the club, and especially the country club, is the product of democracy, and at the same time is a revolt against and a negation of democracy. It is a banding together for the purpose of making available to the group facilities which previously had been the privilege of the wealthy aristocrat. And, almost in the same hour, it is a denial of the spirit of democracy, since a small group sets itself apart from the majority, building, as it were, a wall around its pastimes, and making admission thereto more or less difficult according to the temper and the social requirements of its members. Socially speaking, the spirit of Boston in the '70s and '80s was far removed from the spreadeagle democracy of which the United States so cried aloud, and of which it was so proud." Prior to World War I, the rise of country and golf clubs and the growth of golf itself would express the conflicting trends of democracy and equality along with elitism and social exclusion.

By 1900 it was already clear that golf had become the dominant sport at American country clubs and that the game's popularity had spread beyond the ranks of the nation's elite classes. Even as many of the nation's wealthiest citizens took up the sport at exclusive clubs at Brookline, Massachusetts; Newport, Rhode Island; Shinnecock Hills, New York; and other affluent communities, golf's long-term future in the United States depended greatly on its popularity among middle- and upper-middle class families. To be successful, the golf clubs of the pre–World War I era had to address a number of issues, and while they had the examples of the pioneering institutions to emulate, each association faced its own set of circumstances and its own challenges. Every club had to choose a location convenient to its members' homes, establish rules and policies for membership and management of its financial affairs and facilities, schedule social and recreational activities, design and build a clubhouse, and construct and maintain a golf course. Prior to the arrival of the automobile, members depended on some combination of railroad, streetcar, and horse-drawn carriage for transportation to clubs. Membership policies reflected both social considerations of exclusivity and practical issues of financial solvency. Club founders generally restricted the numbers of members, but often found it necessary to add to the club's roster to pay for improvements to its facilities. Special categories were sometimes created for women, young adults, and public dignitaries the officers wished to honor. Some associations hired a manager to handle financial concerns, while others relied upon a board of governors and committees to keep the club functioning and especially to make critical decisions about raising funds via stock offerings and leasing or purchasing land. To ensure viability, each club required one or two dynamic leaders and many faithful volunteers among the membership. Sound financial management was critical, as was good judgment on policy issues, especially concerning which sports other than golf would be available to members. Tennis proved to be a favorite, while minor pastimes could include billiards, squash, croquet, bowling, trapshooting, archery, swimming, baseball, and even such winter sports as ice skating, tobogganing, curling, skiing, and hockey.

As country clubs opened their doors to women and children during this era, the Victorian American family expanded its domain beyond the home to a new realm in which gender roles would be contested and at least partially redefined. Whatever category of membership women held in particular clubs, their presence raised troublesome questions concerning their proper place in clubhouses and on the golf courses. In particular, the inclusion of females generated conflicts over access to indoor facilities and space and time on the links. Although their primary importance in the early development of country clubs lay in the social sphere, those who were active golfers were determined to be taken seriously as sportswomen as well. Dunn highlighted the central importance of the female presence in the rise of the American country club: "Woman, indeed, is the keynote of their vitality and success. It is strange but true, yet in the spheres to which she has been tradition-ally denied access the country club lets her burst most fully into that one which fifty years ago would have been most impossibly sealed to her—the community of outdoor sports. Her steps in politics have been infantile, in business quite subordinary, while her inroads into letters and art is too old to be historic; but on the golf and tennis field, and as a hunstwoman, she has leaped to equal place with man."

The treatment of women in the earliest and most prestigious American country clubs ranged from total exclusion to varying degrees of acceptance and privileges. A few women played at St. Andrew's in 1889, but shortly after that the club barred them completely. On the other hand, women at Shinnecock Hills were active in organizing major social events and were also regular players. Because of congestion on that club's first twelve-hole course, a separate nine was built for ladies, but dissatisfaction with that solution led to an expansion to a full eighteen holes open to all (although apparently not at all times). At the Onwentsia Club north of Chicago, wid-ows and unmarried women could be elected to full membership, but wives, daughters, and sisters of male members had only limited privileges and ac-cess to the clubhouse and the golf course. The expansion and design of the clubhouse of The Country Club of Brookline in 1905 reflected the practice of gendered space that would become standard in twentieth-century clubs. The Brookline building had a separate ladies' entrance and reception room and a boudoir upstairs, adjacent to the women's locker room. Architects who designed clubhouses often followed this approach by including separate cafes, grills, and lounges for men and women. In 1894 a group of ladies from Morristown, New Jersey, aimed to avoid second-class treatment by founding a club restricted to women—the Morris County Golf Club. But the following year their husbands pressured them to incorporate the club and purchase its grounds, and before long all the officers were male.

The rising popularity of golf in the 1890s and early 1900s for both men and women naturally led to conflicts over the use of country club courses. The pattern was already clear by 1900 when Ruth Underhill, the 1899 USGA women's champion, criticized the policy of excluding women on weekends and holidays. She argued that the more proficient female players should also be permitted to play at those times. She wrote that women "ought not to be turned off the course *en masse* on certain days, as many of the men would like to have done; but instead a certain grade of play on the women's part might be made a basis for their admission." She understood that men did not want to be bothered on their holidays by female beginners, but she also believed that it would be "ungracious and generally hurtful of the game if women of keen interest and enough proficiency in it to entitle them to enter in class B should be shut out." She added (perhaps naively) that "it is not as women that they object to us on the links, but merely as the cause of delay and interruption." Here she may have underestimated the men's general disapproval of females on golf courses, but she remained hopeful that as courses became more crowded "to such women as are fairly entitled to compete with many of the men there will be accorded the privileges they deserve."

But despite Underhill's plea for equal opportunity on the links for women, there is considerable evidence that the men who controlled America's country clubs during the early twentieth century continued to restrict access to their courses to all women whether they were beginners or tournament-caliber players. A survey published in the *New York Times* on July 30, 1916, concluded that most clubs limited play to males on Saturdays, Sundays, and holidays, either all day or during certain prime hours. The writer suggested (perhaps invoking a comparison with suffragettes of that period) that "this may be one of the next points of attack for the ardent feminists, some of whom would doubtless insist that they and their sisters had quite as much right at all times on the links as the mere man." The article did note that there were several clubs with no restrictions on females, but in most of those cases it appeared that there were either very few women who wished to play or they had agreed on rules that gave preference to men using the course. Some clubs also set aside special days for play by women only. In a few extreme cases women had access to club links only a few hours a week. For example, at the elite Garden City Golf Club women could play only on Monday and Friday mornings, provided that they teed off before 11:00 A.M. They were also barred from the clubhouse, but they could sit on its veranda.

⊙ ⊙ ⊙

The American country club of this era was a distinctive institution that evolved according to native circumstances and social trends. It differed significantly from its British counterpart—especially in clubhouse design and course location and layout. As the cultural commentator Gustav Kobbé explained in *Outlook* on June 1, 1901: "Whoever thinks that the country club is an American imitation of something English and had its origin in Anglomania is greatly mistaken." While the first clubs converted country homes and farmhouses for their initial clubhouses, before long many of the most affluent associations and several of more moderate means spent enormous sums on their grounds and especially their buildings. This practice marked a departure from that of Scotland, where most golf courses were built on public lands and were open to the public, and where social clubs of golfers were separate and distinct from the grounds where they played. In the United States even a more modest club such as the one in Hackensack, New Jersey, raised $20,000 for its main building. Theodore A. Havemeyer, former president of the United States Golf Association, warned about the dangers of too many clubs and especially the lavish expenditures by some of them. On January 12, 1897, he fretted in the *New York Times*: "In some cases the game has been regarded as secondary to the club itself, and this cannot help but be detrimental to the best interests of golf. It is a mistake to expend large sums of money upon palatial clubhouses, putting the dollars in the clubhouse and the pennies on the links. Richly furnished clubhouses are not necessary for the enjoyment of golf. The genuine golfer cares far more for a first-class sporting course than he does for elaborate club fixings." But despite this advice, club officers increasingly hired architects to design distinctive clubhouses that could often be quite expensive, even with interior decorations and furnishings that reflected simple country living. Exterior verandas and separate locker and lounging and grill rooms for men and women added to the costs.

Other distinctive features of American golf during these years were the location and physical characteristics of the courses. Whereas in Britain the premier grounds were seaside links, the Atlantic and Pacific coastlines were generally not suitable for golf or were inaccessible to the suburban population. The result was the creation of the inland (or "park") course, constructed out of farmland or hewed out of a primeval forest. The syndicates that built these courses around 1900 invested tens or even hundreds of thousands of dollars on land, improvements, a clubhouse, water systems, and greens and fairway maintenance. Golf course architecture progressed rapidly in the United States, as designers used natural features such as hills and dales, brooks and streams, ponds, lakes, and even rivers, along with artificial hazards they added for extra challenges for players. H. J. Whigham, an Englishman who was United States Amateur champion in 1896 and 1897, noted that the few seaside links in the United States were inferior to those abroad. But he also recognized the necessity of constructing inland courses, often at great expense. He observed in the *New York Times* on December 5, 1897: "The desire, however, to get the best possible golf courses has manifested itself in many cases to a degree that the English golfers would call crazy. The idea of spending a hundred thousand dollars or more on the golf course, as has been done by several clubs here, would never occur to the English mind, one reason being that it would not be necessary. Inland courses, to be brought to perfection, must have water for the greens, and this is expensive, besides the cost of making the greens." Although as an Englishman Whigham did not believe that an American inland course could "ever be made the equal of a North Berwick or St. Andrews" in Great Britain, he did concede that those already built in the interior of the United States "infinitely surpass anything of the same nature in Great Britain, and—what is far more to the point—really present a first-class test of golf." He argued that inland courses fell short of the standard of British seaside links in two respects: the inferiority of the putting greens and the lack of great sand bunkers. As remedies for these deficiencies he recommended that clubs lay out holes with strategically placed sand traps and high grass in the rough.

Although several experts severely criticized many of the first courses, prior to World War I a few pioneering Scottish immigrants significantly raised the standard of American golf architecture. Writing in *Golf* in November 1903, an English visitor, J. A. T. Bramston, described the American courses as "distinctly easy, and rather monotonous," lacking strict requirements and characterized by mediocrity and artificiality. In his view the layouts were too similar, calling for the same shots time after time, with "nothing to make the player exert himself, to draw him out, and compel him to use his judgement." In 1926 an American commentator, Robert Hunter, lambasted the earliest inland course construction in the United States as "so indescribably bad that any one knowing better things must have thought it the work of some maniac with an extremely malicious spirit, determined to deface, with every kind of misshapen erection and eruption known to a depraved mind, those lovely fields and meadows which first caught the eye of our golfers."

Willie Dunn, Thomas Bendelow, and Donald J. Ross were among the most noteworthy of the Scottish golf professionals who contributed innovative features to several distinctive courses during this period. Dunn is best known for his renovation of the Shinnecock Hills course on Long Island during the mid-1890s, but he also recruited many of his friends and relatives from Scotland who later served as golf teachers, greenkeepers, clubmakers, and course designers. Bendelow resigned from a job as a typesetter at the *New York Herald* in 1895 to teach golf to a wealthy family on Long Island and later to join the sporting goods firm of A. G. Spalding and Brothers as a golf consultant. Early in his career he managed the nation's first municipal golf course at Van Cortlandt Park in the Bronx, New York, where he remodeled and expanded its initial layout. Ultimately he designed more than four hundred courses across the country. A Harvard professor persuaded Ross to relocate to Boston in 1898, where he began a long career as the first full-time golf architect in the United States. Ross's designs at four courses at the Pinehurst resort in North Carolina earned him national recognition and an extensive practice.

Most of the early golf courses in the United States were crude layouts that were designed and built quickly and inexpensively. Bendelow was famous for a method that was later ridiculed as "eighteen stakes on a Sunday afternoon." He (and many of his peers) designed a course in a single day by pacing across the chosen ground, placing stakes (more than eighteen) at sites for tees, bunkers, mounds, and greens. Clubs would usually pay only twenty-five dollars for the job, regardless of how long it took. After Bendelow or one of the other designers departed for the next project, the club greenkeeper supervised the actual building of the course. Construction often required painstakingly slow removal of trees and fences, clearing away surface stones, grading the earth, building mounds, seeding fairways and greens, and mowing grass. Laborers using hand tools and mules and horses pulling rudimentary grading and mowing machines did the backbreaking work. Once completed, these early American courses were quite primitive compared to their counterparts in Great Britain. In some cases holes crossed one another, and obstacles such as stone walls, plowed fields, and chasms were treated as natural hazards. Frequently there was little difference between the turf and grass of the fairways and greens.

A few of these early courses achieved distinction and recognition for their special features, and Americans made significant contributions to several of them. Most noteworthy are the British-style seaside links at Shinnecock Hills, the Myopia Hunt Club north of Boston, the Garden City Golf Club on Long Island, and the National Golf Links of America, near Shinnecock Hills. Herbert C. Leeds persuaded the officers of the Myopia Club to replace its first nine-hole layout with a new one that reflected his study of the Shinnecock course. Leeds shaped the greens into rolling surfaces, with none being completely flat. He later supervised the construction of a second nine, and his club was rewarded as host of three national opens over the next eight years. At Garden City, first Devereux Emmet and later early champion Walter J. Travis designed a course that was celebrated for its outstanding turf on both fairways and greens. Travis was a native of Australia who learned to play golf after migrating to the United States. His renovations included rebuilding the greens at Garden City to add more undulations and numerous deep bunkers, especially small pot bunkers. Although he was born in Canada, Charles Blair Macdonald's Scottish heritage and his love of golf motivated him to build a classic seaside links course in the United States. He chose a site on Long Island adjacent to Shinnecock Hills and decided to incorporate elements of famous holes of British courses into his layout. On each hole he offered golfers a fresh mental and physical challenge, with alternative routes of play for both short and long hitters. He spared no expense in hauling in ten thousand loads of topsoil to spread on the grounds and in creating a turf nursery in which he experimented with many types of grasses. He also installed a complete irrigation system for the greens. In the end, Macdonald's National Golf Links revolutionized American golf course architecture. In the opinion of H. J. Whigham, "the main achievement is that a course has been produced where every hole is a good one and presents a new problem. That is something which has never been accomplished, even in Scotland."

⊙ ⊙ ⊙

Another example of the Americanization of golf around the turn of the twentieth century was the adaptation of the sport to the growing vacation habits of the middle and upper classes, especially in the Northeast and the South. Golf courses proliferated at summer colonies and resorts, built by both local residents and hotel owners. While there were numerous places where people of modest means could enjoy golf on rough but still pleasant and playable links, many of the retreats clearly catered to the well-heeled. Managers of the fashionable resorts were quick to see the necessity of building links on their grounds. As early as June 1897 the *New York Times* reported golf courses sprouting in the Berkshires at Lenox and Stockbridge, the White Mountains of New Hampshire, the Adirondacks, and at seaside spots in Rhode Island and New Jersey. That newspaper noted that "it is not unusual to see a hotel advertising golf links as an extra attraction, somewhat similar to the former method of advertising tennis courts." In the White Mountains, golf and baseball dominated the 1900 season. One guest recalled watching the arrival of local boys, ages seven to sixteen, each carrying a tin pail. He explained: "A large pail, filled with many golf balls, might be a necessity, since White Mountain fairways were narrow, the rough was very deep, and many golfers were of suspect talent." A visit in August by famed British champion Harry Vardon spiked interest at hotel courses throughout the region.

During this period many northerners escaped harsh winters by traveling to milder climates in the South. Those already bitten by the golf bug naturally sought chances to play in the states that stretched from the Carolinas to Florida. One of the most successful vacation villages in that region was Pinehurst, North Carolina, a community that first opened for guests in 1896. Pinehurst was founded by a New Englander, James Walker Tufts, a wealthy manufacturer and philanthropist who dreamed of creating a health retreat for recovering consumptives. But when that goal became problematic because of new medical discoveries concerning the contagious properties of tuberculosis, Tufts decided to transform Pinehurst into a recreational winter resort. After a few guests played golf in 1897 on dairy pasture land, Tufts hired a New York doctor the following year to lay out a nine-hole course. Golf exhibitions by Vardon in 1900 had the same effect in promoting golf in North Carolina as they had had in New Hampshire. More significant was the arrival that year of Donald Ross, who was introduced to the Tufts family by their lawyer. Ross's work at Pinehurst earned fame for several of Pinehurst's links and for himself as one of the premier course designers in the United States. After the death of James Tufts in 1902, his son Leonard hired Frank Presbrey, an advertising executive, to promote Pinehurst as a premier vacation destination. Presbrey scheduled glamorous events such as golf tournaments and outings to attract advertising men and their clients to Pinehurst. He also designed attractive advertisements with an engaging product symbol of a young boy carrying a bag of clubs over his shoulder. Prior to World War I, Leonard Tufts decided to sell building plots in the village, and by the 1920s Pinehurst's private homes and hotels were well-known as an exclusive golf community.

◎ ◎ ◎

American inventive genius also profoundly shaped the evolution of golf through the improvement of the game's implements—the ball, tee, and clubs. Coburn Haskell of Cleveland and Bertram Work of the Goodrich Rubber Company together developed the rubber-wound ball in 1898, which replaced the gutta-percha ball (made of a Malay gum extracted from a gutta-percha tree). John Gameter of Goodrich contributed the automatic golf-ball-winding machine. The Staughton Rubber Company then devised an improved cover made of balata, and Jack Jolly came up with the idea for a liquid center for the ball. The coming of the new liquid-centered, rubber-cored ball revolutionized the game during the early 1900s. Due to the availability of rubber and automated production techniques, the new balls were more durable and less expensive than their predecessors. Moreover, increasing the distance of shots put more fun into the game for all, and it contributed to the lengthening and redesign of many courses.

In Britain there was some initial stiff resistance to the introduction of the new American ball, but it was generally grudgingly accepted by the end of 1903. As the noted English golf writer and British Amateur champion Horace Hutchinson explained in *Outing* in October 1903: "The Briton did not want to find the American ball a good one, so he did not find it a good one. Someone said that it had been bounced on the floor of the Stock Exchange and had gone on bounding about there, chucking one member after another under the chin, until it found its way to the fireplace, and from thence up the chimney and never was seen again." The strongest opposition came from two groups: the traditionalists and the professionals. One amateur declared that the new ball "ruins all the links in the country, destroys all science of the game, brings second-class players on a level with the first class, and encourages mediocrity at the expense of genius." British Amateur and Open champion Harold H. Hilton thought it "enabled the rough and tumble golfer of hard hitting propensities to range himself alongside the player who really knows the game, which he never could do with the old gutty." Britain's Professional Golfers' Association (newly organized in 1901) also opposed the new ball because its members believed it "was not conducive to the advancement of golf as *a game of skill*." But they

35

also clearly had a pecuniary interest at stake because the rubber-cored ball lasted longer, did less damage to clubs, and could not be manufactured or repaired in the professional's shop. But in the end the English and Scottish golfers caved in. The marketplace determined the triumph of the Haskell ball, and the prestigious Royal and Ancient Golf Club of St. Andrews voted to take no action on the issue of whether it should endorse or ban the new ball. Hutchinson conceded: "We accept the American invention, as Britons will, of course, with grumbling, but with gratitude down in our hearts." Another British critic, J. A. T. Bramston, concluded in *Golf* in January 1904 that in the opinion of the majority of the English users of the Haskell ball, its advent was a "great crime" because "it has cheapened the game, and made it easier." But he also reassured his fellow countrymen that "golf is too old and too good a game to be affected to any great extent one way or the other by the rough-and-ready transatlantic methods, and the upholders of the real golfing traditions need not fear the influence of that irrepressible and irresistible nation upon this most conservative game of the most conservative section of the English-speaking people." So the rubber-cored ball conquered Great Britain, but in the 1920s and 1930s British authorities permitted their golfers to play with a ball that was one-sixteenth of an inch smaller in diameter than its American counterpart (although equal in weight).

The wooden golf tee was another American innovation, invented and first patented in 1899 by an African American dentist, George Grant. The second black graduate of the Harvard dental school's second class, he became a successful Boston dentist and a pioneer of golf in the meadows of the suburb of Arlington Heights during the 1880s. For centuries golfers had pinched wet sand into a small mound to elevate their ball for tee shots. Annoyed by the trouble of performing this task at every hole, Grant came up with the idea of crafting a wooden peg to support his ball. He found a local company to manufacture his tee and kept bags of them in his homes in Boston and in Arlington Heights, but he never attempted to market his product for commercial gain. That venture fell to another dentist, William Lowell, a white New Jersey golfer who also obtained a patent for a golf tee in 1921. But unlike Grant, Lowell actively promoted his device by paying $1,500 to U.S. Open champion Walter Hagen and trick-shot artist Joe Kirkwood to promote his "Reddy Tee" during their exhibitions in the early 1920s. Lowell failed to earn a financial windfall for his device because of competition and patent lawsuits. But for many years golf historians recognized him as the inventor of the golf tee, when the true credit should have gone to Grant. The American golf tee, like the American golf ball, at first met a cool reception in Great Britain, but by 1927 spectators in the galleries there were scrambling for tees left behind by Bob Jones and other touring American amateurs and professionals.

The British (and especially the Scottish) were more resistant to innovations in club design, especially the Schenectady putter that Walter J. Travis used to win the British Amateur crown in 1904. (It had a shaft in the center of a mallet-shaped head.) In 1910 the Royal and Ancient Golf Club of St. Andrews banned the mallet putter, which set off a storm of indignation in the United States. The following January at its annual meeting, the United States Golf Association refused to support the St. Andrews ruling, indicating its resistance to that body's efforts to standardize the equipment of the game. The *New York Sun* proclaimed: "The time has come for the men of spirit who play golf in America to revolt against the tyranny of the Royal and Ancient Golf Club of St. Andrews if the mallet-headed putter suits them. . . . We trust the free and independent American golfers will stand for their rights and never bow the knee to St. Andrews." In the January 14, 1911, *Harper's Weekly,* Leighton Calkins called on Americans to formulate their own set of golf rules, following the example of tennis, which had separate governing codes on each side of the Atlantic. In 1917, the Western Golf Association created some excitement when it changed the stymie rule by providing that the ball nearest the hole should be played first when both balls were on the putting green. In instituting this regulation, that association broke with the code of Scottish authorities and also acted without the approval of the USGA. In later years the stymie rule, the balanced set of clubs, and steel shafts would also create much controversy. The USGA and the Royal and Ancient club agreed on a uniform set of rules in 1952, but that era of good feelings ended in the 1960s as the two bodies parted ways on regulations pertaining to flagsticks, unplayable lies, and out of bounds.

Charles Blair Macdonald and a few other Scottish Americans initially resisted some of the minor rule changes and innovations in equipment. Macdonald in particular fought the modifications that allowed the wiping of balls on muddy greens, the granting of improved lies under certain conditions, the abolition of the stymie, and even the passing of the tradition of wearing red coats during play. On the other hand, he did endorse limiting the number of clubs, the out-of-bounds rule, and the new rubber-cored ball. In the opinion of Herbert Warren Wind, who believed that moderate revision was a healthy sign for the sport in America, "Macdonald's blind allegiance to the way he had been taught the game at St. Andrews was not going to help the sport find roots in America." In his autobiography, written near the end of his long career in golf, Macdonald conceded that the changes wrought by Americans had not greatly violated the essence of the Scottish sport. He concluded:

> When one considers how golf has been introduced on virgin soil 3,000 miles from the fountain-head, among people who had been taught from the time of the Revolution that they were a law unto themselves and resented any enthrallment which might be dictated by the mother country, it is really extraordinary how well the game has established itself in harmony with most that was best in it in its Scotch home. Here and there there have been dissentions, but when all is said and done there are only a few unimportant diversions from the established game as fathered by the Royal and Ancient Golf Club of St. Andrews; notably, the use of the Schenectady putter and steel shafts, both of which are infinitesimally unimportant. There are a few rules of which the interpretation varies somewhat, but this also matters little.

During the late nineteenth and early twentieth centuries, an American version of golf rooted itself in the United States. While it clearly borrowed much from Scottish and English models, the game across the Atlantic featured new elements that contrasted sharply with British forms. Most notable were the distinctive types of country and golf clubs, with their lavish clubhouses and inland park courses. Innovations in balls and clubs threatened the supremacy of the arbiters of golf in Britain. But its future prospects depended greatly on whether it could increase its acceptance among the middle and lower classes—those who could not afford to join expensive private clubs. To achieve greater appeal it needed the publicity provided by star performers and presidents prior to World War I.

NATIONALISM, EARLY CHAMPIONS, AND WAR

On Saturday afternoon, September 20, 1913, Francis Ouimet rolled in a nine-inch putt on the eighteenth green of The Country Club at Brookline, Massachusetts, to win the nineteenth open championship of the United States Golf Association. It was an improbable achievement, to say the least, and it proved to be a pivotal moment in the history of American golf. Ouimet was just twenty years of age, and his caddie, little Eddie Lowery, was a ten-year-old who had played hooky from school all week. The pair had defeated the two best golfers in the world, the visiting Englishmen Harry Vardon and Ted Ray, in an eighteen-hole playoff round. The miserable wet weather over the last few days of the championship and the pressure of the competition had not broken Ouimet's concentration or diminished his skill as he became the first amateur to win the U.S. Open in one of the most dramatic upsets in American sports history. The next day's *New York Times* reported: "Thousands of dripping rubber-coated spectators massed about Ouimet, who was hoisted to shoulders while cheer after cheer rang out in his honor. Excited women tore bunches of flowers from their bodices and hurled them at the youthful winner; hundreds of men strove to pat him on the back or shake his hand." Jerome Travers, the reigning U.S. Amateur champion and the winner of the U.S. Open in 1915, later recalled that American golf in the years between 1912 and 1914 required "only a spark to set off a conflagration which would mean that the crest had been reached. . . . And that spark flared up in this three-year period through the medium of a calm-visaged, stoical young man who dropped into this picture from a clear sky suddenly, dramatically, spectacularly."

During the formative years of American golf, national and international amateur and professional tournaments greatly increased participation and public interest in the game in the United States. Three major factors contributed to the heightened excitement over these events: the competition between amateur and professional players, the international rivalry between British and United States sportsmen, and the emergence of native stars. While some deplored the rising trend of professionalism in sports in general and golf in particular, the majority of participants were curious to witness exhibitions and tournament play by the most talented men. On October 6, 1900, in reporting Vardon's victory in the U.S. Open, the *Chicago Tribune* editorialized that professionalism would injure golf in the United States, believing that it would "tend to discourage amateurs rather than to induce them to make better and more useful efforts." It fretted that "the real trouble with professionalism in all games is that it tends to make them simply spectacles and deprives the amateur of personal participation and active interest in them." But just the opposite proved to be true in the early twentieth century, as country club and municipal course hackers became inspired by brilliant performances by both amateurs and professionals.

Competition between the best amateur and professional golfers from Great Britain and the United States was keen in the early 1900s, even though the level of skill was far higher in Great Britain than across the Atlantic. At the turn of the twentieth century the Anglo-American sports rivalry already had a fifty-year history, especially in yachting, horse racing, cricket, and prize fighting. During the 1850s a surprising triumph by John C. Stevens in a royal yacht race earned him a trophy that he then offered for international competition as the America's Cup. American horsemen also took native thoroughbreds to England to compete with mixed results in British stakes races, and all-star English cricket elevens showcased their national game to North Americans. In 1860, just prior to the Civil War, a bare-knuckle prizefight between the American John C. Heenan and the Englishman Tom Sayers created a sensation when the bout ended in a disputed decision and a riot. During the early 1900s the modern Olympic Games renewed the transatlantic sports rivalry through track and field events. As golf grew in popularity in the United States, it was only natural that Americans would try to beat the British at one of their own games.

But in order to defeat the British, the Americans had to develop champions of their own. Immigrants from Scotland and England who journeyed to the New World as professionals helped to cultivate a crop of talented golfers in the United States prior to World War I, even as they dominated the first U.S. Open Championships. As the standard of play among the most skilled of the native-born golfers rose dramatically, a few separated themselves from the rest of the pack to gain national and even international acclaim. The three who earned the greatest notoriety were Walter J.

Travis, Jerome D. Travers, and Francis Ouimet. Travis was an Australian immigrant who became known as the "Old Man" because he took up the sport in his mid-thirties. Travers was a native New Yorker who was raised in an upper-class family. Ouimet rose from humble origins to capture the nation's greatest golf prize as a young man. They came from very different backgrounds, but the achievements of each man boosted the sport significantly in the United States prior to 1917.

The golfer who first captured the imagination of the American sporting public and who paved the way for the exploits of Travis, Travers, and Ouimet was a British champion who barnstormed through the United States in 1900. Harry Vardon was a native of the Isle of Jersey who rose from obscurity to win three British Open titles in the late 1890s. His achievements caught the eye of the American sporting goods magnate Albert G. Spalding, a former star baseball player and club executive whose company manufactured golf clubs and balls. Spalding saw the marketing potential of using a superstar to promote a new product—a brand new golf ball made of gutta-percha to be named the "Vardon Flyer." Vardon declined Spalding's offer of a percentage of sales but accepted a flat fee of two thousand pounds ($10,000) for ten months of work, with the opportunity to augment his income through side purses in matches and fees from $200 to $250 for each personal appearance. As soon as he stepped off his steamship in New York City in early February, the American press in general and the golfing community in particular welcomed him as a celebrity, and over the year they treated him to rave reviews and lavish parties and dinners.

Vardon's exhibition tour across the country was a stunning success, as he awed spectators and reporters with his booming drives, crisp and accurate iron play, and deft touch on the greens. Most of his matches were against the better ball of two or even three opponents, who played against him as a team. Many of his challengers were immigrant Scotsmen who were local professionals and skilled enough to test Vardon's talents. He also played a few featured singles events against such stars as current U.S. Open champion Willie Smith. Even though Vardon was unfamiliar with the American courses and generally did not have time for practice rounds, he still broke the course record for nearly half of the clubs he visited. He also sustained only one defeat in the eighty-eight matches on his tour, losing to Alex Findlay in Miami on fairways of dirt and greens of oiled and rolled sand.

During 1900, Vardon had two other goals besides completing his promotional tour for Spalding's new golf ball: a successful defense of his British Open crown in June and a victory in the U.S. Open in October. Accordingly he sailed back across the Atlantic in May to prepare for the tournament at St. Andrews in Scotland. There he faced an old rival and two-time British Open titleholder John Henry ("J. H.") Taylor. Perhaps because he was fatigued by his long travels and emotionally drained after a visit with his estranged wife back in England, Vardon faded badly in his confrontation with Taylor. He finished second, eight strokes behind Taylor, who had now matched Vardon's three British Open Championships. With Vardon, Taylor, Willie Smith, and a few Scottish professionals as contestants, the 1900 U.S. Open Championship generated far more publicity and excitement than the first five national events. The weather cooperated nicely for the two-day, seventy-two-hole competition held at the Chicago Golf Club in Wheaton, Illinois, on October 4 and 5. The players did not disappoint the hundreds of spectators who took packed trains from Chicago and the society ladies who arrived in handsome carriages in fancy gowns. The largest gallery ever assembled for a golf tournament in the United States watched Vardon take a one-stroke lead after the first day's thirty-six holes (157–58). On the following day Vardon was able to extend his lead to two strokes, defeating Taylor by a combined score of 313 to 315, despite shooting a disappointing 80 on the final round. At the closing ceremony Vardon received the championship medal and $150 in gold, while Taylor also received $150 in gold for second place. Charles B. Macdonald, president of the Chicago Golf Club and one of the pioneers of American golf, carted off the medal for the amateur with the lowest score, far back of the leaders with a 352.

When Vardon sailed back to England in December, he could reflect on a spectacular year that was marred only by his loss to Taylor in the British Open in June. But personally and professionally he had scored triumph after triumph and had earned a U.S. Open crown and considerable income. Vardon's tour also gave a huge boost to golf in the United States, inspiring countless youth (including the seven-year-old Ouimet) and older men and women to try the game. It also led directly to the founding of hundreds of new clubs and the construction of many private and public courses. Spalding's company also benefited from the increased sale of golf clubs, but the "Vardon Flyer" ball was soon surpassed by the much livelier new rubber-cored ball invented by Coburn Haskell. From the viewpoint of American sporting pride the example of an Englishman traveling to the United States to capture a national trophy inevitably motivated sportsmen to return the favor by winning British Amateur and Open titles.

Ironically, the first American to meet that challenge was a native of Australia and an immigrant who became a naturalized citizen of the United

States as an adult. Walter J. Travis was born in 1862 and educated in schools in Melbourne. As a teenager he found work with an iron manufacturer in that city and accepted a post at its New York City branch in 1886. Ten years later while on a business trip to England he observed some men playing golf, and when he later learned that a few of his friends intended to start a golf club near his home on Long Island, he decided to purchase a set of clubs. Although he was not initially impressed with the game, after his return in 1896 he joined the newly formed Oakland Golf Club of Bayside, New York. Before long he became obsessed with the sport, but, lacking access to any professional instruction, he taught himself the rudiments of golf by poring over the first instructional books and by practicing and experimenting with his woods and irons. Thus at the age of thirty-four he began a golfing journey that would earn him high honors as a regional, national, and international champion.

During the late 1890s, Travis's rise to golfing prominence was meteoric, as he won several local and regional titles and reached the semifinal round of the 1898 U.S. Amateur Championship, losing to a Scottish immigrant, Findlay Douglas. It was a remarkable achievement for a man who had taken up the game a mere two years earlier. The following year he again lost in the semifinals to Douglas, but by then he had established himself as a major force in the American golfing world. Early in 1900 he relocated his family from Flushing to a small house just a short bicycle ride from the Garden City Golf Club.

By the early 1900s, Travis was known as the "Old Man" as a tribute to his prowess in a sport where most of the competitors were much younger. Short of stature and slender of physique, he weighed less than 140 pounds. Never a long hitter off the tees, he more than made up for his lack of length with accurate iron shots and a deadly short game. He frequently demoralized opponents with his uncanny ability to drop long putts. They also found him to be a courteous but silent competitor who preferred to concentrate entirely on the match at hand and not indulge in any socializing on the course. With a poker face and a long black cigar constantly in his hand or his mouth, he was very tough to beat. Sportswriter Grantland Rice lauded him as perhaps the most consistent golfer of his era. George W. Adair, an astute student of golf of that period, declared that "Mr. Travis could have beaten any golfer that ever lived over a course where the fairway was ten yards wide with a stiff wind blowing." In 1901 he followed up his first national amateur title with a successful defense at Atlantic City, and although he failed to make it three in a row in 1902, he did return to win another national crown at the

Nassau Country Club in 1903. Although he was medalist in the qualifying rounds each year from 1906 to 1908, he never won another U.S. Amateur Championship.

The high point of Travis's career and the first victory by an American in a British national championship was his win at the British Amateur tournament at the Royal St. George's Golf Club in Sandwich, England, in early June 1904. His week of competition began with a frigid reception and several unpleasant incidents before it ended with a satisfying triumph that deflated his hosts but thrilled his compatriots. His experiences were all the more unsettling because of the warm hospitality he had enjoyed three years earlier during a tour in 1901. He and his traveling companions were unable to obtain rooms at the hotel where the other contestants were staying. He was more annoyed and insulted when tournament officials did not provide him with a locker, which forced him to change his clothes in a common hallway and store his clubs in the professional's shop. On the course he was assigned an incompetent caddie, whom he described as a "natural-born idiot, and cross-eyed at that" and who was "too nervous to think of performing the customary duty of teeing a ball, and rarely knew where it went on any shot." Travis's requests for a replacement were ignored. Many years later, writing in the August 7, 1920, issue of *American Golfer,* he recalled that he and his friends "had to flock together, inside and outside, and not a finger was lifted nor a single step taken by a soul to make us escape the uncomfortable feeling that we were pariahs."

In the final round of the tournament Travis's opponent was Edward "Ted" Blackwell, who was famous for his long booming drives but who proved to be too erratic to defeat his relentless rival. Travis closed out the match and won the championship on the fifteenth hole of the afternoon round, 4 and 3. The crowd reacted with a telling silence and then a grudging acceptance and appreciation of Travis's skill and achievement as he became the first foreigner to win the British Amateur. The British press and leading players praised Travis's performance while American golfers and newspapers crowed over his historic achievement. From his castle in Scotland, Andrew Carnegie wrote to Travis: "Now you are among the immortals," and he described his win as "a bloodless victory which causes no tears, that makes us all happy." On June 4, 1904, the *New York Times* reflected: "No international sporting event for a long time has created the widespread interest that has been excited by Travis's victory." It added that the greatest point was that "an American . . . has met the best golfers that England and Scotland can muster on their own ground and beaten them at their own game."

A noteworthy element of Travis's triumph was his Schenectady putter, which generated substantial controversy within the British golf establishment before it was banned in 1910 by the Royal and Ancient Golf Club of St. Andrews. The center-shafted, mallet-headed club took its name from the town where it was invented in 1901 by Arthur T. Knight, an employee of General Electric. Travis had already used it in the 1902 U.S. Open at Garden City but decided to try it at Sandwich in 1904 only after he became discouraged by his poor play in practice with other putters. After a friend suggested that he switch to the Schenectady putter, his magical touch on the greens returned. Ironically, after his victory in the British Amateur he was never able to use the club effectively again. But that made no difference to the Royal and Ancient Club, the governing body of golf in Britain, which outlawed it despite the protests of Travis and others. In 1911 the USGA's Rules Committee rejected that ruling and allowed the Schenectady putter to be used in American tournaments. In 1920 Travis designed a modified version to be manufactured and named after him by the Spalding company. The Royal and Ancient Club finally dropped its prohibition in 1951.

In his later years Travis continued to play a reduced schedule of tournament golf, but he devoted most of his energy to writing, editing, and golf course design. It was only fitting that the "Old Man" ended his competitive career at the age of fifty-three with a thirty-foot putt that won the 1915 amateur championship of the Metropolitan (N.Y.) Golf Association. In 1908 he founded and edited the *American Golfer*, a periodical filled with instruction, reports on clubs and courses from across the nation, accounts of major matches, and foreign (mostly British) articles. After he sold his interest in that magazine in 1920 he worked as a stockbroker but continued his labors as a golf course architect. His career in that field began in 1899 with the Ekwanok links in Vermont. The most noteworthy of the fifty courses he designed or modified are the Essex County Club in Manchester, Massachusetts; Cape Arundel in Maine; Lookout Point in Niagara Falls, Canada; Garden City, Long Island; and Pinehurst #2 (with Donald Ross). He died in 1927.

Jerome D. Travers succeeded Travis as the next celebrated American golfer. While the two rivals differed dramatically in age and personal background, they shared much in common (besides the similarity of their last names) in their physical characteristics, style of play, and temperament. Twenty-five years younger than Travis and born into an affluent family, Travers had the advantage of learning the game at an earlier age and in a privileged household and country club setting. Yet the Old Man and his youthful challenger were strikingly similar in their slight stature, accurate iron play, passion for practice, superb putting, and intense powers of concentration. Between 1904 and 1915 the two contested many memorable matches, alternating victories at the sectional, state, and national levels. In the end, Travers wound up with one more national amateur title and one U.S. Open Championship, but he never equaled Travis's triumph in Britain.

Born in 1887, Travers took his first swings as a boy on his father's estate at Oyster Bay, Long Island. In the summer of 1904 he attracted national attention with a birdie on the twenty-first hole and a stirring come-from-behind win over Travis in the final of the Nassau Invitation tournament. It was his first confrontation with Travis in a rivalry that would continue for eleven years. The following year he became Long Island champion and in 1906 he won his first major crown in the Metropolitan (N.Y.) Golf Association championship. Four U.S. Amateur titles followed in 1907, 1908, 1912, and 1913. His greatest success came at the 1915 U.S. Open at the Baltusrol Golf Club in Springfield, New Jersey, which he won by one stroke. He then retired from championship competition and became a wealthy cotton broker on Wall Street during World War I and the roaring 1920s. The stock market crash and the ensuing Great Depression wiped out his wealth, and he spent the rest of his life in obscurity. He died in 1951.

While the championships won by Travis and Travers earned them considerable fame in the United States, and while Johnny McDermott became the first native-born American to win the U.S. Open in 1911 (he repeated the feat in 1912), the most celebrated early American golf hero was Francis Ouimet. His stunning victory in the 1913 U.S. Open was one of the greatest sports stories of the twentieth century and a pivotal event in the democratization of golf in the United States. It captured the imagination of the American people because it had all the elements of the American Dream: a young man, barely past boyhood and adolescence, from a lower-class family, playing as an amateur against the best professional golfers in the world (including two famous Englishmen), defeating his rivals with a spectacular, pressure-packed performance. The setting at The Country Club of Brookline, Massachusetts, only added to his achievement, for it showed the nation that a lad of humble origins who grew up in a modest house across the street from the swanky golf course could surpass men of privilege to reach the pinnacle of American golf. British golf writer Henry Leach later remembered the reaction to Ouimet's feat in the *American Golfer* in August 1916: "I found that the Americans also believed in fairies. It was when the full romance of a newly elevated hero, with all its glow and colour was being presented to the people. It was the epic of Francis Ouimet."

Francis Ouimet was born in 1893 into a family that had no connection or appreciation for the Scottish game that was growing in popularity in Massachusetts during the early 1900s. His father, Arthur, was a French-Canadian Catholic immigrant who struggled to support his wife and four children as gardener and handyman for the affluent citizens of Brookline. Although Arthur encouraged his sons to work as caddies at The Country Club to bring home extra money, he strongly opposed their playing the game for recreation. As a schoolboy Francis had to cope with his father's overt hostility as he honed his skills to become one of the most talented young golfers in his region. It appears that his Irish mother, the former Mary Ellen Burke, was more supportive. Francis's formal introduction to golf as a boy came through his work as a caddie, which enabled him to learn the game well enough to win tournaments in high school. At sixteen he was the Brookline High School golf team captain and number one player, and he led his squad to a state high school championship as well as capturing the individual Boston Interscholastic Championship. After he completed his junior year of high school he faced a personal and family crisis. The rules of the USGA prohibited amateurs from working as caddies after they reached the age of sixteen. Eager to enter state and national amateur tournaments and under great pressure from his father to find a job, he quit school and found work as a stockboy in a Boston dry goods store. At eighteen he found a better position in the Boston sporting goods store of Wright and Ditson. Its founder was George Wright, a former major league baseball star (and future member of the Hall of Fame) who was also one of the pioneers of golf in Boston. With Wright's encouragement the young Ouimet won the 1913 Massachusetts State Amateur Championship in June after barely surviving the second round when his opponent missed an eighteen-inch putt that would have eliminated him. In early September of that year he surprised the golf world by nearly winning the gold medal for lowest qualifying round in the national amateur tournament. He lost in the second round to the defending champion, Jerome Travers, who would go on to capture the 1913 title as well. But Ouimet's sparkling performance had caught the eye of prominent golf writers, including Bernard Darwin of England, who called him "the find of the tournament."

The 1913 U.S. Open was scheduled for two weeks later at The Country Club in Brookline, and the president of the USGA, Robert Watson, was so impressed with Ouimet's play at Garden City that he persuaded George Wright to give him some extra time off from his clerkship so he could compete on the course that he knew so well. Ouimet's challenge was for-

midable because the field at The Country Club featured such luminaries as
the legendary Harry Vardon, British Open champion Ted Ray, the French
professional Louis Tellier, Wilfred Reid from England, two-time defending
champion John J. McDermott, and a novice named Walter Hagen. Ouimet's first task was to find a caddie for his qualifying round, and only a few
minutes before his starting time he selected a pint-sized ten-year-old named
Eddie Lowery. Eddie and his brother Jack had played hooky from school
the day before to watch Ouimet practice, but after a truant officer visited
their home that evening, their mother made them promise they would go to
school the next day. Jack followed his mother's orders, but Eddie skipped off
to the golf course in Brookline, persuaded Ouimet to allow him to carry his
bag, and thus became an important character in the story that soon became
part of American golf folklore. On Tuesday, September 16, Ouimet scored
a respectable 152 for thirty-six holes, placing fifth among the qualifiers
for the championship of seventy-two holes scheduled for Thursday and
Friday. Sportswriters and fans rooting for an American victory fretted that
the Englishmen Ray, Vardon, and Reid headed the list.

On the first day of the main event, Ouimet recovered from a shaky first
round of 77 to close with a 74 for a total of 151, which left him four shots
behind Reid and Vardon and two behind Ray. On Friday morning, a soak-
ing, all-day rain created miserably wet conditions for all the contestants, but
Ouimet's 74 for his third round kept him in contention. In the afternoon a
bad first nine on his final round (43) put him on the brink of elimination.
As he and Lowery approached the fifteenth tee they learned that Vardon
and Ray had tied for the lead with total scores of 304. Ouimet needed to
play one under par for the remaining four holes to join the Englishmen in a
playoff the next day. A miraculous chip on the fifteenth hole and a nine-foot
par putt on the sixteenth green kept him in contention. On the seventeenth
a twenty-foot putt gave him the birdie he needed to tie Vardon and Ray,
and on the eighteenth he steadied his nerves and sank a five-foot putt for
the par that secured his place in the playoff.

On Saturday morning, September 20th, the rains continued as Ouimet
and his two English opponents approached the first tee for their ten o'clock
starting time. At the beginning of the tournament Lowery had prophesied
that Ouimet would score a 72 for one round of the championship, and this
would be his last chance. The trio closely contested the first nine holes,
and at the turn they were all tied with 38 strokes each. At the short tenth
hole Ouimet took a one-shot lead with a par three. On the twelfth Ouimet
gained another stroke on both men with a par four, but on the thirteenth

Left to right: Harry Vardon, Francis Ouimet, Edward Ray (Ted Ray). Ouimet won the 1913 U.S. Open Championship, held at The Country Club (Original Course), Brookline, Mass. Photo is by George S. Pietzcker, St. Louis, Mo. AP/WIDE WORLD PHOTOS.

Vardon got one stroke back on the leader with a birdie three. All three scored bogey fives for the fourteenth, but on the fifteenth Ray dropped out of contention with a double bogey six. Ouimet and Vardon both parred the short sixteenth, but on the seventeenth hole Ouimet repeated his stunning performance of the day before with a birdie three, as the Englishmen both carded fives. A safe four on the finishing hole for Ouimet earned him the title and fulfilled his caddie's prediction of a round of 72. A double bogey for Vardon on the eighteenth dropped him to a 77, while a finishing birdie for Ray still left him last with a 78.

A scene of jubilation greeted the new young champion as he walked off the eighteenth green to a thunderous ovation by thousands of drenched spectators who fully grasped the magnitude of the moment for American golf. So did sportswriters on both sides of the Atlantic. During the celebration, members of the crowd spontaneously offered Ouimet money, which he refused, citing his amateur standing. But he did ask some friends to pass a hat around for a collection for his caddie that netted Lowery more than a hundred dollars—a small fortune for a ten-year-old boy in 1913. As Ouimet accepted his trophy, he humbly expressed his surprise over his victory, but he also pointedly remarked: "I simply tried my best to keep this cup from going to our friends across the water." He added: "I am very glad to have been the agency for keeping the cup in America." The next day a *New York Times* editorial proclaimed Ouimet's triumph as "substantial and astonishing, something to crow about . . . moderately." It also called the outcome "an awful blow to British golfing pride, worse even than the triumph on English soil in the amateur championship games of Mr. Travis a few years ago." From the English side the immediate reaction was one of stunned disbelief followed by a realization of what Ouimet's achievement meant for the growing Anglo-American golf rivalry. In the *American Golfer* in October 1913, the English writer Leach grudgingly admitted that "a new era has begun since the twentieth of September." He explained: "America has graduated now as a first-class golfing power. I am glad of it; it is all for the good of the game, and Francis Ouimet, besides having achieved immortal fame among golfers, has done something splendid for the good of that game."

Francis Ouimet (horseshoe in hand) being carried by celebrants after winning the 1913 U.S. Open at The Country Club (Original Course), Brookline, Mass. His caddie, Eddie Lowery, is pictured in front. Copyright Unknown/Courtesy USGA Archives.

Ouimet's victory in 1913 gained him lifelong honors as an American sports icon, but while it remained the high point of his golfing career, he did win other foreign and American titles. In 1914 he played poorly in British competitions, but he captured the French amateur national crown just weeks before the beginning of World War I. That summer he achieved one of his lifelong goals when he won the USGA's national amateur championship—a feat he repeated seventeen years later in 1931. In 1916 he found himself in the midst of a controversy when the USGA declared him to be a professional and banned him from amateur tournaments because of his connection with his new sporting goods company, Ouimet and Sullivan. Ouimet defied the USGA by playing and winning the Western Golf Association's Championship in 1917. Later that year he enlisted in the army, and in January 1918 he regained his amateur status when the USGA ruled that Ouimet had severed his ties to his sporting goods firm when he began his military service.

◎ ◎ ◎

During the years that immediately preceded American entry into the First World War, golf professionals residing in the United States founded an organization that would profoundly shape the future of the sport in the nation. The men who launched the Professional Golfers' Association of America (PGA) in 1916 were mostly transplanted British players who were keenly aware of the long-standing prejudice against professionalism in sports in the United States, especially in golf. The USGA had struggled with the issue of defining amateurism since its inception, and in 1915 and 1916 it once again revisited this thorny issue when it rewrote sections of its bylaws and voided Ouimet's amateur standing. Writing in the January 1917 issue of *Golf Illustrated* in defense of the USGA's action against Ouimet, Charles B. Macdonald underscored the ideal of amateur athletics even as he recognized that professionals had the right to form their own association. He explained: "In this game where we leave our studies, our courts, our counting houses and our offices for rest and recreation to enspirit [*sic*] us to do that which we are trying to do in this world in the noblest manner, there should be nothing of materialism, which I consider professionalism resembles. Those who wish to play the materialistic side of the game are perfectly at liberty to create their own association, to bring their own friends with them, to play their own game, and to do whatever they please, but why try to sully the United States Golf Association which was born honestly and faithfully to keep pure an ideal game?"

On January 17, 1916, a group of professional and amateur golfers initiated the planning of the PGA at a luncheon in New York City hosted by Rodman Wanamaker, a wealthy department store magnate. The purpose of the gathering was to form a national association of professional golfers that would address several of their problems, including their lack of control over open tournaments and especially their desire to secure suitable club positions for professionals who were seeking employment. The meeting appointed a committee of seven professionals who were instructed to draw up a constitution and bylaws. Not surprisingly, that committee then decided to model the new organization after the charter and rules of the Professional Golfers' Association of Great Britain. The American PGA's committee chair, James Hepburn of the National Golf Links of America, had been secretary of the British PGA for twelve years. In February, a subcommittee announced the organization's purposes, which included promoting golf (including greenkeeping and course architecture), protecting the mutual interests of members, scheduling meetings and tournaments, establishing a benevolent fund for relief of deserving members, and helping members find employment at clubs. That body also established six classes of membership, with the right to vote at PGA meetings restricted to those in Class A (professional golfers with club affiliations). In April, the PGA's organizational committee elected eighty-two charter members and announced plans for a preliminary tournament to be held at Van Cortlandt Park in July and the first official PGA Championship for the Rodman Wanamaker trophy to be held in the fall. One year later the PGA formally adopted a permanent constitution and listed a membership of nearly four hundred, most of whom were club professionals. It also announced that it had taken over the placement of professionals at clubs, which had formerly been supervised by the USGA, and that it had gained a voice in the selection of courses for the U.S. Open.

The PGA held its inaugural championship in mid-October 1916 at the Siwanoy Country Club in Bronxville, New York. Wanamaker contributed prize money of $2,580 (with first place worth $500) plus a silver trophy. Thirty-two men from regional medal play competitions qualified for the five match play rounds. The tournament provided plenty of thrills for American golf enthusiasts, as the winner was not determined until the final stroke on the thirty-sixth green of the last contest. "Long" Jim Barnes holed a pressure-packed four-foot putt to earn a narrow 1–up victory over Jock Hutchison, who had just missed sinking a putt only inches farther from the cup than Barnes's. Barnes was an Englishman and Hutchison hailed from Scotland, but both held positions at American country clubs. The victor earned $500, a diamond studded gold medal, the silver trophy, and the title. Barnes repeated as PGA titleholder in 1919 (no championships were held during the war years), and he added a U.S. Open title in 1921 and a British Open crown in 1925.

◎ ◎ ◎

Although the male champions attracted most of the attention of American golfing enthusiasts prior to World War I, the most talented female golfers were also competing for honors on the nation's fairways and greens. Analysts of early women's golf believed that its popularity was due at least in part to its competitive aspect, both for individuals against the course and ultimately even against men. In 1900, Lilian Brooks, a leading early player, viewed the rise of women's golf as a "'sign of the times,' a significant indication of the steady march of progress, that men and women are constantly drawing comparisons between each other." For Brooks, bicycling for women was a refreshing and relaxing recreation, but was not as appealing as a competitive game like golf. She explained that the advantages males had over females in sports were not just a matter of superior strength: "Men have played games all their lives—they and their fathers before them. They have competed all their lives, and will go on competing to the end. Life is the same old question of the 'survival of the fittest.' ... In consequence, in golf, as in every contest, men have the advantage over women of familiarity with competitive play." Over the next few decades the leading female golfers would labor mightily to overcome the physical and cultural handicaps they experienced as they tried to narrow the gap between themselves and the premier male players. But even an average female country club player could enjoy a friendly match against a man using the handicap system.

For the championship caliber female golfers, the ultimate challenge was direct competition against men, without using handicap strokes. In June 1917 in *Golf Illustrated*, U.S. Women's Amateur champion Alexa Stirling argued that at the club and possibly even at the local and regional levels the most talented women should be allowed to compete directly against men. In "A Plea for the Woman Expert," Stirling maintained that each club should allow special privileges to its best female golfers, including the chance to play for "all the club trophies." Participation in men's tournaments, she explained, "would do no harm unless it hurt the dignity of any of such as happened to be beaten by any of the women. If it did, the plan would be an excellent lesson in chivalry, and golf would have proved its possibilities as a moral force in the community!"

As girls and young women flocked to the links in the 1890s and early 1900s, those who were the most talented and the most competitive by temperament entered club, regional, state, and national tournaments. The fact that these championships were inaugurated so early in golf's history in the United States testifies both to the sport's popularity and its acceptance as an appropriate activity for competition by ladies. Although the best female golfers in the 1890s regularly carded scores of over 100 strokes for eighteen holes, the standard of play improved dramatically after the turn of the century. By the World War I era the leading women's scores ranged in the upper 70s to low 80s. By the Roaring Twenties the ladies who were national champions were celebrities in the golfing world, symbols of the Age of the New Woman.

The Shinnecock Hills club of Long Island, New York, was among the first to actively promote women's golf, and its pioneering female players dominated the first national amateur championships sponsored by the USGA. In 1895 Lucy Barnes (Mrs. Charles S. Brown) carried off the inaugural trophy, needing 132 strokes for the eighteen-hole event, held at the Meadow Brook Club in Hempstead, Long Island. Although she scored an eleven on the first hole and a fourteen on the seventeenth, she was still able to edge out the runner-up by two shots. The following year Beatrix Hoyt won the national women's title, bettering Mrs. Brown's total by 37 strokes in carding a respectable 95. Hoyt was only sixteen years old and held the honor of being the youngest USGA women's champion until 1971, when Laura Baugh displaced her. Hoyt was representative of many young women of the privileged classes in the United States who took up golf in the 1890s. The granddaughter of Salmon P. Chase, Lincoln's secretary of the treasury and later chief justice of the United States, she started playing at the Westchester Country Club in 1895. In June of the following year she went to Shinnecock, where she shot a 45 and broke the record for the nine-hole ladies course at that fashionable summer colony. Her score of 97 on the eighteen-hole men's course at Shinnecock set a women's record, preparing her for the three national titles she captured between 1896 and 1898. She competed for two more years before retiring in 1900 at the ripe old age of twenty.

Harriot Sumner Curtis and Margaret Curtis were golfing sisters from a prominent Massachusetts family who were early national champions, social reformers, and founders of the Curtis Cup for international women's golf competition. They were the ninth and tenth children (and the fourth and fifth daughters) of Colonel Greeley Stevenson Curtis and Harriot Appleton Curtis. Their father had served in the cavalry during the Civil War and retired early to a life of leisure filled with horses, yachts, and country club life; their mother was the daughter of a financier, congressman, and industrialist. Harriot and Margaret shared athletic childhoods, competing with their older brothers and sisters in baseball, tennis, golf, and many other games at their family's estate at Manchester, Massachusetts. They shared a special connection to the nation's golf pioneers, for their second cousin, Laurence Curtis, was an early advocate of the sport at The Country Club of Brookline, a founder of the USGA, and its second president. With Laurence's encouragement the girls learned to play golf in the 1890s at the Essex County Club.

Although Harriot was soon overshadowed by her younger sister, she was the first to bring golfing honors to her family when she won the 1906 women's national amateur championship. The following year she lost to Margaret in the only all-sister final in the history of the championship. While she never captured another national trophy, she maintained a keen interest in the game for the rest of her long life. Outside the world of sports she followed a path typical of many upper-class women in the Progressive Era who never married but who devoted their lives to social reform work. Harriot's calling was civil rights, as she served as dean of women for the Hampton Institute, a predominantly African American college in Virginia. She died in 1974.

Perhaps because she was the youngest child in a high-achieving family, Margaret was the most successful sportswoman of the clan and one of the most talented multisport athletes of the early decades of the twentieth century. She added national amateur women's titles in 1911 and 1912 to her 1907 victory, and she also shared the 1908 United States women's doubles tennis championship with her partner, Evelyn Sears. The latter feat earned her the distinction of being the only woman to hold national crowns in golf and tennis in the same year, since the tennis final preceded the 1908 golf championship. Like her sister, Margaret was an energetic woman who remained single all of her life and who devoted herself to improving the lives of those less fortunate. In 1904 she enrolled in the first class of the School of Social Work at Simmons College, which prepared her for a position with the Associated Charities of Boston. During World War I she traveled to Paris, where she worked for a Red Cross agency that assisted war refugees. After the war she devoted herself to child health clinics and aid to refugees in eastern Europe and Greece. During World War II she answered yet another call to duty as she volunteered to be Massachusetts's chief of salvage operations for the War Production Board. She died in 1965.

Margaret Curtis, Sallie Ainslee, and Harriot Curtis on the grounds of the Midlothian
Golf Club, Midlothian, Ill., during the 1907 U.S. Women's Amateur Championship.
Margaret Curtis won the title. SDN-006006, *Chicago Daily News* negatives collection,
Chicago History Museum.

Perhaps the most lasting contribution to golf by the Curtis sisters was the
Curtis Cup. The origins of this event may be traced back to the spring of
1905, when a group of American women journeyed to England to participate
in the British women's championship. While there, Harriot and Margaret
played in an informal international challenge between ladies from Great
Britain and the United States. Although the British side trounced the American ladies by a score of six matches to one, the experience made a lasting
impression on the Curtis sisters and motivated them to propose a regular
event between women golfers from both sides of the Atlantic. In 1927 they
purchased a trophy in Boston and offered it as a prize for the competition,
but a series of delays over arrangements delayed the inaugural match until
May 1932, at Wentworth, England. For her championships, her founding
of the Curtis Cup, her work in fostering junior girls' golf in Massachusetts,
and her donations of golf balls for patients' use in recreational therapy in
veterans hospitals, Margaret received the 1957 USGA Bob Jones Award for
"distinguished sportsmanship in golf."

A star of ladies' golf of the World War I era was Alexa Stirling, of Atlanta,

Georgia. A three-time national women's champion, she was tutored as a girl by a Scottish professional, Stewart Maiden, and she was also a childhood playmate of Bob Jones. At the age of twelve she defeated Jones (age seven) and a few other playmates in an informal children's tournament, but the boy scorekeeper gave the cup to Jones instead of to Stirling. He explained

Alexa Stirling on the grounds of the Onwentsia Country Club in Lake Forest, Ill., 1915. She won the U.S. Women's Amateur Championship in 1916, 1919, and 1920. SDN-060500, *Chicago Daily News* negatives collection, Chicago History Museum.

in March 1917 in *Golf Illustrated*: "We couldn't have a girl beat us." Jones kept the cup; years later he admitted that it rightfully belonged to Alexa, but joked that he wouldn't give it back because "the statute of limitations has run against her claim." As a youth, Stirling played many rounds of thirty-six holes with Jones and Perry Adair (another child prodigy), carrying fifteen clubs without a caddie. Although Stirling was cheated out of a cup at age twelve, she won a far more valuable prize in 1916—the jeweled trophy given by the USGA to the women's national amateur champion. During the war she served in the motor corps as a driver, advancing from sergeant to lieutenant. Although the USGA suspended championship competition for two years, she performed patriotic duty by participating in many four-ball benefit matches for the Red Cross with Jones, Adair, and Elaine Rosenthal. After the war she added two more national titles in 1919 and 1920 and won other regional championships through the 1920s, averaging close to eighty strokes per round. A multitalented woman, she also worked in New York in the bond business and found time to play the violin, which she had learned as a child and which she credited with helping her golf game by strengthening her hands and wrists. In 1925 she married W. G. Fraser, moved to Ottawa, Ontario, Canada, and raised three children. In 1950 she was named one of North America's six greatest female golfers and was elected to the Ladies Professional Golfers' Association Hall of Fame.

National and international sporting competitions between Americans and Englishmen first excited public interest in the mid-1800s, and once golf took root in the United States in the 1880s and 1890s, a keen rivalry soon developed between players from both sides of the Atlantic. Harry Vardon's tour and triumph in the U.S. Open in 1900 and his return with Ted Ray in 1913 generated enormous publicity for the Scottish pastime in the United States. Even though Walter Travis was a transplanted Australian, the American golfing fraternity claimed his epic victory in the British Amateur Championship in England in 1904 as a triumph for Uncle Sam, because Travis had learned to play the game in the United States. But American golf really came of age at The Country Club of Brookline, Massachusetts on September 20th, 1913, when a young amateur, Francis Ouimet, conquered two celebrated English professionals to win his nation's open title. Three years later native professionals launched the PGA. The example of the amateur men inspired athletic-minded females to improve their skills on fairways and greens, with Beatrix Hoyt, the Curtis sisters, and Alexa Stirling leading the way. American championship golf for both sexes was off to a rousing start prior to World War I.

◎ ◎ ◎

As golf gained in popularity during its formative years in the United States, a few presidents took up the sport with enthusiasm, even as they fretted over how the masses might view their participation in a pastime that had strong associations with the privileged classes. But presidential golf turned out to be a positive force in the democratization of the sport in America, as the examples of William Howard Taft and Woodrow Wilson inspired countless novices to try the Scottish game. While World War I temporarily slowed the progress of the sport in the United States, it also provided an opportunity for golfers to combine their patriotism with their favorite pastime through charitable events.

Between the 1890s and World War I, the chief executives had to weigh the positive and negative political fallout of playing golf, including the opportunity to help promote the Scottish game in America. William McKinley was the first American president to try the game of golf, but his first outings were unsuccessful and he lost interest in the sport. Taft and Wilson were the first two presidents to play golf with a passion; both did so to improve their health and for recreation and diversion from the burdens and pressures of office. These two pioneering golfing presidents set a precedent for their successors, most of whom were also ardent linksmen, albeit of widely differing talents. Over the remainder of the twentieth century the nation's chief executives would also exhibit varying patterns of combining golf with work.

When McKinley's assassination elevated Theodore Roosevelt to the White House in the fall of 1901, the nation gained a chief executive who was an energetic and exuberant boxer, outdoorsman, horseback rider, big game hunter, and tennis player—but not a golfer. Roosevelt had tried the game in the 1890s and had even been a member of the Oyster Bay Golf Club near his home on the north shore of Long Island. But he dismissed the sport as "too tame," and he was uncomfortable when his hand-picked successor for the Republican Party's nomination for the presidency in 1908, William Howard Taft, was ridiculed in the press for his obsession with golf. Taft had started playing the game in 1894 at his summer home in Murray Bay, Quebec, with the encouragement of his younger brother Henry, who was one of the first members of the St. Andrew's Golf Club in Yonkers, New York. Weighing in at around 350 pounds and squatting awkwardly with his driver at the tee, Taft was an ideal subject for fat jokes and especially for lampooning by cartoonists and photographers. Roosevelt was concerned that Taft would look ridiculous in these pictures, and he also worried about the potential political impact of Taft's playing a game still popularly associated with rich plutocrats. As Taft campaigned across the country, Roosevelt sent him some public relations advice. He wrote: "It would seem incredible that anyone would care one way or the other about your playing golf, but I have received literally hundreds of letters from the West protesting about it. I myself play tennis, but that game is a little more familiar; besides, you never saw a photograph of me playing tennis. I'm careful about that; photographs on horseback, yes; tennis, no. And golf is fatal."

But Taft loved to play golf and he sensed correctly that the sport would not prove to be fatal for his or his successors' presidential ambitions. He ignored Roosevelt's warnings and persisted in playing golf during breaks in his campaign schedule. In January 1909 after his election as president, he praised golf as a game for the people and not just for the plutocrats. In a letter to the St. Andrew's Golf Club on the occasion of its twentieth anniversary, he stated: "Preceding the late election campaign there were many of my sympathizers and supporters who deprecated its becoming known that I was addicted to golf, as an evidence of aristocratic tendencies and a desire to play only a rich man's game. You know and I know that there is nothing more democratic than golf; that there is nothing which furnishes a greater test of character and self-restraint, nothing which puts one more on an equality with one's fellows or, I may say, puts one lower than one's fellows than the game of golf." As president, Taft played golf most afternoons, scoring mostly in the 90s and low 100s. His contemporaries viewed him as competent on the links, although modern historians rate him as one of the worst of the twentieth-century presidential players. In an often-told tale on foreign policy matters, Taft became furious when an aide suggested that he meet with the president of Chile during his visit to Washington. Taft retorted: "I'll be damned if I will give up my game of golf to see this fellow." Satirists had a field day with Taft's golf obsession. The humorist Finley Peter Dunne's popular character, Mr. Dooley, quoted Taft: "Golf is th' thing I like best next t' leavin' Washington!"

Although satirists, cartoonists, and the press in general made fun of Taft's passion for golf, there is considerable evidence that his example significantly boosted the popularity of the game among the general public during his term of office. On August 8, 1909, the *New York Times* reported "an unprecedented congestion of players on the city's golf courses," with the numbers doubling since Taft's election. That paper thought that the increase in golfers "is indicative that Americans are imitative in their patriotism, and diligently

President William H. Taft on the golf links, Hot Springs, Va., December 30, 1908. Library of Congress, Prints and Photographs Division, LC-USZ62-41721 DLC.

follow the examples set by the head of the Nation." The following year, Walter J. Travis also credited the latest golf boom to Taft's influence. During his final months in office Taft also contributed to the movement for more municipal golf courses by making several pleas for the construction of new public links in Philadelphia and Washington, D.C.

When Woodrow Wilson took the oath of office in March 1913 as President of the United States, the nation gained a Democratic administration with new domestic and foreign policies, but its new chief executive shared and even exceeded Taft's devotion to golf. While in the White House, Wilson played the game even more frequently than his predecessor, but in his case practice did not make perfect, for Wilson was a chronic duffer whose average score for eighteen holes was probably around 115. Like Taft, Wilson took to the links for health and escape from the burdens of office, but unlike Taft his obsession with golf did no damage to his public image. News reporters were much kinder to Wilson on golf matters, perhaps because presidential golf was now taken for granted, or perhaps because they respected Wilson more than Taft as a hard worker, a scholar, and a statesman.

Wilson's love affair with golf began late in life, in 1898, at the age of forty-two, while he was a professor at Princeton. Wilson played golf most weekday mornings and Saturday afternoons, but never on Sunday, throughout the year. Cold or wet weather rarely deterred him. His regular playing partner was his physician, Dr. Cary T. Grayson. But in 1915 the regular twosome of Wilson and Grayson became a threesome when Wilson fell in love with an attractive widow, Edith Bolling Galt. Wilson's first wife, Ellen Axson Wilson, had died a few months earlier, and he suffered from severe bouts of melancholy and loneliness until he met Galt. This presidential storybook romance of love at first sight blossomed on the golf course. After her marriage to the president, Edith Galt Wilson gained the distinction of being the inaugural first lady to play golf.

Remarkably, Wilson doggedly kept to his golf routine despite numerous moments of high drama during his two terms in the White House. Those included conflicts and military intervention in Mexico, his election to a second term, German submarine attacks that cost American lives, and the final confrontation with Germany that led to the United States's entry into the First World War. Early in February 1917, Edith Wilson suggested that Wilson continue his golf even as he and his aides debated the proper response to Germany's resumption of submarine attacks on neutral shipping. In his diary, Colonel Edward House, Wilson's closest adviser, recalled that Mrs. Wilson asked whether House thought that "it would look badly if the President went on the links." House replied: "I thought the American people would feel that he should not do anything so trivial at such a time." But Wilson did play golf that fateful spring, including an early morning round on the Saturday he drafted the message in which he asked Congress to declare war on Germany. His wartime golfing does not seem to have provoked any outcry from the American people. Wilson, Grayson, and Edith kept playing, although now they were joined by an expanded secret service detail, with agents hiding in the woods, keeping out of sight of the presidential party. In the end it was Wilson's trip to Europe after the Armistice in November 1918 that sharply curtailed his time on the links. In France early in 1919 he was able to play only two rounds as he negotiated the Treaty of Versailles with French, British, and Italian leaders, and after his return he was preoccupied with his campaign for ratification of the Treaty. In September a paralyzing stroke crippled him and ended his days on the fairways and greens.

◎ ◎ ◎

During the early decades of American golf, the nation fought two wars. The Spanish-American War of 1898 was brief and posed few if any problems for the game that was still in its infancy in the United States, but World War I (called the "Great War" in its time) lasted much longer and was far more challenging to the sport on both sides of the Atlantic. The war emergency raised major issues among the Anglo-American golfing fraternity concerning the propriety of indulging in their favorite pastime at a time of immense carnage and suffering. But the conflict also provided the opportunity for national and regional associations and individual clubs to use golf as a means of promoting physical fitness, preparedness, and patriotism, especially through fundraising events to support the Red Cross and other charities. Some army officials also believed that golf in military camps could help with the training of troops. When the war ended in November 1918, American golfers had endured the trials of the conflict quite well and were poised to begin a decade of dramatic growth.

Although the United States did not enter the Great War until April 1917, from the beginning of the fighting Americans were well aware of the devastating impact of the combat on British society, including its effects on golf. In October 1914, Henry Leach, the British correspondent for the *American Golfer*, reported the grim news from London. Many English and Scottish men had enlisted in the armed services, major tournaments (including the British Open) had been canceled, golf periodicals had gone out of business, and links had been turned into military camps. Leach was hopeful that a special bond would develop between the golf communities in America and Britain. He wrote: "We, England and America, are the two greatest powers of the golfing world; no other is to be compared to us. Certainly our enemy is one of the least of the golfing countries though she may be no worse for that. The point is that golf is a freemasonry, a brotherhood if ever there was one. We in this game do understand one another." He asked: "Give your sympathy to us and not to our enemies. We deserve it." His plea was answered, for during the war the newly formed Professional Golfers' Association (PGA) of America did assist Great Britain's professional golfers, and in 1920 the latter group offered a prize medal for competition in the PGA Championship in recognition of American assistance during the Great War.

World War I was the first great military conflict of the United States in the twentieth century, and during that trial its citizens weighed the proper role of athletics in American society in wartime. It was a subject that would be revisited during World War II and to a lesser extent during the Korean and Vietnam wars. Sports in general in 1917 benefited from a federal government policy that supported athletics "as a great builder of material for the army as well as a necessary requisite for men already in the service." Golf in particular was thought to be an ideal activity for middle-aged men who were not subject to the draft but who still wished to get themselves into shape should they be called for some kind of service in the future. On April 15, 1917, the *New York Times* explained: "The great benefit that golf can accomplish . . . is to bring business men out of their offices and fit them for marches and military manoeuvres [*sic*] perhaps better than any other sport these men could take up." In January 1918 *Golf Illustrated* commended the federal government for permitting both baseball and golf to continue during the war emergency. It remarked that officials "early realized that though baseball was and always will be the *national* game, golf is essentially the *game* of the nation, and as such must be preserved at all costs." That journal argued that golf was for all age groups, was especially valuable for those who managed the business of war, and would prove useful "to give back health to those golfers of a military age who will be invalided [*sic*] home from France."

Thousands of young American golfers from public and private courses and clubs did heed the call to duty, from such celebrated stars as Francis Ouimet to college athletes, country club members, and obscure duffers. Charlie Lanigan was a former Harvard baseball captain and golfer who used golf metaphors in a letter to a friend to explain his challenge as an officer in a field artillery unit in France. He wrote that "it's a hard course, full of water hazards and bunkers and ditches, and you've got to play the ball where it lays. There is one advantage here, though, Grand Army rule 716 allows the use of dynamite, so when in doubt we don't lift and lose two, but just blast." Country clubs across the nation suspended the dues of those who volunteered to serve, and at the end of the war they welcomed back those who returned safely and dedicated memorials to those who sacrificed their lives for the cause. The Country Club of Brookline even adopted a rule to expel members who were citizens of nations at war with the United States, but the club's records do not indicate that there were any such men.

Shortly after President Woodrow Wilson asked Congress to declare war against Germany in April 1917, representatives from national associations in golf, tennis, and amateur and intercollegiate athletics agreed to cancel all championship competitions for that year. It was the sense of these officials that holding national tournaments might "interfere with a man's first duty to his country," but that scheduling lesser events would keep the spirit of athletics alive in the nation and also aid the Red Cross through fundraising. The group's formal resolution affirmed that "the youth of the nation should be encouraged to become physically fit and mentally alert, through the stimulus of athletic competition ... but that by reason of the state of war now existing it is not advisable to hold championship events at any date subsequent to a call of the Government for volunteers or the enactment and operation of a bill for compulsory service." It also recommended substituting certificates in place of the usual prizes or medals given to the winners of special tournaments arranged as patriotic demonstrations for the benefit of the Red Cross.

The USGA honored the patriotic policy and canceled its national open, amateur, and women's tournaments for the duration of the war. Instead, it arranged a "Liberty Tournament" on July 4, 1917, across the country in which 485 clubs representing forty-four states participated. The event raised more than $72,000 for the purchase of ambulances to be used in France. The USGA also organized a Patriotic Open in June to replace its regular open competition. The PGA supported the patriotic golf movement by encouraging its members to offer their services free of charge for charitable wartime exhibitions. By the end of the year the *Times* estimated that all national, regional, and local special events had raised about $180,000 for the war relief fund. But while there was great general satisfaction with the new wartime policy in 1917, there were at least a few dissidents who argued for a resumption of championship tournament play in 1918, at least at a local level. 1917 and 1918 were banner years for golf exhibitions staged to raise money for the Red Cross and other wartime charities. Francis Ouimet, Chick Evans, Walter Hagen, Jim Barnes, Jock Hutchison, and the young Bob Jones were the leading stars of this touring road show. One day before the Armistice, two aging stars of the early years of American golf, Findlay Douglas and Walter Travis, played a charity exhibition match, won by Travis. Afterwards, at an auction, the controversial Schenectady putter Travis had used in winning the 1904 British Amateur Championship went for $1,700. The funds benefited the wartime relief cause, and the lucky high bidder got a priceless item. In addition to hosting charitable special events, country clubs could also display their patriotism and aid the wartime cause in a variety of ways. These included remitting dues for members who enlisted in the armed services of the United States, growing vegetables or keeping sheep on their courses, conserving coal by closing their clubhouses in the winter, and by opening their links to servicemen who were convalescing.

By 1918 it was evident that golf had served the nation quite well as a means of both patriotic expression and fundraising, and officials in both the War Department and the USGA were also weighing its merits as an appropriate recreation for men in the armed forces. In the fall, the Commission on Training Camp Activities of the War Department endorsed the introduction of golf in military cantonments, having "conclusive evidence that golf provides a form of recreational activity which plays an important part in counteracting the tension of intensive training." The War Department planned to lay out nine-hole courses near the bases. The policy was endorsed by the USGA, which urged its member clubs to assist by providing clubs, balls, and other equipment. Some also envisioned golf as a beneficial activity for injured soldiers recovering from their wounds. Golf also became popular for servicemen who remained in France after the war ended. In April 1919, Sergeant William Rautenbush won the golf championship of the American Expeditionary Forces over Lieutenant James W. Hubbell. The victor was a member of the Garfield Golf Club of Chicago, while his opponent was a former Harvard player and intercollegiate eastern champion.

With the return of peace in November 1918, golf officials in the United States looked forward to resuming regular championship tournaments. They memorialized those golfers who had made the ultimate sacrifice, and they took great satisfaction in the charitable work accomplished by the nation's players and clubs. The *Times* estimated that about 15 percent of the members of private clubs served in the armed forces. In January 1919 the USGA reported that 7,359 men representing 287 clubs had enlisted in the army or navy. Among those golfers killed in action was William R. Cottrell, the professional at the Plymouth Country Club in Massachusetts. A native of England (and still a British subject) who had emigrated to the United States in January 1914, he nevertheless accepted the American draft. He died on October 6, 1918, two days after his twenty-seventh birthday, a casualty of the battle of Meuse, Argonne. Others served the cause by raising nearly half a million dollars for the Red Cross and two or three hundred thousand dollars for other wartime relief funds in 1918.

With an avid player as president and commander-in-chief, the United States and its golfing community both survived the emergency of the Great

War. Future presidents (especially Dwight D. Eisenhower) would equal or even surpass Wilson in their devotion to golf, and World War II would present even greater challenges for the nation and for the sport. But in the short run, the return of peace in 1918 witnessed the beginning of a new round of growth for American golf, with sharp increases in country club memberships and new heroes. The first golden age of golf lay ahead.

A GAME FOR
THE PEOPLE

On June 26, 1910, the *New York Times* magazine section featured a satirical article about male and female golfers on the public course in Van Cortlandt Park in the Bronx in New York City. The author believed that the reader would find it hard "to keep from laughing outright at the self-conscious man who tries the game for the first time." He added: "If he is a large man dressed in the up-to-date golfing attire which only the veriest novice affects, it is all the more pitiful." The writer could also not resist ridiculing "the woman golfer," whom he believed was "not popular on the links." While he conceded that "occasionally a fairly good player commands admiration," he noted that "for the most part they are barely tolerated." He explained that "the average woman with a golf club is a source of terror and vexation to male players. Most of them attire themselves as if for a promenade down Broadway. . . . The daintily attired creature gets the ball out of the trap regardless of the number of strokes, and then sits calmly down and shakes the sand out of her four-and-a-halfs. She handles her clubs exactly like a broom and pushes the ball before her."

In the long run, the advent of municipal golf courses was the most critical factor in the democratization of American golf. Beginning in the mid-1890s, crusaders for golf for the people struggled mightily to convince public officials and skeptical citizens and taxpayers that the new Scottish game was not simply a pastime for the idle rich and that towns and cities should provide courses for the masses. The crowds of white, middle-class men and women who trekked to the first public links before World War I (many of whom arrived before sunrise on holidays and weekends) proved that golf was far more than a passing fad. Youth from a variety of lower-class urban ethnic and racial groups gained their first exposure to golf through their work as caddies on both public and private courses.

The creation and early popularity of municipal golf courses reflected a variety of new cultural trends in the United States during the period between the 1890s and 1930. Among these were the rise of a new and rapidly growing middle class, a pervasive culture of mass consumerism based on rising disposable income, increasing leisure time, and changing attitudes toward work and recreation that made sports more acceptable and even desirable for Americans. More specifically, the golf mania of this period and especially the proliferation of suburban country clubs for the more affluent class profoundly influenced urban residents who wished to play the Scottish game but who were unwilling or financially unable to join private golf clubs. Among the nation's new middle classes were hundreds of thousands of golfers who patronized public links prior to 1920. They were shopkeepers, skilled craftsmen, factory owners, lawyers, doctors, engineers, journalists, middle managers, salespeople, secretaries, entertainers, and a host of other professional and white-collar employees who had benefited from the rapid growth of corporate capitalism during the late nineteenth century. They were eager patrons of the new culture of consumerism, happily purchasing a vast array of goods produced at affordable prices by modern industry and aggressively promoted by advertisers.

The rapid growth of suburban golf clubs between the 1890s and World War I provided a powerful model for city dwellers who became fascinated by the new Scottish sport but who required land accessible by mass transit for public golf grounds. In part, no doubt, these men and women were emulating more upscale suburbanites in taking up golf, but to a significant degree they were also fascinated by the game itself—its test of character, the opportunity it provided for wholesome and healthy exercise for people of all ages and degrees of athletic talent, and the experience it provided for city folk who enjoyed walking for several hours through a scenic stretch of countryside. But while a few chose to remain city residents and commute outward to suburban clubs, the vast majority of metropolitan golfers needed a more convenient place to play.

The campaign to build golf courses open to all citizens grew out of the crusade to construct public parks in American cities, which began with the planning and opening of Central Park in New York City in the late 1850s. After the Civil War, officials in Boston, Philadelphia, Chicago, and numerous other metropolises followed New York's example and dedicated space for parks, which they hoped would benefit their urban population. Initially, upper- and middle-class reformers persuaded government leaders to support and develop parks, but by the late 1800s representatives for workers and immigrants were also clamoring for facilities that would serve the needs of the poor. Those who spearheaded the first waves of agitation for public parks believed they would provide order for both the urban landscape and metropolitan society, which was fragmented and plagued with a number of social problems. In particular, the champions of public parks believed they would bring badly needed open space and a rural environment to urban residents who craved some contact with the fresh air of the countryside. They also argued that parks would bring innumerable health benefits to congested, disease-ridden population centers, acting as the "lungs of the cit-ies." Moreover, in their view parks would alleviate class conflict by bringing residents from different social strata together. They also thought that the new facilities would elevate public morality by providing the urban masses with a setting more conducive to virtue than the saloons, brothels, theaters, and other centers of vice downtown. Finally, they wished to protect pre-cious public land for the benefit of future generations, stimulate the local economy, boost real estate values, and raise the prestige of their town by building a first class park for their people.

During the late 1800s and early 1900s, upscale reformers, public officials (especially park commissioners), and advocates for the interests of workers, immigrants, and other groups (including golfers) debated three major issues. The first two were related, for they concerned the location of the first mu-nicipal parks and the classes that would benefit most from their construction. When Central Park opened in Manhattan in the late 1850s, it was on the northern periphery of the city. It is not surprising considering the explosive urban growth after the Civil War that major metropolitan governments chose to place their parks on the outskirts of urban development in suburban regions near the residences of the wealthier citizens. Naturally, the upper and middle classes made more use of the new space than the immigrant poor and other lower-class urban dwellers. That pattern also raised issues of fairness of access when private clubs (including several golf associations) requested privileges to use public parks for their pastimes. An even more troublesome question concerned the activities that park officials deemed appropriate for these new municipal facilities. During the early 1900s many commissioners were still enforcing the restrictions implemented by Frederick Law Olmsted for Central Park and widely copied after the Civil War. Olmsted had decreed that public parks were suitable only for quiet, "receptive" recreation, not "exertive" or active amusements. His park designs featured pedestrian paths and carriage roads where visitors could view beautiful landscapes and scenic vistas. He frowned upon active sports in parks, limiting ball playing to chil-dren. "Keep off the grass" signs sprouted on lawns, which were provided for observation and perhaps for picnics but were off limits for baseball, cricket, or other such athletic pastimes.

The pioneers of early American municipal golf had to persuade park commissioners and managers that some of their precious real estate should be reserved for courses. Thomas Bendelow was a Scottish immigrant and early designer and promoter of public golf links who encountered initial resistance to his cause. In *The American City* of July 1916 he recalled that some commissioners opposed the use of parks for golf, "believing that golfers had no right there whatever, that golf was a rich man's game." Bendelow responded that their parks' "miles of beautiful roads" with their "beautiful effects" were "for the cultured classes who had the esthetic taste to appreciate such things; that the miles of the fine roads which they had built through the parks could be used only by the wealthier people who had equipages in which they could ride; and that the artisan and his family were really not looked after at all." He explained that "the keep-off-the-grass signs forever barred them from utilizing the great open spaces in public parks for recreation and should a poor man with his family come into a park and the children attempt to play ball, the brave defender of park rule, if true to this oath of office, would have to stop them." Bendelow knew that the first requirement for municipal golf was to persuade the officials that it was acceptable to play on the lawns. Once they conceded that point, he and others would convince the more liberal-minded commissioners that all classes would benefit from golf courses built on public land. Prior to World War I, daily newspapers and golfing periodicals actively supported their construction. In 1913 one writer declared: "Public interest should now be developed in golf and public links as a national asset, a builder of better and hardier citizens . . . golf is and ought to be brought within the reach of all poor or rich, as a mental and physical developer, and in the interest of a better and saner citizenship."

New York City built the nation's first public golf course of nine holes in 1895 at Van Cortlandt Park in the Bronx, and its founding and early history illustrate many themes and issues that would concern other municipal links that opened in the United States prior to World War I. The first was the question of private use of public land, for the original impetus for the creation of the Van Cortlandt grounds came from a group of affluent residents of suburban Riverdale in the northwest Bronx. They had searched the surrounding region in vain for a suitable site available at a modest rental, and then as a last resort petitioned New York City parks commissioner James Roosevelt to include golf in his plans for developing Van Cortlandt

Park. The gentlemen also hoped to gain permission to establish a private club there. Roosevelt favored the idea of public links in general "if they will make the new parks known to the public and bring crowds to them on holidays," but he denied their request to have a private club on public land. The petitioners then organized themselves into the Mosholu Golf Club and played two or three afternoons a week on the Van Cortlandt links until the crowds forced them to relocate. In 1896 the superintendent of New York City's parks announced that the use of the course by private clubs would be regulated and that "no club is going to have a monopoly of the Van Cortlandt Park links for any special day or days." An exception was made for an amateur public golf tournament sponsored by the St. Andrew's Golf Club in late November 1896.

Roosevelt wasted no time in getting the nine-hole course ready for at least rough play during the late spring and summer of 1895, at a cost of about five hundred dollars. Play was free of charge and open to all who obtained permits at Central Park. The city's policy of free admission no doubt partly explains its popularity, to the point where the *New York Times* suggested that the Park Commission should institute a modest fee that "might happily serve to keep away the pestilential dubbers who block the links and chop the turf with borrowed clubs." Initially the course was open on Sundays, but a ruling by the city's corporation counsel against Sabbath

SECOND ROUND OF MATCH PLAY FOR THE HERALD CUP.
Raynor Godwin Misses Put for a Half with H. E. Brown at Fifteenth Hole, on Van Cortlandt Park Links.

Van Cortlandt Park Golf Course, Bronx, N.Y., 1899. Title under illustration reads: "Second Round of Match Play for the Herald Cup." Copyright Unknown/Courtesy USGA Archives.

sports closed the Van Cortlandt links on the Lord's day until that ban was lifted a few years later. Although there was no green fee, caddies at first charged the highest prices they could get from the eager golfers. A new rule instituted in 1899 entitled them to twenty-five cents for carrying a bag for nine holes—as compared to fifteen cents at private clubs. Thursday afternoons soon became "ladies day," but the presence of so many women on Saturday afternoons prompted some discussion of an issue that was also becoming controversial among private clubs—the banning of females on weekends. That rule would allow businessmen to have exclusive use of the course during the only leisure time they had during the week.

The Van Cortlandt facility was an immediate success, attracting large crowds on holidays, Saturdays, and Sundays after Sabbath restrictions were ended, despite some price gouging by caddies, poor greens, and chaotic, even dangerous, playing conditions. In the May 1934 *American Golfer*, the prominent golf writer H. B. Martin remembered that Van Cortlandt was "the recruiting ground for more followers of the game than any other course in the country," adding that it "probably enjoyed in its time the patronage of more famous personages, people prominent in the public eye, than any other single golf playground." As he reminisced about his early golf at Van Cortlandt as a cub reporter, Martin recalled in particular its popularity for middle-class professionals, especially night workers, including "authors, newspaper writers, editors, artists, both comic and serious, actors, ball players, champions of the ring." Others who patronized the course included ministers of the gospel, doctors, lawyers, and college professors. In June 1903 Arthur Ruhl of *Outing* called this course "the house of the Philistine," but he also praised it for its pretty setting and its accessibility. He noted its popularity among actors, newspapermen, and others who played a round before going to work in the evening.

While the players at Van Cortlandt were mostly from the middle classes, the caddies were mainly lower-class and immigrant youth who knew and cared little about golf etiquette. Golfers who took the train up to Van Cortlandt Park in the Bronx in Manhattan encountered "a small army of yelling, howling caddies," and "many a scrap ensued between the rival caddies as to who should secure the opportunity of chasing the ball over the links." In 1899 a new regulation forced the caddies to wear badges and to go out on the course in order. But the new rules apparently did little good, for on March 18, 1900, the *New York Times* reported that "those urchins roam unrestricted, intent upon fleecing every strange golfer out of as much money as can be extorted, while cases have often occurred where balls were purposely not found that had been driven into high grass or into a woody section. An unemployed confederate keeps his eye on the spot, however, and when the player has passed from sight the ball is picked up, and perhaps sold for a dime to the very man who lost it." A decade later not much had changed. On June 26, 1910, the *New York Times* reported: "Many of the boys who hang around the links are not caddies in any sense of the word. Most of them are Italian boys who play truant from school and spend their time on the links waiting every opportunity to steal a ball when a player is not looking."

On holidays and weekends the wait on the first tee at Van Cortlandt could be lengthy, and once on the links the men and women struggled with the rough and uneven greens and the danger of being struck by a shot. On March 12, 1899, the *New York Times* described a common scene: "Players who had just driven from the tee found others following before they had reached the green, and amid the mass of flying balls, wild shouts of warning, and inextricable confusion which sometimes occurred, it is a wonder that serious accidents were averted and that any genuine enjoyment was obtained." In *Outing*, Ruhl speculated that a golfer's view of the degree of congestion on the course depended "on the number of times you are hit." He explained: "If you are hit, say three times, in making the circuit of the eighteen holes, and also lose half a dozen balls, the course is disgustingly overcrowded. If you don't lose any balls, beat the man you've picked up as a partner while waiting in line at the first tee, and manage in a polite and accidental way to send a low hard drive into the back of the player ahead of you sometime during the day, you will find the course not half bad."

The enthusiasm for public golf at Van Cortlandt Park persuaded the parks commissioners to enlarge the course into a full eighteen-hole facility of 5,960 yards with a new golf house complete with 150 lockers for men and women. They also planned more links in other locations in New York City. The construction of links at Pelham Bay Park in the northeast Bronx in the early 1900s gave the region's golfers an additional outlet. That facility was initiated at the request of three hundred members of the New York Athletic Club, who had a summer facility nearby at Travers Island. Construction problems delayed its opening until the spring of 1901, although the course initially was in rough condition. During the early 1900s New York City's golfers could also play at a course in Forest Hills, Queens, and in the spring of 1914 construction began on the Mosholu links in the Bronx, which added eighteen more holes to Van Cortlandt Park. Just prior to the American entry into World War I a season golf permit in New York City cost one dollar, and 6,600 people purchased one in 1914.

74

Boston was the second city to open municipal links, although a few golf-ers tried out the game on part of that town's public grounds in 1890—five years before the inaugural of New York City's Van Cortlandt Park. George Wright, an early star of baseball's National League and a sporting goods merchant, obtained permission for his customers who purchased golf clubs to test them on a section of Boston's Franklin Park. After six years of ex-perimental play (which included some heated conflicts between golfers and park patrons) the parks commissioners approved construction of a nine-hole course, which was ready by the fall of 1896. Golfers were required to orga-nize a club and choose officers to obtain permits to play and were charged fifteen cents for one round or twenty-five cents for eighteen holes. Willie Campbell, a Scottish immigrant, became its first professional. After his untimely death in November 1900, his wife was appointed superintendent of the Franklin Park courses, thereby becoming the first woman to earn employment as a golf professional in the United States. Ironically, despite the heavy demand for play, the town closed the course on holidays and Saturday afternoons in the summer because of the danger posed by errant shots to the crowds who flocked to the park during those prime times. In 1900 as many as 350 players teed off in one day. In 1901, large crowds and "continual grumbling . . . concerning the beginners and other 'duffers' who repeatedly pulled and sliced their ball, and disregarded the etiquette of the game to an alarming extent" motivated the commissioners to lay out a six-hole course for novices inside the regular links. A new clubhouse also opened that year at Franklin Park, but complaints continued about poor management and too little attention paid to rules. *Golf* magazine noted approvingly that "public golf links are becoming as necessary to cities as public libraries," adding that "it would be a happy idea to have at least one member of the board of park commissioners a practical golfer." During the early 1900s patronage of the Franklin Park links rose dramatically, reaching a peak attendance of 47,469 in 1902. The decline to 15,632 in 1907 may be explained in part by beginners who elected to join private clubs in the vicinity or who became discouraged by the crowded and sometimes unruly conditions on the course. But the next year witnessed a reversal of the trend, with the number of golfers at Franklin Park increasing over the next six years to more than 23,000 in 1913.

In Chicago in 1899, professors and students at the University of Chicago led the movement for a public nine-hole links in Jackson Park, the site of the 1893 World Columbian Exposition. On Memorial Day 1901, more than 750 people jammed onto the 1,700-yard, nine-hole course, with some latecomers waiting up to two hours to tee off in the afternoon. On May 31st, the *Chicago Tribune* described the gathering as a "heterogeneous mixture from the little tadpole golfer, with his natty sweater and kindergarten clubs, to the man in his office suit who made the rounds with a driver and a cigar." It also noted "the family party with the mother striving hard to show the girls how the ball should be hit." In 1902 a supplementary course of nine holes (1,900 yards) opened in the southwest corner of Jackson Park. Three years later the South Park commissioners planned a new course of eighteen holes (6,190 yards) and the lengthening of the old "practice course" to 2,800 yards. Crowds continued to flock to Jackson Park during the early 1900s, and the facilities improved significantly in 1907 with the construction of a new locker room and showers. There were 1,700 applicants for the 821 lockers that were allotted to three or four occupants each. In 1911 Bendelow redesigned the Jackson Park public links, which by 1913 constituted two courses of nine and eighteen holes. As early as 1902, residents of Chicago's West Side were agitating for the city's West Park Board to build a nine-hole course in Garfield Park, replacing a half-mile cement bicycle track, as the golf fever superseded the cycling craze of the 1890s. Their goal was real-

Golfers line up to play at Jackson Park Public Golf Links, Chicago, 1919. Copyright Unknown/Courtesy USGA Archives.

Golfer and caddie Devine Kober, winner of a caddie championship, on the grounds of the Jackson Park Golf Course, Chicago, Ill., 1908. SDN-054341, *Chicago Daily News* negatives collection, Chicago History Museum.

ized, as *Golf* magazine explained in December 1906: "The supplanting of the cycle track by the golf links is an indication of the fickle-ness—or would you call it progress?—of the American people in their attitude toward sport. Unquestionably the proper thing is being done in razing the track, but a decade ago it would have been a sacrilege." But the huge throngs that turned out at Garfield Park on Memorial Day 1911 created up to a seven-hour wait to tee off and led to a call for a full eighteen-hole links. In 1913 Chicago also constructed a new eighteen-hole municipal course at Marquette Park, thanks in large part to the efforts of John Barton Payne, president of the South Parks Commission. Payne believed that golf was a better sport for the average citizen than baseball or football and proclaimed: "I do not believe the parks board could do anything of greater general benefit to the people of Chicago than to install golf courses where the man who cannot afford to belong to a club can play. It is not only a recreative game, but one which makes for better health, better thinking ability and better self-control for every man or woman who plays it earnestly." In 1917 the courses at Marquette Park and Jackson Park attracted 364,491 golfers.

In Pittsburgh, as in New York City, the first steps toward a municipal golf course began with a private club gaining permission to use park land for their sport. But in Pittsburgh's case the shift toward a facility that was open to the general public took longer and became more of a political reform issue. In 1896, wealthy residents of Pittsburgh's East End obtained the approval of the city's director of public works to lay out a golf course on sixty acres of Schenley Park. Their exclusive Pittsburgh Golf Club maintained the links, discouraged use by nonmembers, and built a sumptuous clubhouse on adjacent private property. Its privileges became a political issue in 1906 when the town's two city councils questioned its control of a golf course on public property. But four years passed before a new mayor ordered his public works director to open the Schenley course to the public, appointed city officials to monitor play, constructed a caddie shack, and urged that city residents take up the sport. Two years later the city built a public clubhouse at a cost of $10,000, and at its dedication a councilman declared that "the man who makes $2 a day is just as welcome here as any millionaire." Demand was so great that the following year the city expanded the building to include more lockers and hot and cold showers. Not surprisingly, the elite of the Pittsburgh Golf Club abandoned their former playground, but even though there was no fee to play a round, it appears that relatively few steelworkers or other lower-income people appeared on the course. Instead, middle-class residents of the adjoining neighborhoods of Pittsburgh's East End took advantage of the new facility.

Philadelphia was one of the last major eastern cities to build a municipal golf course. Resistance by the town's Fairmount Park commissioners delayed action until just prior to World War I. Harry Vardon's tour of the United States in 1900 sparked some early interest in laying out a course in Fairmount Park, but thirteen years later the public golf forces were still battling the city. In 1913 they recruited President William Howard Taft to write a letter to lobby the Fairmount Park commissioners to authorize construction of the links. Taft was an avid golfer who argued for a "freer use of public parks by the people." He stated: "Golf is not a mere plaything of faddists, as some suppose, nor is it a rich man's game." But the commissioners rejected the scheme, arguing that there was "no available space" in Fairmount Park (despite its 3,400 acres) and that "it was unfair to the poorer classes of the city for the authorities to fence off any section of the Park as a links." Instead, they asked the town's councils to appropriate funds to build a free eighteen-hole golf course in Cobb's Creek Park. That facility opened three years later, but by 1917 it was already being criticized for its high fees and mismanagement. The *American Golfer* reported that it was mostly used by those who had been members of other clubs but who preferred Cobb's Creek because it was less expensive than the other organizations.

Prior to World War I, public officials from Baltimore, Cincinnati, St. Louis, Providence, Indianapolis, Syracuse, Milwaukee, Newark, and other major American cities followed these examples of New York City, Boston, Chicago, Pittsburgh, and Philadelphia, as municipal golf courses multiplied across the nation. On April 13, 1913, the *New York Times* reported: "A great wave of agitation for public golf links is sweeping through the United States, and in such decisive fashion as to make it only a matter of time when each city of large size will have a course of its own for the rank and file . . . the man of means in golf is not to be the only one to enjoy the many fascinations of the royal and ancient game." That paper explained that the main beneficiaries would be "office and store assistants, clerks, workingmen, and a host of others," provided that public courses were accessible to all with nominal fees charged. It also argued that the links were not more expensive to maintain than regular parks and also provided "enjoyment of a healthful nature which cannot be obtained in regular parks, where people may walk on concrete and must touch nothing." The following year, sixty-three municipal links had regularly organized clubs on their grounds, and fifty of them founded the Association of Public Golf Clubs to improve the existing public golf courses and promote the construction of new ones.

⊚ ⊚ ⊚

In the fall of 1896, John Shippen, Jr., scored a 78 on the Shinnecock Hills golf course to tie for the lead after the first round of the second annual United States Open Championship. While Shippen's feat was impressive in its own right, what made it even more remarkable was that he was the sixteen-year-old son of an African American schoolteacher and Presbyterian missionary at the Shinnecock Indian reservation in Southampton, Long Island. Born in Washington, D.C. in 1879, as a youth he moved to Long Island with his family. Shinnecock's professional, Willie Dunn, had recruited Shippen and several local Indians to caddie for the club members. Some of these boys had demonstrated some talent for the game, and Dunn showed a special interest in Shippen. Before long the boy was serving as a teaching assistant to Dunn and also worked as a starter for tournaments, repaired clubs, and helped with course maintenance. All the while he honed his golf skills. Shippen's chance for golf immortality arrived when the first president of the United States Golf Association and its championship director, the sugar magnate and millionaire Theodore A. Havemeyer, permitted Shippen and his friend Oscar Bunn (a Shinnecock Indian) to compete over the objections of several others in the field of mostly English and Scottish professionals. Shippen's partner for the first eighteen holes was Charles B. Macdonald, the founder of the Chicago Golf Club and a former U.S. Amateur champion. (Macdonald withdrew after scoring an 83.) On the second day Shippen remained in contention until he carded a disastrous eleven on the thirteenth hole. Years later he recalled: "It was a little, easy par four. I'd played it many times and I knew I just had to stay on the right side of the fairway with my drive. Well, I played it too far to the right and the ball landed in a sand road. Bad trouble in those days before sand wedges. I kept hitting the ball along the road, unable to lift it out of the sand, and wound up with an unbelievable eleven for the hole. I've wished a hundred times I could have played that little par four again. It sure would have been something to win that day." Instead he had to settle for a prize of ten dollars and a place in history as the first African American to earn money as a participant in a U.S. Open. His combined score of 159 placed him in a tie for fifth place—seven strokes behind James Foulis, the winner. Shippen played in four more U.S. Open Championships, the last one in 1913 when Francis Ouimet stunned the golf world with his memorable triumph.

As a young man, Shippen worked as a golf instructor at a series of white country clubs, but after World War I he found employment at several African American golf associations as the sport became increasingly segregated. His early positions included terms at the Maidstone Club at East Hampton, Long Island, the Aronimink Golf Club near Philadelphia, the Spring Lake Golf & Country Club in New Jersey, and the Marine and Field Club in Brooklyn, New York. He returned briefly to Shinnecock Hills as a greenkeeper and then became course maintenance foreman at the nearby National Golf Links of America. After the war he tried a civil service position in Washington, D.C. in the federal public works department, but during the 1920s he returned to his lifelong love of golf as instructor for two black-operated organizations—the Citizens Golf Club in Washington and the National Capitol Country Club in Laurel, Maryland. His final position was at the Shady Rest Golf and Country Club in Scotch Plains, New Jersey, where he remained from 1932 to 1964. There, during the hard times of the Great Depression and for decades afterward, he pieced together a living by giving lessons, repairing clubs, selling equipment, and playing in matches.

Over his lifetime he made the transition from a partial acceptance in the world of white country club life and competition to the segregated Jim Crow status of black golf. He also lived to see the imported Scottish game of his youth become part of the mainstream of twentieth-century American athletics for both races. He is now recognized as the first golf professional native to the United States.

While the overwhelming majority of the first generation of American golfers were of white, Anglo-Saxon Protestant heritage, some were members of minority racial and ethnic groups. Although John Shippen, Jr.'s experience was hardly typical of the lives of African Americans of his generation, he and a few other hardy players pioneered the sport for blacks in the United States. The early twentieth century was an era of black accommodation to white racism in sports, as African American athletes struggled but failed to gain the opportunity to compete with whites on equal terms. With only a few exceptions, black individuals and teams wound up in segregated clubs, leagues, and tournaments in baseball, football, basketball, tennis, and other sports. In golf, the poverty of the majority of black Americans of this period led many of them to work as laborers on courses and as caddies. Several later distinguished themselves as skilled players, architects, and organizers of clubs and national associations. In short, the black presence on American links does not date from the heroics of Tiger Woods or the achievements of his predecessors like Charles Sifford during the 1960s and 1970s. Rather, it extends back more than a century to the dawn of American golf.

Black caddies carried the bags of white golfers in both the North and South during this era, on private and public courses and also at resorts. Since the black population of the nation was still concentrated in the South, their appearance on golf courses was more common in that region. Children as young as eight or nine years old shouldered one or two bags over miles of links, sometimes covering eighteen holes more than once a day. Often poorly fed, ill-clad, and even barefoot, they were paid a pittance and some-times had to turn over a part of their earnings to the caddie master at the end of the day. But caddying did provide the opportunity to learn to play golf, because during the hours of waiting to be called to the first tee a boy could practice with a few old clubs and balls. Also, most clubs permitted caddies to play the course on Mondays, and some even scheduled special caddie tournaments. All the premier black players of this period started out as caddies, as they keenly observed the strokes of the best golfers and prac-ticed to improve their own game. Yet the boys could never forget that they were viewed as a servile class. For example, at Pinehurst, North Carolina, the Winter Golf League of Advertising Interests introduced a tradition in 1905 that provided amusement for white guests while it symbolized and showcased black subservience. At the end of the group's stay at Pinehurst, its president drove a golf ball off a five-dollar gold piece. The prize coin went to the black caddie who could outrun and outfight his peers to retrieve the ball.

As countless African American youth mastered the rudiments of golf as caddies and grounds maintenance workers, they sought access to courses and tournaments where they could enjoy the game and perfect their skills. Admission to municipal courses was generally open in northern and midwestern cities, but not in the border states or the South. Even in the North equal opportunity was sometimes denied, especially in cases of interracial competition on public grounds. Walter Speedy was a Chicagoan who had a running battle with that city's officials over black participation in public links tournaments. Born in Louisiana in 1878, he moved to Chicago around

African American children playing golf, c. 1905. Library of Congress, Prints and Photographs Division, Detroit Publishing Company Collection.

82

1900 and became one of the first African Americans to play on the Jackson Park public links. In 1910 Speedy and three other blacks were barred from a competition at Jackson Park. The four sued park officials; the outcome of their case is not known. Five years later Speedy and several of his friends organized the Alpha Golf Club and held Chicago's first African American golf tournament at the Marquette Golf Course. Speedy earned some respect after he won the tournament and the right to compete, along with three other black golfers, against the best white players from Jackson Park. In 1918 two black golfers performed well in the Amateur Golf Tournament in Jackson Park, but the following year entrance requirements were changed to include membership in a "regularly organized golf club." The black players met this requirement by founding the Windy City Golf Association, but in 1920 a further restriction mandated that the club be affiliated with the Western Golf Association. Since that organization would not admit the Windy City group, the black golfers were barred from the annual citywide tournament in 1921 by the Chicago Parks Department. Speedy and his friends sought legal relief in the courts, but their request for an injunction was denied. On July 16, 1921, the black-owned *Chicago Defender* blamed the Jackson Park Golf Club for "this latest form of jim-crowism" and concluded that "it is barely possible if they [the black golfers] were not quite so good this senseless opposition would be less pronounced." The following year that newspaper sponsored a national golf tournament, managed by the Windy City Golf Association, open to all amateurs regardless of race.

A few African American golfers fought for the right of equal opportunity in amateur events sponsored by the USGA. In 1928 in Philadelphia, Robert "Pat" Ball and Elmer Stout entered the National Public Links tournament. They became mired in a legal controversy after they were disqualified following the preliminary round for alleged scorecard violations. The two men filed for an injunction in a city court, charging racial discrimination by their accusers and requesting reinstatement in the tournament. The judge ruled in their favor, finding no evidence of rules violations but also exonerating the USGA of any involvement with racist actions. Ball and Stout then chose to withdraw from the event because they did not wish to force the USGA to reschedule several rounds of match play that had been completed while the judge was deciding their case.

In two border cities the major racial issue on municipal golf courses was not access to tournaments, but rather the more basic right to play on those grounds. The post–World War I period witnessed several challenges to the policy of racial segregation on municipal courses in St. Louis and

Washington, D.C. In a 1917 report, the St. Louis planning commission recommended segregated use of public recreational facilities, including the Forest Park golf course. That year the commissioner of parks refused a request from three black players that they be allowed to play at Forest Park one day a week or certain hours on a few days. Instead, he ruled that they would have to wait until a separate course could be built. Another request in 1922 led to a new policy the following year that reserved public golf links on Monday mornings from 6:00 A.M. to 12:00 noon "for the exclusive use and enjoyment of colored persons." A local newspaper reported that "on occasions the 27 holes . . . have been given over to a solitary Negro golfer." Even when whites protested that they would be unable to play on Labor Day morning, the commissioner refused to change the rules. In the nation's capital during the early 1920s, Lt. Col. Clarence O. Sherrill, a North Carolinian, was in charge of the district's parks and public buildings. He decreed that blacks were permitted to play the East Potomac Park Golf Course exclusively after 3:00 P.M. each Tuesday and the three-hole West Potomac course after noon on Wednesdays. In 1925 Washington's African American golfers gained the exclusive right to use the Lincoln Memorial Golf Course but were no longer welcome on the other public links in that city. On June 8, 1925, the *Baltimore Afro-American* criticized middle-class blacks "in high business and professional circles" who "have adopted 'Jim Crow' golf as a sport and are submitting gleefully to segregation on account of race and are making ineffective the protests of others against other forms of segregation and discrimination." That paper specifically blamed Sherrill for the segregationist policy at the Lincoln Memorial course. It urged the black golfing community to fight "to remove every vestige of discrimination and to get rid of Colonel Sherrill." It also charged that black acceptance of his decree "puts him in position to say that he is giving the colored people what they want."

By the end of World War I, many towns had provided municipal golf courses for the masses, and thousands of middle- and working-class caddies and players had learned the rudiments of the sport on these grounds. Early in its history American golf had demonstrated an impressive degree of democratization, which extended to immigrant and African American youth. While black players were frequently not welcome on links in border states and the Deep South, they were beginning their long campaign for equal access to public courses. The 1920s would witness spectacular gains for the sport in the United States for the country club set and more modest growth for black and white golfers on public grounds.

FIRST GOLDEN AGE

In January 1919, Sam Solomon of the *American Golfer* reflected on the views of pessimists who doubted that Americans would retain the same passion for sports after the Great War that they had displayed in the more innocent times before the horrific conflict. He remarked: "We are told that sport, of all things, will not be the same again, that men will be too busy, too earnest, too serious, and too mindful of past griefs to strike a ball with a club as was their wont and try to guide it to a little hole in earth. . . . In such a programme, the gloomy ones murmur, there is no room for such as golf." But the columnist rejected these doomsday predictions. While he conceded that in mankind there may be an instinct for war, he also believed that "there is another and a stronger for the happy arts of peace." He explained: "To shoot with a gun in battle may be at times a fine and splendid thing, but yet we know that when the world is set to right it is a finer thing to tap a little ball upon a sunny putting-green." Another writer in that journal quoted "Colonel Bogey," who had just returned from the war, grieving for lost sons: "Thank God the war is over and our Golf Family can return to peaceful pursuits, with a new zest and a new spirit borne of the tribulations through which we have passed."

The optimists turned out to be right, for the decade of the 1920s witnessed a remarkable boom in sports in general in the United States, including golf. Often labeled the "Golden Age," it featured such heroes as Babe Ruth in baseball, Jack Dempsey in boxing, Red Grange in football, and Bill Tilden in tennis. In golf the legendary exploits of Walter Hagen, Gene Sarazen, and Bob Jones captured the nation's imagination, but more important for the rapid growth of the Scottish pastime in America were the prosperous times that benefited the upper and middle classes. The most important of these developments were increased leisure time, mass production of automobiles that facilitated new rounds of suburbanization, a business culture that embraced golf, the proliferation of private country clubs in suburbs and small towns, a dramatic increase in the number of municipal courses, and growing participation by ethnic and racial minorities and women.

As early as the spring of 1920, evidence abounded that pointed to a resurgence of interest in golf, despite the setbacks of the war and the added disadvantage of Prohibition, which threatened to curtail revenues at country clubs. New private and public clubs and courses were sprouting around the nation; manufacturers of clubs, bags, balls, and clothing were barely keeping up with the demand; hackers were playing many more rounds; and attendance was increasing at annual meetings of golf associations. The decision of many states to continue the wartime experiment of daylight saving time also benefited businessmen, who used the extra sunshine to complete a full round of golf after work. While estimates of the total number of private and public courses and players during the 1920s vary considerably, it appears that the number of links increased from about 2,000 in 1923 to 3,500 in 1925 to 5,800 in 1930. Apparently there were between one and two million Americans who played at least a few rounds of golf a year during that period.

Politicians and presidents kept golf in the public eye, and after the precedents of Taft and Wilson they no longer had to worry that frequenting the links would alienate voters. According to the *American Golfer*, "no congressman today would think of foregoing his golf for fear of public disfavor. Golf bags in the Senate and House office buildings are as common as brief cases, lame ducks, and lobbyists. Even the House and Senate pages turn out players of ability." The three presidents of this decade included an avid golfer of modest ability (Warren G. Harding), a hopeless incompetent who despised the game and played only a few rounds as chief executive (Calvin Coolidge), and a nonparticipant (Herbert Hoover).

While presidential duffers played only a minor role in promoting the game in the United States during the 1920s, the exploits of the golfing heroes of this age had a far greater impact. "Sir Walter" Hagen (or more simply, "The Haig"), Gene Sarazen ("The Squire"), and Bob Jones (the "Emperor") dominated the decade at home and also abroad in the British Isles, where they combined for seven British Open titles. But while the three champions shared the sporting headlines with their thrilling victories and boosted American pride, they differed dramatically in their social class backgrounds and their personalities. Hagen came from a working-class family of German descent, took up the game as a caddie, and became one of America's first home-grown golf professionals. A flamboyant character and an elegant dresser, he was also an intense competitor who won titles despite

86

his reputation as a late-night bon vivant. The son of an Italian immigrant, Sarazen also learned the sport as a caddie. On the other hand, Jones was born into a moderately affluent Georgia family and learned to play at a country club. An amateur throughout his tournament career, he was a modest young man who was adored by the public for both his accomplishments on the links and his devotion to his family.

Born in 1892 in Rochester, New York, Hagen was the son of a blacksmith. He started playing golf at the age of four with an old club given to him by a family friend, began caddying at seven, and thereafter spent his spare time at the pro shop of the Rochester Country Club. A talented athlete who loved all sports, he later had a chance for a baseball tryout with the Philadelphia Phillies. After dropping out of school at twelve, he chose to concentrate on golf, and by his fifteenth birthday he was regularly breaking 80 on the Rochester course. He so impressed the club's pro that he earned a promotion from caddie to assistant professional. That position launched his career, for it gave him the opportunity to learn how to make and repair clubs, supervise the course, and play many more practice rounds. He first gained national attention at Brookline during the 1913 United States Open, when as a twenty-year-old novice he finished just three strokes behind Ouimet, Vardon, and Ray. Just one year later he won his first major championship with a win in the United States Open, a feat he repeated in 1919. But it was his five PGA titles, including four consecutive (1921, 1924–1927), and his four British Open crowns (1922, 1924, 1928, 1929) that made him the darling of the American golfing fraternity. He was the first native-born American to win the coveted British Open title. (Jock Hutchison, a resident of the United States, was the British Open champion in 1921, but he was born in St. Andrews, Scotland.) News of Hagen's first British Open victory in 1922 touched off wild celebrations in the United States that culminated in a grand reception in New York City followed by a lavish dinner at the Westchester-Biltmore Country Club in Rye, Westchester County. On June 24, 1922, the *New York Times* described Hagen as "indisputably the finest overseas player who ever contested for the British Open championship" and labeled his achievement "an American victory outright." But his triumph also elevated him to international stardom, for in the words of Grantland Rice: "Hagen is better known today outside the United States than Babe Ruth, and only a Dempsey covers a greater range."

Hagen's significance for golf during the Roaring Twenties transcended his numerous major and lesser titles. As a showman he reflected the spirit of his age, and his exciting and aggressive style of play no doubt helped to popularize golf enormously. But he also helped to revolutionize the status of the golf professional in the United States in two ways. He was the first to make a good living exclusively through playing tournaments and exhibition matches, as opposed to giving lessons and selling equipment at a country club. He won five Professional Golfers' Association titles. Secondly, he helped to elevate the social status of golf professionals by demanding equal treatment and accommodations at country clubs for both amateurs and professionals, especially in Great Britain. Although it took a while to completely break down the social customs that discriminated against golf professionals, Hagen's objections and occasional antics certainly blazed the way.

Among the golf professionals of the 1920s, Gene Sarazen was Hagen's greatest rival. Born Eugenio Saraceni in Harrison, New York, in 1902, he changed his name when he was about sixteen years old because "it looked and sounded like it should be on a violin, not a golf club." The son of a carpenter who struggled with his business but still wanted his son to follow his trade, Sarazen began caddying at the age of eight near his home at the Larchmont Country Club. Francis Ouimet's thrilling victory in the 1913 U.S. Open inspired Sarazen to improve his game, and he switched to the Apawamis Club in Rye, New York. During World War I he dropped out of school to work with his father as a carpenter's helper, and in 1918 he barely survived a bout with pneumonia. In 1921 he secured his first job as a golf professional in Titusville, Pennsylvania, and early in 1922 he moved to a new position at the Highland Country Club in Pittsburgh. That year he stunned the sports world by winning both the U.S. Open at the Skokie Country Club in Glencoe, Illinois, and the PGA Championship at the Oakmont Country Club in Oakmont, Pennsylvania. Only twenty years old (the second youngest to capture the U.S. Open crown), Sarazen cashed in on his fame by playing lucrative exhibition matches, opening a golf correspondence school in New York, signing an endorsement contract with the Wilson Sporting Goods company, filming short movies, and agreeing to become the professional at the Briarcliff Lodge resort in Westchester County, New York. All in all, it was a spectacular beginning for a young golfer who stood barely five feet five inches tall and who came from an immigrant Italian family. In 1923 he added a second PGA Championship, but he achieved true stardom during the Depression decade of the 1930s, winning his second U.S. Open and the British Open in 1932, his third PGA title in 1933, and the new Masters Tournament in 1935. The last achievement earned him the distinction of becoming the first golfer to win all four of the modern era's major tournaments.

The man who would eclipse both Sarazen and Hagen in the world of golf was Robert Tyre Jones, Jr., who was born on St. Patrick's Day, March 17, 1902, and named after his grandfather. His father, Robert Purmedus Jones, was a successful corporate lawyer in Atlanta. Each summer beginning in 1907 he rented a house on the outskirts of the city near the East Lake Country Club's golf course. Although young Bobby had a sickly childhood, by the time the family began making its annual pilgrimages to the countryside he was well enough to swing a golf club. Before long he was hooked on the game and began playing regularly with his parents and friends. At the age of nine he won the junior championship of the Atlanta Athletic Club, a feat that drew national attention and got his picture published in the *American Golfer.* Childhood play and competitions with the rising stars Perry Adair and Alexa Stirling helped him to hone his skills. In 1916, at the age of fourteen, the child prodigy from Atlanta qualified for the United States Amateur Championship, losing in the third round of match play to the defending champion, Robert Gardner. During World War I young Bob was a popular figure touring the country for Red Cross charity exhibition matches. As a young man after the war he came close to winning major championships, but his inexperience and lack of maturity held him back. On July 18, 1926, a writer for the *New York Times* recalled that back in 1920 young Bob was "a fretful, impetuous youth—golf's bad boy, a lovable, forgivable bad boy," who was then "a headstrong, petulant youth, easily provoked and prone to fly off the handle at any minute."

As he grew into young manhood Jones developed more discipline and poise, perhaps simply because he was older and perhaps because he chose to pursue higher education and training for the law even as he compiled his remarkable record on the links. During the 1920s he completed undergraduate and master's degrees in engineering at Georgia Tech and a second bachelor's degree in the humanities at Harvard, followed by legal studies at Emory University, which enabled him to pass the bar exam in Georgia. His competitive career was launched to superstardom with his victory in the 1923 U.S. Open. The following year he won the first of his five U.S. Amateur Championships, but it was his back-to-back triumphs in the British Open in 1926 and 1927 that captured the hearts of the American public. In 1926 New York City welcomed the conquering hero with a three-hour celebration that featured a confetti parade, speeches by Mayor Jimmy Walker and dignitaries from Atlanta, and a gala reception, dinner, and dance at the Hotel Vanderbilt. As always, Jones responded briefly with humble remarks in which he thanked those who were honoring him. But those festivities hardly matched those of the summer of 1930, as Jones was in the process of winning all four major championships that would later be known as the "Grand Slam" of golf. After his victories in the British Amateur and Open events he returned to New York City to an even grander ticker tape parade in early July. At City Hall, Mayor Walker stated that Jones's British titles "probably would increase the demand for municipal golf courses so that our youngsters will have a chance to grow up and be champions." Jones hardly had time to savor his accomplishments, for he had to travel to Minneapolis, Minnesota, for his next challenge, the U.S. Open. After winning that championship he boarded a train for Atlanta, where an estimated 125,000 cheering citizens greeted his convertible amidst a snowstorm of confetti. According to the Associated Press's account of July 15, 1930, the parade on July 14 was "decidedly democratic" and included "soldiers in olive drab," a "brilliantly costumed drum and bugle corps," and "pretty women golfers in a huge white tallyho [pleasure coach]." The reception was also racially inclusive, although the newspaper account reveals the current status of the black population in golf. The reporter noted: "It was a big day for the Negro caddies. Each division carried a banner in typical language of the dark skinned bag carriers. . . . To them he is the greatest man in the world and they'd caddy for him for 'nuffin' just to brag to their friends."

In the fall of 1930 Jones completed his historical cycle by winning his fifth U.S. Amateur title, which he added to his one British Amateur, four U.S. Open, and three British Open titles. He then retired from competitive golf and signed a contract to make instructional golf films, thereby giving up his amateur status. He had a reached the pinnacle of golf, and there were no more worlds for him to conquer. A June 2, 1930, editorial in the *New York Times* titled "More than a Golfer" suggested that the key to Jones's success was that he had finally achieved "self-mastery." It explained: "Today he is not only a model of sportsmanship in his bearing, but a man whose poise and self-control are never shaken by the slings and arrows of outrageous fortune on the golf links." That newspaper concluded that Jones had become an international figure as the "finest golfer who ever lived" and that "he is as much loved as a man as he is admired and wondered at as a golfer."

During the 1920s, Hagen, Sarazen, and Jones also played instrumental roles in establishing American hegemony over Great Britain in two international series—the Walker and Ryder Cups. The Walker Cup takes its name from its trophy's donor, George Herbert Walker, president of the USGA in 1920. (He was also the maternal grandfather of the forty-first president of the United States, George Herbert Walker Bush.) An internationalist, Walker initially promoted a plan to invite all golf-playing nations to select a team of amateurs, in the hope that golf competition might help foster better international relations after the bloodbath of the Great War. He enlisted the support of the USGA, but a disappointing response to his proposal resulted in the revamped bilateral contest between players representing the United States and Great Britain (including all of Ireland). Delegates from the USGA and the Royal and Ancient Golf Club of St. Andrews agreed to a match play format of four foursomes and eight singles, with the first event scheduled for August 1922 at the National Golf Links at Southampton, Long Island. The Walker Cup was held annually for three years before switching to a biennial schedule beginning in 1926. With Jones, Ouimet, and other stars recruited for the American side, the United States contingent won the first nine challenges, until the British finally turned the tables with a victory in 1938.

The Ryder Cup was the brainchild of an English sportsman who earned a fortune selling penny packets of seeds to his country's gardeners and who became enthralled with golf in his middle age. Samuel Ryder was a spectator who witnessed an unofficial match between American and British professionals in Wentworth, England, in 1926. Impressed with their play and especially their camaraderie, he offered a small gold cup with a golfing figure atop the lid as the trophy for a series of biennial challenges between teams from the United States and Great Britain. As was the case with the Walker Cup, the outcome would be decided by a match play format of four foursomes and eight singles. Although the British visitors lost the first event in June 1927 at the Worcester Country Club in Massachusetts, in May 1929 they rebounded with a narrow win at Moortown, Leeds, England. The two nations then alternated victories on their own soil until 1937, when the United States professionals finally defeated their British opponents on their home turf at Southport, England.

Through their success in the Walker and Ryder Cup competitions and with twelve British Open and six British Amateur crowns won between the two world wars, American golfers had clearly achieved mastery over their British adversaries. Hagen's four British Open titles and Jones's two British Open Championships and one British Amateur victory signaled the American ascendancy. As early as 1923, veteran British golfer Harry Hilton conceded: "There can be no doubt that the American player of the game has somewhat rudely annexed that presumptive hereditary right of ours. . . . To put the matter in the very plainest of language, American players of the present day are better golfers than their British cousins."

◉ ◉ ◉

At the heart of the golf boom of the 1920s was the increase in the number of country clubs for the upper and middle classes, which both reflected and reinforced the latest rounds of suburbanization outside of the nation's major cities. While golf was naturally at the center of these associations, social life and amenities took on new significance. The result was often lavish spending on luxurious clubhouses and extravagant parties and other special events, which placed the clubs under a burden of debt that would force many of them to the brink of bankruptcy during the financial crisis of the 1930s. But in the short run the good times rolled on, as successful country clubs spurred a boom in residential real estate values in adjacent districts. In numerous cases older clubs were forced to relocate because of rising property taxes on their appreciating acreage. But even as they moved farther outward from the city center they attracted real estate developers who began the building process anew. As Charles Phelps Cushing explained on February 12, 1921, in an article in the *American Golfer*: "Wherever you go in America, 'the country club district' spells a high-class residential neighborhood—and corresponding high taxes." The pressure of higher taxes would generally lead to a rise in dues and often to relocation to lower the costs for members. Golf architect and developer Tom Bendelow's company promoted golf course construction as a positive force in improving the quality of suburban planning. A pamphlet that advertised the company's services noted that golf courses invariably led to both increased land values and also better features, such as wider streets, good pavements, artistic lighting, large lots, and zoning. Writing in *Golf Illustrated* in April 1923, Louis Kibbe described how golf courses became "community builders," proclaiming that "the town that does not boast of a golf course is set down as a curiosity along with rail fences, log cabins, and other relics of bygone ages." Country clubs had become the advance guard for "the marching phalanx of suburban home builders."

A key component of the suburban culture that featured golf courses and residential subdivisions was the support that the business world provided for golf in the 1920s. Although this trend dated back to the prewar period, it came of age in the prosperity of the decade when American companies enjoyed great prestige. Upper-echelon executives and middle managers who loved golf realized its potential to seal deals. A May 1921 article in *Golf Illustrated* quoted an "enterprising business man in his early thirties" who had resolved to take up golf. He confessed: "Honestly, you are out of it nowadays unless you do. Everyone who is anybody seems to be playing and even in business the big men behind the enterprises are encouraging their subordinates to cultivate an acquaintance with the game. Apparently golf is a common ground upon which businessmen can meet. Moreover, when they wish to close an important transaction there seems to be nothing like a game of golf to pave the way. The value of this is seen on every hand—and think of the splendid exercise."

While the decade of the 1920s witnessed many examples of upscale country clubs with clubhouses that cost hundreds of thousands of dollars, there were also hundreds of golf clubs in cities and small towns designed for families of more modest means. In the September 5, 1925, *American Golfer*, Grantland Rice quoted commentator George Ade, who had remarked that "little towns and villages had shackled prohibition on the big cities, and the big cities in turn had shackled golf on the smaller towns." Rice reported that almost every town in the country with eight to ten thousand inhabitants had a golf course, "but when the towns and villages of 800 and 1,000 lay out their nine-hole battle ground the national aspect of the game is fixed for all time." He used the example of Sheffield, Illinois, where the chauffeur for one of the town's bankers became the architect for the first nine holes, building greens for less than fifty dollars each at the start. For Rice, the course in Sheffield was "one of the great boons to village life," because "here the leading banker, butcher, groceryman, etc. all meet in a friendly four-ball match in the great democracy of the game." He concluded: "No social lines are thought of as long as each player as a good sportsman plays the game." In the August 1930 *American Golfer*, journalist Peter Holt echoed these sentiments about the sport in small towns: "It is democratic golf in which the banker rubs shoulders with the farmer and the merchant meets the local garage owner and . . . learns a little of his fellow and his problems and benefits his community thereby."

◎ ◎ ◎

The return of peace after World War I and the prosperity of the 1920s for many Americans generated new waves of enthusiasm for golf and led to fresh calls for municipal sponsorship of expanded and new courses. Supporters of public golf links pointed to the game's popularity, its health benefits, and especially its potential for expanding American democracy in the realm of recreation. As town and city administrators grappled with difficult issues of acquiring adequate land and financing construction and maintenance costs, private individuals experimented with semipublic daily-fee courses that could earn a profit as they met the ever-growing demand for affordable golf. On municipal courses players organized their own clubs and at the national level the United States Golf Association recognized the grassroots movement by sponsoring the first Public Links Championship.

During the 1920s, champions of municipal golf extolled the sport's democratic and social class attributes, and they insisted that no American city could consider itself first-class unless it had at least one public course. In the May 1922 *Golf Illustrated*, Sylvanus P. Jermain instructed public officials that the establishment of golf grounds was "one of the best expressions of American democracy." He argued that public golf "makes a common privilege of an otherwise especial privilege. It is a wisely established 'social safety valve' and reaches deep into fundamental things concerning equality of opportunity. It 'gives the lie direct' to the demagogue when he yelps that 'golf is a rich man's game.' It absolutely removes one of the sharpest contrasts that create social discontent and turmoil." To promote the game, he opposed charging a fee for play, but he did support requiring a permit. He concluded with a patriotic reference to the Great War and his home city of Toledo, Ohio: "We sent the flower of our American youth to other lands to fight and to die 'to make democracy safe Over There.' In Toledo we have had these scarred but youthful veterans building public golf courses, their own playgrounds, to keep democracy safe 'Over Here.'" On February 12, 1921, the *American Golfer* noted that municipal golf courses offered competition to some private country clubs, and asked: "What place that makes bold to describe itself as a 'city' is today without a first class municipal golf course? Or, if it is a city of much size, two or three courses?"

Celebrated sportsmen and writers reported on the "golf bugs" from all classes who were passionate about their pastime and willing to wait hours in line, even in the cold and the rain, for their chance to tee off. On June 12, 1920, Grantland Rice wrote in the *American Golfer*: "It is around the public golf course that you get your cross-sections of humanity. Old and young, men and women, some without collars, wearing suspenders, others driving up in big touring cars, but all golf lovers of the same 100 per cent caliber." On September 4th of that year the *American Golfer* praised public golf as a great asset to Indianapolis, which boasted more golf links per thousand of population than any other American city. That journal noted that when that city's first municipal course was laid out around 1900, some citizens thought that golf was a game for the rich only. It explained: "There are those who think so yet, but now most of the players on the municipal links are 'regular guys'—men of all occupations, rich and poor alike, male and female, youth and old age, all in a melting pot of genuine sportsmanship." It concluded that "the municipal golf links are a measure of democracy. And of course the democratic spirit is there." In the July 1924 *World's Work*, the legendary former Yale football coach and sportswriter Walter Camp severely criticized private country clubs for "plunging into an orgy of spending" that excluded middle-class people from membership. He insisted that "*golf is not a rich man's game*. It sprang from common folk and the figures of municipal golf carry out that fact." He continued: "Golf is the people's game. It should be a game any one can afford to play." Perhaps he overstated his case a bit when he proclaimed: "Every American should be entitled to the rights of life, liberty, and the pursuit of golf balls. I submit the above as a vitally necessary change in our American Constitution, a change that must come, if we are to live up to our best ideals of sportsmanship and healthful sports for all." In the July 7, 1923, *Colliers*, he cited a national survey that listed only eighty five municipal golf courses in forty-five cities in the United States. He blamed this paltry number on the inaction of the men who administered public playgrounds, who he thought "have been guilty of almost criminal negligence and stupidity in their blind lack of recognition of the necessity for building first-class municipal courses." He concluded that golfers "who are temporarily stymied in their approach to the green of a comfortable bank account, need the healthful sport that golf has to offer." Public golf courses were the remedy.

While the support of prominent golf and sports journalists for municipal golf was helpful in the campaign for public courses during the 1920s, most important were the views of town and city administrators—especially planners and parks commissioners and board members. The vast majority of that influential group believed that a municipal course was a valuable and necessary asset for their community. In 1928 the *Knoxville Journal* maintained that tax funds that provided fire and police protection, public schools, libraries, and other services could also subsidize a golf course. It grounded its argument on the social class issue: "The project for a municipal golf course is an excellent thing. The idea that such a course caters to the pleasures of the rich at the expense of the poor taxpayers is an utterly ridiculous one. . . . Golf is not an expensive game when public courses are available. It can be as much a poor man's game as any sport or recreation can be." One year later, Knoxville's superintendent of the Bureau of Recreation reported that the brand-new course had paid all expenses, including rental and taxes, and showed a profit in its first year of operation.

Financial issues provided the greatest challenge for city officials as they struggled to build and maintain courses at a reasonable cost to their taxpayers. Most communities used public bond sales to pay for the initial purchase of land and construction expenses, while some relied upon special assessment charges against property owners adjacent to the course. Other towns benefited from private gifts of land or fundraising projects. Generally these public links were expected to be self-supporting through green fees that would generate adequate revenue to pay for maintenance and perhaps even part of the outstanding debt. By 1924 virtually all municipal courses charged a green fee that ranged from ten cents to one dollar per day, and between one and ten dollars for a season's pass for residents. The exceptions of free play included the links in Baltimore, Buffalo, Chicago, Memphis, Milwaukee, Omaha, Sacramento, St. Louis, and San Antonio. Locker rentals ranging from five to ten dollars per year provided additional funds.

The campaign launched by sportswriters, city bureaucrats, and editorialists during the 1920s for municipal golf courses generally succeeded, as several hundred new facilities opened during that decade. Still, the growth of private country club links far exceeded that of the public courses during that prosperous era. It is difficult if not impossible to compile an accurate total of municipal golf courses during these years, but a review of several surveys and estimates shows that the number increased from about 60 in 1921 to 140 in 1924 to 201 in 1927 to 291 in 1930. (It is likely that the true total is higher for each year.) In 1930 the highest concentration of public golf courses was in the midwestern states of Illinois, Michigan, Indiana, and Ohio. About half of all municipal links in the nation were in cities with 100,000 or more residents. By way of comparison, a leading annual survey of golf courses shows that the total number of private and public golf courses in the United States skyrocketed from 1,903 in 1923 to 5,856 in 1930. (Two other publications listed the total in 1930 as 4,669 and 4,262.) These figures reveal the huge increase in country clubs and semipublic daily-fee links and the far more modest growth of municipal facilities, which constituted only about 5 to 10 percent of the grand total of courses.

In many American cities, golfers who patronized municipal courses organized public golf clubs to foster social contacts among the players, to establish a fair handicap system and conduct tournaments, to lobby for improvements on their links, and to promote their sport. Public golfers in New York City founded the Municipal Golf Association of New York in 1922, which was designed to serve the same function for public golf as the Metropolitan Golf Association did for the private country clubs. In particular, its officers aimed not only to hold tournaments, but more importantly to press the city administration to change the financial system that directed green fees into a general city sinking fund instead of course improvements. At the national level the United States Golf Association acknowledged and supported the rise of municipal golf by creating a Public Links section and by scheduling the first Amateur Public Links Championship of the United States in the fall of 1922 at Ottawa Park in Toledo, Ohio. In this inaugural event Edward R. Held from Forest Park Club in St. Louis defeated Richard Walsh of New York by a score of 6 and 5 in the thirty-six-hole match play final. In its report in October 1922, *Golf Illustrated* praised the public links movement and the action of the USGA in preserving and extending the Scottish tradition of democratic golf. It endorsed its goal "to allay social discontent and turmoil and refute the demagogue and agitator when they harangue that 'golf is a rich man's game.'" It concluded: "It cannot be too often emphasized nor deeply taken to heart what it all means in the preservation of democracy." That journal linked the American municipal golf movement to the much older Scottish practice of building most of the courses on public lands and opening them to all social classes.

The 1920s also witnessed the growth of modest semipublic and daily-fee courses to meet the demand for golfers who could not afford to join private country clubs. In New England, about 60 nine-hole courses provided recreation at a modest price of twenty-five to forty dollars per year for dues, with no special assessments and no professionals other than a greenkeeper. During these years Chicago became a center for semipublic "pay as you play" courses, in large part due to the demand for grounds by local business and trade golf associations. An editorial in the July 26, 1924, *American Golfer* explained that the Scottish sport had grown so popular that many businesses and vocations had a golf association that scheduled one or more tournaments a year. In the Windy City a prominent golfer and businessman even stated that he would pay an additional five hundred dollars per year to any employee who played golf. But private clubs were becoming more inclined to deny trade associations access to their links because of added congestion. As a result the Chicago Daily Fee Golf Association was founded to provide these trade associations and individuals the opportunity to play golf at a reasonable price. Nine new eighteen-hole courses opened for public play, with a charge of one dollar for weekdays and two dollars for weekends and holidays. In the Chicago area that year there were twenty-nine public golf courses, including the municipal links. Nationwide there were about seven hundred daily-fee public courses in 1931, most of them built after 1925.

⊙ ⊙ ⊙

The decade of the 1920s brought new rounds of democratization of golf among religious, ethnic, and racial minorities from a diverse range of social classes and both sexes in the United States. But even as Jews and African Americans continued to face antisemitism and racism, both elevated their standing in the American golfing community. For the former group, German Jews earned increasing respect through the expansion of country clubs, while for blacks, enhanced status was achieved through both individual contributions and the establishment of their own clubs and associations. Both groups built upon their earlier initiation into the world of American golf prior to 1920. In the meantime, a few celebrated female players elevated women's golf in America through their sterling exploits in championship competition.

Although few of the southern and eastern European newcomers who poured into the nation's seaports between 1880 and World War I could afford to play golf, even on public courses, thousands of descendants of earlier migrants to American shores took up the sport with a passion. Among them were wealthy German Jews, who were excluded from gentile country clubs and the most fashionable resorts. During the early 1900s affluent German Jews founded their own country clubs to showcase their economic success and to counter the stereotype of Jews as weaklings who were obsessed with making money but indifferent to physical activity. They hoped to use golf and other upper-class sports to show that they subscribed to the new American cult of athletics and thus to elevate their social standing and gain acceptance and equal treatment in mainstream American culture. But even as they built lavish clubhouses and constructed well-groomed courses, they achieved little progress in gaining admission to gentile clubs or in reducing the level of antisemitism in American society.

The interest of German Jews in golf dates from the early years of the sport's development in the United States in the late 1890s and early 1900s. Shut out of admission to the leading upper-class country clubs, they founded their own in the suburbs of New York City; Chicago; Philadelphia; Baltimore; Washington, D.C.; St. Louis; Pittsburgh; Montgomery, Alabama, and many other cities across the nation.

Among the first were New York's Century Club (1898) and Inwood Country Club (1901), Baltimore's Suburban Club (1900), and Chicago's Ravisloe Country Club (1901). The Inwood Club rose from humble beginnings to become one of the premier organizations of the 1920s and the site of the 1923 U.S. Open Championship, where Bob Jones won his first national title. It was formed by eighty men who rented a potato field and laid out a rough first course. Fifty resigned after the first season, but the club struggled along until its officers purchased its property in 1915 and fashioned the land into a championship-caliber links. In Baltimore, German Jews who were members of the city's urban Phoenix Club sought a rural retreat where they could amuse themselves with the newly popular game of golf. They held the grand opening of their Suburban Club in November 1901. Officials of Chicago's Ravisloe Club leased 101 acres at Homewood on the Illinois Central railroad line and had a nine-hole course ready for play by September 1901. One year later its roster of 150 was full, with a waiting list, and it was planning to spend $15,000 on a clubhouse and add another nine holes. Ravisloe's charter members were prominent in Chicago's business, civic, and social life. In 1911 it celebrated its tenth anniversary with an invitation tournament that included players from prominent Jewish clubs from around the United States. In 1907 the Philmont Country Club outside of Philadelphia had five hundred members ("the leading Hebrews of the city"), a nine-hole course, eight tennis courts, and a baseball field. Its professional was John Reid, Jr., the son of the "father" of American golf.

Of the dozens of Jewish country clubs launched in the United States during this era, the Lake Shore Country Club of Chicago may serve as an example of the wealth of its predominantly German Jewish membership and the lavish scale of its operation. In 1908, prominent Jews from Chicago followed the success of the Ravisloe Club by founding the Lake Shore Country Club on three hundred acres of the city's North Shore, overlooking Lake Michigan and straddling the border of Highland Park and Glencoe. In 1901 a suburban newspaper editorial offered a welcome to "Hebrews" who were moving into the North Shore region despite objections by local residents. The paper stated: "Tastes do differ, but why object to the sons and daughters of Abraham. We don't object to them, rather we commend them, for they pay their bills one hundred cents on the dollar every time and pay promptly and cheerfully any obligations they make. That kind of thing goes a great way with us." The Lake Shore Club spent $750,000 on its course, clubhouse, and locker rooms. It also promoted the development of Highland Park and Glencoe as a Jewish summer colony, and it enrolled some of the richest and most powerful men in Chicago's German Jewish community and in the city itself. For example, one of its members, Julius Rosenwald, was president of Sears, Roebuck and was reputedly the wealthiest man in Chicago. He was also well-known as a leading philanthropist, and his club demonstrated its patriotism during World War I by raising $30,000 at a charity golf tournament to benefit the Red Cross.

During these years Jews frequently encountered resistance at golf resorts and were sometimes barred from tournaments. They could not purchase property at Pinehurst, North Carolina, and after World War I Pinehurst's manager dropped "suspiciously Hebraic names" from its mailing list to invited guests. But some Jews did apparently slip through the system. A 1920 memo from a guest suggested that Boston visitors believed that Pinehurst had too many "Hebrews." But after arriving the guest expressed surprised "to find that there are so few." In Chicago in 1921 the Women's Western Golf Association excluded Jewish clubs from full membership, which prompted them to withdraw from the organization. Two years later it barred Jewish women from a tournament, even though there were several talented local Jewish female players. On July 16, 1923, the *Jewish Daily Forward* regretted that antisemitism had "infected the sports world—that phase of American life wherein Americans have always maintained that racial intolerance is not to be found."

The prosperity of the 1920s witnessed even greater spending by old and new Jewish country clubs, especially those on the outskirts of New York City and Los Angeles. An annual survey of Jewish country clubs and sport participation published in 1926 in the magazine the *American Hebrew* listed fifty-eight country clubs in twenty states that were owned and operated by predominantly Jewish memberships. Not surprisingly, New York had the greatest number with twenty, while metropolitan Chicago had seven. Philadelphia's Philmont Club boasted the largest membership, with 938 on its rolls. In 1924 it added a second eighteen-hole course and also a polo team. In certain cities eastern European Jews founded their own country clubs when they were denied admission to German Jewish associations. A case in point occurred in Baltimore, where affluent Russian Jews launched the Woodholme Country Club in 1927. One early member recalled: "I didn't want to go over to the Suburban Club because I felt like I wasn't wanted. Our generation as a group felt that way." While there were smaller concentrations of Jews in the South and West, Jewish clubs also thrived in Cincinnati, Cleveland, St. Louis, Kansas City, Miami, Montgomery, New Orleans, and San Antonio.

Many of the nation's wealthiest German Jews were businessmen and professionals in New York City and Los Angeles, and the clubs they founded and joined displayed their wealth and social aspirations. In 1925 in Westchester County north of New York City, the Progress Club bought a 205–acre estate with grounds that featured a white stone mansion of more than forty rooms, which was remodeled as a richly appointed clubhouse. The facilities for members included two golf courses, an outdoor swimming pool, a fishing pond, a field for polo, five guest cottages, and a sixty-car stone garage. Across the continent, Los Angeles's elite German Jews established the Hillcrest Country Club in 1920 on a 142–acre enclave just south of Beverly Hills. Although Los Angeles's German Jews had considerable success in gaining acceptance into that city's gentile social world prior to World War I, after that war they encountered increasing restrictions by country clubs, in part because of negative reactions to eastern European Jews associated with the motion picture industry. Their reaction was the founding of Hillcrest, complete with a golf course, tennis courts, and a palatial clubhouse. Ironically, during the 1920s the German Jews of Hillcrest followed their gentile counterparts in discriminating against Jews of eastern European ancestry, even barring such Hollywood studio moguls as Louis B. Mayer, the Warner brothers, and Adolph Zukor. But during the Great Depression a looming bankruptcy forced Hillcrest to open its doors to these Hollywood Jews and to take on a more eastern European Jewish character.

⊚ ⊚ ⊚

While affluent northern and midwestern German Jews emulated the Protestant elite by founding country clubs, at the opposite end of the social scale were those African American youngsters who learned to play golf as caddies on courses in the South. A few of them became expert professionals, landscape architects, and pioneers of the nation's first all-black clubs. Among these trailblazers of African American golf were Ralph Dawkins, Joseph Bartholomew, and Dewey Brown. Dawkins learned to play golf as a caddie at the Florida Country Club in Jacksonville, then won the Florida state junior golf tournament in 1928. He later competed in state tournaments and became the teaching professional at the Lincoln Golf and Country Club in Jacksonville. Born in New Orleans in 1881, Bartholomew learned to play as a caddie at the Audubon Golf Course. In 1922 his reputation as an accomplished player, teacher, clubmaker, greenkeeper, and landscaper landed him a choice assignment from the prestigious Metairie Golf Club to build a new eighteen-hole course. That achievement led to other assignments in constructing public links in New Orleans, including Pontchartrain Park, which was later renamed the Joseph M. Bartholomew, Sr. Municipal Golf Course in his honor. Ironically, because of his race Bartholomew was not permitted to play golf on any of the private courses he built early in his career. Later in life he became a successful general contractor, and in 1972, just a few months after his death in 1971, he was honored as the first African American to be inducted into the New Orleans Sports Hall of Fame. Dewey Brown was born in 1898 in North Carolina, but his golf career began in New Jersey after his family migrated north. As a boy he too worked as a caddie and groundskeeper, beginning at the Madison Golf Club. But his true talents lay in clubmaking, which he learned under the tutelage of Tom Hucknell at the Morris County Golf Club. After World War I Brown worked for several years as assistant to the club professional at Shawnee-on-the-Delaware in Pennsylvania, and he also held positions at the Baltusrol Golf Club in Springfield and the Hollywood Golf Club, both in New Jersey. In 1928 Brown became the first African American member of the Professional Golfers' Association (PGA), but in 1934 that organization withdrew his eligibility, apparently because it received information that the light-skinned Brown was actually of black ancestry. In the mid-1960s his application for reinstatement was approved. After World War II he bought, managed, and served as the club professional for the Cedar River House and Golf Club at Indian Lake, New York, in the Adirondack Mountains. He died in 1973.

By the 1920s thousands of African Americans were active golfers on public courses in northern and western cities, and a few from the black middle and upper classes were already forming private clubs and playing on their own grounds. The black press took notice and devoted some of the space in its sports pages to highlight growing African American participation and achievements on the links. In 1926 William de Hart Hubbard (a gold medalist in the long jump at the 1924 Olympic Games) wrote a column for the *Pittsburgh Courier* in which he noted that previously, few blacks enjoyed the game because of lack of money and white racism. But now, he argued, public courses had opened the game for the poorer classes. He explained: "Our people have responded. Go to Chicago, Detroit, Cleveland or any city with a public course and you will see colored players enjoying the game. They are not yet as proficient as their white brethren, but they are progressing rapidly. The colored man is taking up golf and he is bound to develop some star players." He also noted with approval the surprisingly good performance of black youths in a public links caddie tournament. He predicted it would not be long before there were some "top notch" black players, but he doubted whether they would get the chance to compete in the major tournaments. He predicted correctly that "we will probably have to have colored golf tournaments just as we now have colored tennis championships, and baseball championships." Between the World Wars the black press continued to actively promote African American golf through the publication of articles about club news and golf instruction, tournaments, prominent players, and racial issues of segregation.

Although African Americans organized golf clubs prior to World War I, they generally did not own their own grounds, but rather used public courses for their sport. But by the 1920s a critical mass of middle-class black golfers had the means and the opportunity to purchase land and to manage their own associations. During that decade there were at least fourteen black golf clubs in eight states and the District of Columbia, although not all owned their own links. The largest concentration was in Washington, D.C., with three, while others were launched in Massachusetts, New York, New Jersey, Pennsylvania, Maryland, Virginia, Florida, and Illinois. The Shady Rest Club in New Jersey was organized in 1921 after a group of black golfers purchased the white-owned Westfield Country Club. Shady Rest was likely the first organization founded by African Americans that featured a clubhouse and the range of sports generally associated with white country clubs during this era. It became a social and cultural center for prosperous blacks during the 1920s, hosting tournaments, concerts, and meetings for the African American community, including such intellectuals and writers as W. E. B. DuBois. To a small degree it also served the needs of less privileged blacks in that it opened its doors to visitors on Saturdays for a seventy-five-cent admission fee. It survived a divisive struggle for control in 1925 between factions based in New York and New Jersey, but in the Depression of the early 1930s Shady Rest became the property of the township of Scotch Plains. Yet it remained a black organization until 1963, when it was opened to the public as the Scotch Hills Country Club. For its final thirty years it was also the home course of John Shippen, Jr., discussed previously.

The Mapledale Country Club had a much shorter and more troubled history than its New Jersey counterpart, and it represents one of the many attempts to form black-owned golf associations that failed within a few years. Located twenty-five miles outside Boston, it was the brainchild of Robert H. Hawkins. Established in 1926 on the former estate of a prominent physician, it had a clubhouse, a nine-hole course, and tennis courts. It was also the site of three national black open golf championships. But Hawkins's dreams were dashed when the local black community did not enroll in sufficient numbers to keep his club solvent, perhaps because of its distance from Boston or criticism of his management of club affairs. Hawkins lost $25,000 of his personal investment and gave up his venture in 1929. On March 31st of that year his club changed its name to the Stow Golf and County Club and opened its links to all races.

The flurry of activity in founding black golf clubs naturally led to a movement to launch the first African American national golf organization. In this Jim Crow era of American sports, racial discrimination by whites barred blacks from competing in the major baseball, football, and basketball leagues and in golf and tennis tournaments. The only alternative was to follow the example of the Negro Leagues in baseball and create an all-black golf association. A group of black players took the first steps in that direction in 1925 in Washington, D.C. by founding the United States Colored Golf Association (USCGA), also known as the Colored Golfers Association. On Labor Day weekend that year the Shady Rest Club hosted an open "international" golf championship, with Harry Jackson and John Shippen (both based in Washington, D.C.) the victor and runner-up, respectively. Over the next few years the USCGA changed its name to the United Golfers Association (UGA) and held its next three tournaments at the Mapledale Country Club before the competition returned to Shady Rest in 1929. The UGA consisted of regional organizations of black golfers, including the Eastern Golfers Association, and it periodically coordinated the scheduling of their competitions. Besides Jackson and Shippen, Robert "Pat" Ball, Walter Speedy, Henry Johnson, and Porter Washington vied for the title of best black golfer in the United States during the late 1920s. By the end of the decade the annual UGA tournament was recognized as the "Negro National Open" and was a major sporting and social event for the elite

of the black community. These competitions also promoted comparable tournaments at the state and regional levels.

◎ ◎ ◎

The Golden Age of sport in the 1920s also featured an extraordinary increase in girls' and women's athletics, which had important consequences for American golf. It was an era that brought new fashions and new standards of beauty for women, more physically demanding styles of dancing, and more acceptance of female sexuality. The press adored such sporting heroines as Gertrude Ederle in swimming and Helen Wills in tennis and championed more active lives for both sexes. Although affluent women did not gain equal treatment in country clubs during that decade, they became more prominent both on the courses and in the clubhouses. Meanwhile their middle-class counterparts took advantage of the growing number of municipal and daily-fee courses. Newspapers and magazines also expanded their coverage of ladies championship tournaments.

The premier golfing woman of the 1920s—the "female Bob Jones" as she was then called—was Glenna Collett, a six-time national amateur champion. Like the Curtis sisters and Alexa Stirling, she was raised in an affluent family and enjoyed an active, athletic girlhood. Born in 1903, as a youngster she loved playing baseball with her brother's team in Providence, Rhode Island, until she was nearly fourteen. Then her mother intervened and suggested that she "take up a game more becoming a young girl." First she tried tennis, but a trip with her father to the Metacomet Golf Club changed

The Citizens' Golf Club of Washington, D.C., was an African American association founded during the early 1920s. John Shippen was its golf professional between 1921 and 1927. General Research and Reference Division, Schomburg Center for Research in Black Culture, the New York Public Library, Astor, Lenox and Tilden Foundations.

her life. After smashing a few tee shots she had found her calling, and with her father's encouragement she began lessons with a Scottish professional in New Haven, Alex Smith. During World War I she was enthralled while watching a Red Cross four-ball exhibition match at her home club that featured Bob Jones, Perry Adair, Alexa Stirling, and Elaine Rosenthal. While most of the gallery followed the young phenom Jones around the links, Glenna was mesmerized by the women—especially Stirling, whose poise under fire greatly impressed her. After a few years of practice and mixed success in tournaments, she dropped her plans to pursue a college education in 1921 to devote her energies full time to championship golf.

Collett's dedication to golf paid off, for over the next decade she dominated the sport among the ladies. She symbolized the new American woman in the Roaring Twenties with her competitive success, her attractiveness, and her grace and style under pressure. In 1922, at the age of nineteen, she won her first national women's amateur title, defeating Mrs. William A. Gavin. Two years later she triumphed in fifty-nine out of sixty matches, but lost a semifinal contest in the women's national championship to Mary K. Browne. Undaunted, she returned to capture five more U.S. Women's Amateur trophies in 1925, 1928, 1929, 1930, and 1935. The last crown was particularly satisfying, for Collett had taken several years off from championship competition to marry and bear two children. In the final she defeated the teenage prodigy Patty Berg with a long, dramatic putt on the thirty-fourth hole. The only blemish on her superlative record is that she was never able to defeat her nemesis from Great Britain, Joyce Wethered. Their most memorable match occurred in 1929 in the thirty-six-hole final of the British Ladies Amateur Championship at St. Andrews. Collett took the early lead in the morning round on that day, but in the afternoon Wethered passed her and won the title with a long putt on the seventeenth hole, much to the delight of the cheering crowd of Scottish spectators. In 1965 the USGA honored her with the Bob Jones Award for sportsmanship, and in 1975 she was inducted into the World Golf Hall of Fame. She died in 1989.

Another star female golfer of the 1920s was Marion Hollins, who gained fame both as the national amateur women's champion in 1921 and also as a founder of several distinctive courses on both the east and west coasts. Her first project was to plan a golf course designed and built for women only—the Women's National Golf and Tennis Club at Glen Head, Long Island. Her goal was "to create a course that would bring out the best in women's golf without sacrificing length or hazards." She argued that such a course "should not be of the usual standard type designed for men because it is impossible for most women players, despite the great advance made by their sex during the past few seasons, to cope with a man's course on equal terms with par or even with bogey." She then toured Great Britain to photograph and sketch famous holes that would serve as models for many on her new links. After returning home she hired golf architect Devereux Emmet, assisted by Charles Blair Macdonald and Seth Raynor, to plan the final layout. The average length of Alexa Stirling's tee shots (about 175 yards) was used as the standard for the placement of fairway hazards. The course opened on Memorial Day 1924, and it lasted seventeen years until it merged with a nearby all-male club on the eve of World War II. Hollins later relocated to California, where she made a fortune in oil exploration and played key roles in the designing of the Cypress Point course on the Monterey Peninsula and the Pasatiempo links near Santa Cruz.

Although the overwhelming majority of early American female golfers were Protestant or Catholic white girls and women, a small minority were Jewish or African American. While these two groups were from opposite ends of the social scale, their participation does suggest the widespread appeal of golf during its formative years in the United States. From the early 1900s through the 1920s golf was the most popular sport among wealthy Jewish country club women. Jewish newspapers and magazines such as the *American Hebrew* published detailed and illustrated accounts of their exploits on the links, highlighting their championships won in local and regional competitions. Significantly, coverage of their achievements also often included references to their families and their memberships in exclusive clubs. A recurrent theme was that their success on the golf course did not preclude fulfilling family lives shared with husbands and children. But it was also true that most if not all of the most talented female golfers learned the game before they married. The premier female Jewish golfer of this era was Elaine Rosenthal Reinhart of Chicago's Ravisloe Country Club. A three-time Women's Western Golf Association champion between 1917 and 1925, she gained national attention during World War I when she toured the United States as part of a celebrity golf foursome that gave exhibition matches to raise money for the Red Cross.

The participation of privileged Jewish women in early American golf is certainly understandable given their social and economic status, but much more surprising is the role of African American females. A few photographs showing black girls and young women holding golf clubs and an instructional essay in an African American west coast newspaper provide fragmentary evidence of a black female interest in golf prior to 1930. In 1925, Elise

Johnson McDougald, a Harlem elementary school principal, published an article in which she referred to a small privileged black upper class that enjoyed the "luxuries of well-appointed homes, modest motors, tennis, golf and country clubs, trips to Europe and California." By the end of that decade there were a number of black women golfers who were proficient enough to gain recognition in African American newspapers. Women played an important role in the first black golf clubs, but it was not until 1930 that the United Golfers Association held its first female championship, won by Marie Thompson.

During the Roaring Twenties American golf experienced its first golden age as amateur and professional champions, the country club set, and patrons of public courses propelled their favorite pastime to new heights of popularity. Most of the best golfers were from the privileged or middle classes, but a few (most notably Hagen and Sarazen), were raised in ethnic, working-class families. Others who were outsiders to the white Anglo-Saxon establishment (especially Jews and African Americans) also became enthusiastic participants, even though private country clubs excluded them. The brilliant play of Glenna Collett, Marion Hollins, Alexa Stirling, and Elaine Rosenthal during the 1920s signaled the arrival of women's golf during the Era of the New Woman and the Golden Age of sport. The ladies had certainly come a long way since the days of country club women at Shinnecock Hills and Morris County, and their performances far surpassed the early tournament play of such pioneers as Beatrix Hoyt and Harriot and Margaret Curtis. On private and public courses women were also demanding equal respect and fair treatment, including the right to play on holidays and weekends and to wear appropriate and comfortable clothes as they stroked and putted their way around the courses. But despite a good start, in 1930 American women still had a long way to go to realize their goals of equal opportunity and full participation in the Scottish sport that had swept the nation in the preceding decades. All these groups helped to advance the sport in the United States before the Great Depression brought the good times to an abrupt end.

DEPRESSION
AND WAR

In a sobering piece published in the *American Mer-cury* in February 1933, Kenneth P. Kempton outlined the daunting financial predicament that threatened his posh White Brook Country Club. Although he probably used a fictitious title to conceal its identity, its plight was no fabrication and certainly was shared by many other private golf organizations across the nation. He explained: "We have a $50,000 house equipped with every known convenience and luxury; we have a championship course offering fresh beauties, fresh challenges to skill, on every tee; we have a practice green, tennis courts, a skating rink, a swimming pool, a toboggan run—all the trimmings. But at this moment we have less than half the income necessary to save the club from collapse and dissolution." After much soul-searching the members decided to follow the advice of an old-timer. He told them: "Golf is not a rich man's game. Go ahead and laugh. But any game, to be worth while, must be a poor man's game, not loading a man down with costly stuff that takes his mind off the prime essential—to hit the ball like merry hell." They followed his recommendations and drastically cut their expenses, keeping the course open by shutting down the clubhouse, firing most of the employees, and requiring members to carry their own bags and do most of the groundskeeping. Some no doubt chose to give up the sport, at least for the time being. As one pundit wrote in a satirical piece in the same magazine in August 1934, one positive benefit of the hard times was the decline in golf. He remarked: "God sent that blessing in disguise, the Depression, to turn men from such follies as golfing, stock-broking and marathon dancing back to honest, healthy occupations like farming and road building."

For the American people in general and for golfers in particular the contrasts between the 1930s and the 1920s were striking. As the Great Depression swelled the ranks of the unemployed and compelled men and women to think foremost about their families' survival, sports naturally receded in importance. Yet the severe economic downtown carried important consequences for both private and public golfers. As many country clubs faced retrenchment or even dissolution, some of their members sought less expensive ways of enjoying their favorite pastime on municipal or daily-fee courses. As more players crowded onto these grounds, city, state, and federal work relief programs hired an army of laborers to upgrade existing links and build hundreds of new ones. The result was an increase in popular participation on public courses and the expansion of public golf facilities for the enjoyment of present and future generations. Thus the great cloud of the country's economic crisis contained a silver lining for the lovers of the Scottish sport. Further, even through the hard times Gene Sarazen and other champions of the decade provided thrilling competition that provided escapist entertainment for millions of Americans who welcomed some diversion from their everyday woes. Yet as the prospects for American golf brightened with the revival of the economy after 1938, a new challenge arose in December 1941 with the entry of the United States into World War II.

Considering the proliferation of posh country clubs and their extravagant spending on clubhouses, courses, and social events during the 1920s, it is not surprising that most of them experienced a critical financial crisis during the early 1930s as members resigned and waiting lists vanished. In responding to economic pressures, many clubs adopted measures that had a democratizing effect on memberships and social policies. John Kieran explained on July 30, 1933, in the *New York Times*: "Golf went democratic even before the national political tide turned in that direction at the Presidential polls in 1932. In the great boom period in this country, the simple pastime fostered by the thrifty inhabitants of the seacoast of Scotland was converted into a luxurious game garnished with gorgeous appointments and surroundings. Golf went gayly beyond the golf standard. It was resting in splendor on the platinum peak when the earthquake hit Wall Street. After that the deluge!" Kieran conceded that the "staid, old-line golf clubs . . . weathered the financial storms of the last few years fairly well." He argued that they never were very expensive and carried no vast overhead. But what, he asked, was the fate of a golfer in a club "who was plodding the links carrying a pergola, a tiled swimming pool, a gaudy garden, an extensive social program and a luxurious clubhouse on his back, financially speaking?" He answered: "The story is told in the vast number of resignations from membership lists and the march of many of these clubs into involuntary bankruptcy. Those that are still staggering along are, for the most part, in a desperate condition."

Clubs facing large deficits or even financial ruin tried a variety of remedies to restore themselves to solvency. Many of these had the effect of extending playing privileges to classes of people who would have been denied entrance during the more flush times. Some organizations created new categories of "house" or "associate" memberships through policies that reduced annual dues, lowered or abolished initiation fees, and waived requirements that new members purchase an expensive bond or stock certificate. Although in some cases these new members faced restrictions on playing times, they also paid a lower green fee for each round, especially during weekdays. Some suggested that clubs actively recruit "social" members at a nominal fee who would share all the privileges except golf, and also seek out more female players (and dues payers). Clubs also lowered the price of food, and after the end of Prohibition in 1933 the sale of alcohol boosted clubhouse income. Caddie fees also declined from about two dollars to one dollar a round, including tip. Lower prices for golf balls and clubs also made membership in a country club more affordable for those middle-class families that were not devastated by the Great Depression. During the 1930s golf journals also devoted much attention to reforming golf club management, improving course maintenance, and eliminating waste and corrupt business practices.

Despite the gloomy news about many golf clubs, during the Depression there were still signs of life among those who remained loyal to country clubs. In 1933 *Time* magazine reported that 25 percent of the nation's golf clubs were bankrupt or had suspended operations, but according to a March 1933 issue of *Golfdom*, that statement was a mistaken reference to the 25 percent decline in the USGA's membership in a little over two years. *Golfdom* countered with the dubious conclusion that "more clubs operated at a profit in 1932 than during any other year of American golf history." It asserted that very few clubs folded completely, "and those were largely of the 9–hole pasture type." It did concede that some country clubs were now operating as daily-fee courses, but it added that "that should arouse more golf interest if properly worked." In December 1937 *Sports Illustrated and the American Golfer* recalled that earlier in the 1930s golf club income declined by up to 65 percent and green committees had to operate with only one-third of the money they had during prosperous times. But now, after a "siege of retrenchment," clubs were becoming profitable again, partly because of new facilities and dances and parties that attracted new members and raised more money. A composite financial analysis of four prominent clubs in the New York City metropolitan district revealed that although the 1929 income of $110,000 had fallen to $40,000 by "mid-depression," it had risen to $87,000 in 1936.

⊚ ⊚ ⊚

While thousands of white-collar players resigned from their clubs and quit the game entirely during the Depression, some sought an escape from their woes on municipal or daily-fee courses, or on grounds built by corporations for their employees. In 1933, average annual compensation for industrial workers in the United States was $1,089, which increased to $1,342 in 1939. Although those incomes were certainly modest, they did enable some wage earners to purchase inexpensive clubs and play rounds on public or company courses. In a few cases blue-collar industrial workers organized golf programs. In Flint, Michigan, machine operators founded an "Overall Club" and began playing on municipal courses in 1925. By 1933, three thousand workers, clerks, and executives from Flint factories competed in twelve leagues, replacing baseball as the sport of choice for these employees. Writing for the *American Golfer* in August 1933, George Hammond reported the democratizing effect: "Executives and office workers and machinists all mingle in the comradeship of golf, and more often than not, the subordinate in the shop is gloriously superior on the links." In Pueblo, Colorado, workers from a fuel and iron company built a rudimentary course on the prairie. George Kirk of the firm's employee service department suggested that "perhaps the depression has helped in giving the game a boost," for the lack of work inspired employees "to turn to wholesome and beneficial use of their leisure time." In Hammond's view, "golf has enabled large numbers of workers to relax and get some fun out of life, in the midst of trying conditions. It has been a saving force in keeping up the morale of the men."

During the 1930s a few major American corporations constructed company golf courses for their employees, two of them in Endicott in upstate New York. George T. Johnson, president of the Endicott-Johnson Company, was an ardent golfer who built a course for his workers and set its green fee at twenty-five cents. To encourage participation he also purchased several thousand golf clubs and bags and sold them to workers for $1.00 a club and $2.50 a bag. A few years later Thomas J. Watson of International Business Machines opened a company country club for his employees in Endicott, requiring only a nominal fee of one dollar and a green fee of twenty-five cents. In April 1941 *Golfdom* explained that his aim was "to make the club the hub around which social life and the recreational activities of the employees would center and to provide recreation for the entire family group." By the eve of World War II golf had become the preferred sport among a wide variety of pastimes available, with more than 1,200 golfers playing 40,000 rounds.

The available statistics on patronage of municipal golf facilities provide only estimates and are probably inaccurate, but they do suggest that millions of golfers continued to play their favorite sport despite the dismal economic conditions. The National Recreation Association's survey of 1930 estimated that 7,520,000 people frequented municipal courses that year. A more scientific survey of 543 municipal and 700 daily-fee facilities conducted in 1931 by *Golfdom* and reported in that magazine in June 1932 counted 24,666,500 rounds played on municipal courses and 9,705,500 rounds on daily-fee links, for a total of 34,372,000. That journal also found that the average fee charged for a round on these courses ranged from fifty-four cents for a weekday on a municipal course to eighty-four cents on a Sunday on a daily-fee course. In September 1931 *Golfdom* reported the opening of hundreds of new municipal or commercial courses, with new opportunities for impoverished farmers who owned land near cities to convert their fields into links. It cited an example of two midwesterners who were barely able to pay the taxes on their property: "They dug up some dough, hired an architect who laid out nine holes and did a good part of their construction work with farm labor under the architect's supervision." In 1931 they were taking in six to seven hundred dollars a week charging fifty cents to a dollar a round. Thus public golf provided one solution to the farm relief problem. When *Golfdom* published another survey of private and public golf in October 1936 its statistics indicated that while "no one doubts that golf slumped seriously during the depression . . . all agree that the past several years have seen the game recover much of the ground it lost." It calculated that as of October 1, 1936, the United States had 3,705 private golf clubs, 1,050 daily-fee courses, and 606 municipal links, for a total of 5,361. It also estimated the number of golfers at 861,000 (private), 203,000 (daily-fee), and 301,000 (municipal), totaling 1,365,000. These men, women, boys, and girls played more than 58 million rounds in 1936, including 31.7 million on private courses, 12.1 million on daily-fee links, and 14.3 million on municipal facilities.

Golfers who could not afford to pay for country club privileges during the Depression still had two options in most communities: the daily-fee or municipal links. Usually the fees were slightly higher in the former (semiprivate) courses, in part because the latter did not have to pay local taxes. Owners and operators of commercial public courses thought these tax exemptions gave cities an unfair advantage in attracting players. Max Ludwig, the owner of a Pennsylvania daily-fee course, raised the issue in a May 1933 article in *Golfdom*. "Is Paternalism in government going too far," he asked, "when the municipalities engage in competition with owners of fee courses and take an 'edge' by subsidies out of taxes paid in part by the fee course owner to his municipal competitor?" Ludwig charged that local governments were building golf courses, maintaining them at a loss, and then were "nonchalantly extracting the difference out of the hides of the genial but long suffering taxpayer." It was especially troubling to owners of daily-fee links in the provinces at a distance from densely populated metropolitan areas. He concluded that while the entrance of government into the business of golf was good for the golfer, "it was a bitter pill for the public golf course owner," especially "if the city-owned course operates at a deficit and he then contributes a share of his tax money to foster golf at less than cost and at the expense of his own business." It would not be the last time that operators of daily-fee facilities would complain about unfair competition from city and county governments.

Golf lovers who refused to be deterred by the hard times flocked to public courses in large numbers during the early 1930s, but as the Depression deepened between 1932 and 1936 patronage at municipal grounds fell 25 percent nationwide and as much as 40 percent in some metropolitan areas. New York City proved to be an exception to the national downward trend of the middle of the decade. In 1934 Gotham's eight public courses recorded a total of 370,580 rounds, with more than 500,000 projected for 1935. By the late 1930s the number on ten courses had swelled to just over 600,000. Other cities also experienced an increase in public golf during these years. For 1938 *Golfdom* reported a 14 percent growth over the previous year for fifty-three municipal courses in thirteen metropolitan districts. A June 2, 1935, *New York Times* account of its city's public golfers divided them into three categories. The first included "the old-timers—the doctors, dentists, small businessmen, brokers and merchants, who have been playing a particular course for years." The second were "recent graduates from the ranks of caddies," who "play a pretty sound game, affect a careless disorder of dress and seem frequently to make a point of going around with as few clubs as possible, perhaps in studied contrast to their less spectacular elders." The third group constituted the novices, both men and women, whose ranks included many bookkeepers and secretaries. Their play featured "wild swings and flying divots"; some had "only the haziest conception of the difference between a golf club and, say, a hockey stick."

During the 1930s golfers also crowded public links in midwestern cities. In Chicago, park authorities struggled with how to cope with the sport's "terrifying popularity." A 1937 survey of Chicago's municipal golfers revealed that the sport was recovering strongly from the Depression. Most of the golfers were in their twenties and thirties, and more than half played all their rounds on the public links. Nearly three-fourths listed amusement or some factor other than health as their primary reason for playing the sport. Cincinnati's director of recreation, Tam Deering, described a "phenomenal increase" in the growth of golf in that city. Deering argued that the golf boom was due only in part to a lowering of fees. More important was a reversal in public opinion. Previously townspeople were hostile to golf because they viewed it as a game of "an exclusive social set" that "involved wearing unusual types of clothes" and as a sport of "the leisure class." But enthusiasts used a newspaper campaign and free group lessons in neighborhoods, factories, department stores, and schools to reverse these attitudes and promote the gospel of golf. As a result "working men, clerks, and those of all ages and groups were taking up municipal golf."

Early in the Great Depression public officials realized that municipal golf courses provided ideal opportunities for emergency relief employment funded by city, state, and especially federal government programs. As golf architect and consultant Robert H. Humphreys explained in 1932, since construction costs had fallen more than 50 percent since the late 1920s, a new facility that charged a nominal green fee could pay off its debt within three or four years. Land was readily available in many cities and towns, and since the proportion of labor to materials was very high, almost all money spent went into relief payrolls. Humphreys concluded: "Through golf construction, an avenue of employment is opened to any man who is able to work." Communities that did not wish to add new courses could hire laborers to upgrade fairways and greens that had deteriorated due to heavy usage and years of neglect.

New York City, the birthplace of municipal golf in the United States, became a prime beneficiary of government funds invested in the expansion and improvement of its ten public courses. In January 1934 *Golf Illustrated* printed a brief editorial on "The Disgrace of Gotham's Public Courses," but three months later it praised the appointments of Robert Moses as the city's new parks commissioner and John R. Van Kleek as supervisor of the golf course renovations. As a June 2, 1935, *New York Times* magazine article reported, the city's Parks Department was "trying to take the mental and physical hazards out of municipal golf." It explained that "the hardy souls who ventured out on those links" encountered "pancake greens, turfless tee and shuttle fairways" that "never saw a bag of fertilizer or a pound of grass seed from one Spring to the next, and a minimum of ten bushels of worms could be gathered on any green at any time." But when Moses took office during the administration of Fiorello La Guardia, "he quickly concluded that the down-at-heels system would be a 'natural' for work relief" because of the high proportion of money that went directly to labor costs. Van Kleek began work in February 1934, and over the next year the city spent $3.5 million, including $2.8 million on an average of 3,800 laborers per week, who applied liberal amounts of fertilizer and grass seed and built bunkers and enlarged tees. It also added nine holes to the La Tourette links, remodeled those at Pelham Bay, Forest Park, and Dyker Beach, and constructed new courses at Split Rock in the Bronx and Kissena in Queens.

Although the federal government's aid to municipal golf courses actually began at the very end of Herbert Hoover's presidency, the major boost to public golf came from Franklin Roosevelt's New Deal. In 1932, under Hoover's administration, Congress authorized the Reconstruction Finance Corporation (RFC), which permitted loans to eligible projects (including golf courses) that were economically desirable and "self-liquidating" through fees charged for their use. The advent of Roosevelt's New Deal in March 1933 brought more substantial public relief projects that dramatically aided the cause of municipal golf, especially through its Civil Works Administration (CWA, 1933) and its Works Progress Administration (WPA, 1935). Those agencies financed the building or improving of six hundred courses throughout the nation, beginning in 1934. As early as December 1935, 206 communities in thirty-nine states had new or rebuilt courses, clubhouses, or improved grounds. By October of the following year 247 public golf projects were underway, including seventy-five new courses. By that date the WPA had spent $5.5 million on golf course work, with another million dollars contributed by local sponsors. In one project in Schenectady, in upstate New York, the recruited workers included farmers, chemists and biologists, plumbers, engineers, draftsmen, agriculturists, botanists and landscape architects, and even a modeler. To maximize the relief rolls, much of the work was done by hand labor and simple tools instead of steam-driven machinery. Bob Jones volunteered his services as an advisor to the WPA program and commented: "It will go a long way toward reducing the costs of the game for the average person. That is what is needed to popularize golf." He urged officials to hire "competent golf architects" in laying out new grounds. In the spring of 1936 Jones visited several New York City facilities and singled out the new Split Rock course for special commendation. In its first two years the WPA spent $10.5 million on 368 public golf courses nationwide, including 62 new facilities. Local governments contributed another $1.5 million.

A few of these grounds became celebrated as among the finest in the nation, public or private. Perhaps most noteworthy was the four-course layout at Bethpage State Park, near Farmingdale, Long Island. In 1932 the Long Island State Park Commission had leased 1,368 acres of land in Farmingdale that was the former site of a residential estate that featured an eighteen-hole golf course designed by Devereux Emmet. After acquiring title to the property in 1934, the newly formed Bethpage Park Authority hired the noted golf architect A. W. Tillinghast to renovate the existing course and design three new eighteen-hole layouts, with materials and labor supplied by the CWA. According to *Golfdom*, the four courses at Bethpage constituted "the largest publicly owned golf center in the world." It explained that "Bethpage has become the mecca for a great army of metropolitan golfers who cannot afford private clubs and who find facilities of a private club in a completely democratic atmosphere. In the parking lot fields may be seen cars large and small, antiquated and new; on the golf courses well-to-do people with caddies, playing behind clerks and mechanics carrying their own bags. In the grill and locker rooms, golfers from all walks of life eat, drink and enjoy themselves, brought together by the unique facilities which the park offers." It concluded that "the construction of Bethpage is an accomplishment of the Depression." The most famous of the original four links is the Black Course, which opened in 1936 and was the site of the 1936 U.S. Amateur Public Links Championship and the 2002 U.S. Open. (A fifth Yellow Course opened in 1958).

In late 1936 the Professional Golfers' Association (PGA) announced an ambitious new project to work with the federal government in planning and building another six hundred municipal courses. That organization named Tillinghast as a consultant to inspect proposed new sites. The PGA would also help to assure that "no previously established course or club will suffer in patronage by proximity to the new course." While only a modest number of these courses were ever built, the expansion of facilities and improvements of the mid-1930s dramatically enhanced the status of municipal golf during the Depression. As the *New York Times* affirmed in an editorial on May 3, 1936: "When the economic depression has receded it will not be quite the same America that rises above the waves. Among other things, it will be studded with golf courses. . . . Golf under the WPA has thus the same significance as highways, bridges, dams and land reclamation under PWA [Public Works Administration]. Public Works or Works Progress, they testify to a firm belief in the future of this country and this people. There will be automobiles to drive on arterial roads and over bridges. There will be factories to run by electric power and homes to heat and illuminate. There will be golf links to play on and a nation in the mood to play."

During the Depression some cities were able to finance, construct, and maintain municipal golf courses without the benefit of WPA assistance. Officials in several cities took advantage of the depressed real estate market to purchase large tracts of land for park development. A few courses, such as those in New Haven and San Francisco, opened just prior to the stock market crash but flourished during the 1930s. Others, such as those in San Diego and Galveston, were integral parts of ambitious recreational parkland facilities. Some towns began plans for a public course in 1929 and persevered even as the economy sank. That year in Albany, New York, the mayor announced that considering the popularity of golf it was "imperative" that his city construct a course. Over the next few years a temporary nine opened for play, and in May 1931 work began on the full eighteen-hole layout, which opened the following May.

On the eve of World War II it was obvious that during the Depression municipal golf courses had contributed greatly to the preservation and even expansion of the sport in the United States during trying times. As A. T. Comstock explained in *Golfdom* in August 1939, the first challenge was to convince the people "that golf was a legitimate business for a city to engage in," because managers of private and public fee courses felt "the municipal course was a menace to their well-being." But Comstock argued: "It is most fortunate for golf, and I mean the welfare of the sport as a whole, that the municipal courses were ready and fully established when the depression years of the 'thirties' arrived." In his view the municipal courses gave the former country club members a chance to continue playing golf, "and some day will return these players to the private clubs and fee courses, and promote a new crop." He doubted whether the public links in any way cut into the business of the private or fee courses, stating: "If the cheaper municipal golf had not been available the golf would just not have been played." In the end he was certain that the thousands of new golfers created through the municipal links would become "the legitimate game for the private and fee courses and they will flock to them in droves."

◎ ◎ ◎

During the Depression, championship competition provided escapist entertainment for America's golfing public, as new stars sought to fill the void left by the retirement of Bob Jones. But even as he exited center stage, Jones remained in the limelight through his role as a founder of the Augusta National Golf Club and its signature event—the Masters Invitational Tournament. During the early 1930s Jones's departure from the golfing scene and the slumping economy sharply reduced interest (and gate receipts) at the U.S. Open, professional tournaments, and national amateur events. Next came a time of transition, as Gene Sarazen, a hero of the golden age of the 1920s, returned to form with four major titles between 1932 and 1935. The end of the decade witnessed a rejuvenated PGA tour and the emergence of new stars who would dominate the nation's golfing scene during and especially after World War II—Sam Snead, Byron Nelson, and Ben Hogan.

Jones's great gift to the world of golf was the course that he and Alister MacKenzie built for the Augusta National Golf Club. In an interview with a reporter published in the *New York Times* on August 7, 1932, Jones explained that his goal was to construct a layout that would "afford plenty of trials and tribulations" for skilled players, but at the same time would "give pleasure to golf's lame, halt, and blind—the high handicap players who pay the freight charges and get least for their money." Each hole was designed to both test the mettle of the most gifted amateurs and professionals and also offer an alternative route for average golfers who simply wished to keep their balls in play. Jones and MacKenzie also sharply contoured the greens to make birdies difficult. The course opened in December 1932, and in 1934 the Augusta National Golf Club hosted an invitational event that soon became known as the Masters. Horton Smith captured the first title with a one-stroke victory over Craig Wood.

1932 was a year of misery for President Herbert Hoover, the Republican Party, and many ordinary Americans who were jobless or homeless, but it was time of triumph for Gene Sarazen, who returned to glory with victories at the British Open and U.S. Open. His success at the British Open was particularly satisfying because of several previous poor performances dating back to 1923. At Prince's Golf Club at Sandwich, England, he used a new sand wedge he had recently designed and hired an aging caddie, Skip Daniels, who helped him lead all four rounds en route to a record score of 283. A few months later at the Fresh Meadow Country Club on Long Island, New York, he won his second U.S. Open. Trailing by five shots after 36 holes, he charged back to win with final rounds of 70 (including a 32 on the back nine) and 66.

Over the next three years Sarazen maintained his pre-eminence among the nation's professional golfers. He earned his third PGA crown in 1933 at the Blue Mound Country Club in Milwaukee, Wisconsin. But it was at the Masters in 1935 that Sarazen put his name in the pantheon of golf heroes when he hit a shot that many believe remains the most spectacular stroke ever played in the long and storied history of the game—the "shot heard round the world." In the final round he came to the 485–yard fifteenth hole three shots behind the leader, Craig Wood, who was already in the clubhouse. A fine drive down the right side left him with a 235–yard second shot over a pond. Playing boldly, he struck his spoon (three-wood) perfectly. His ball carried the pond, landed on the front of the green, and rolled straight into the hole for a deuce and an incredible double-eagle. He followed that feat with three solid pars that gained him a tie with Wood. The next day he easily defeated Wood by five strokes in their playoff, and thereby became the first golfer to win the modern career Grand Slam (Masters, U.S. Open, British Open, PGA Championship).

Although Sarazen would not win another major title, he and his fellow professional golfers benefited enormously from the increasing number of events and the greater prize money beginning in 1937. The man who was primarily responsible for launching the new era was Fred Corcoran, a rotund storytelling Irishman who became the PGA's traveling tournament director during the 1936–37 winter season. Corcoran was a master at persuading business leaders of municipal Chambers of Commerce and resort publicists that sponsoring a golf tournament would boost corporate sales and attract thousands of tourists to their cities. He was also a fountain of statistics and colorful anecdotes, providing local and national journalists with choice material for their reports and columns. Above all, he recruited talented players, a few of whom blossomed into stars who captivated America's sporting public. His eleven years of tireless work as the PGA tournament manager and three more as its promotional director laid a lucrative foundation for professional golf's next golden age during the 1950s.

Any sport needs attractive characters to boost public interest, and just prior to World War II golf gained a new generation of heroes with the arrival of three men born in 1912: Snead, Nelson, and Hogan. Samuel ("Slammin' Sam") Jackson Snead was born May 27, 1912, in Ashwood, Virginia, near Hot Springs. He learned his sweet swing practicing barefoot in a cow pasture, using limbs or sticks as makeshift clubs. An all-around athlete in high school, after graduation he perfected his game first at jobs at two Hot Springs courses and then at the Greenbrier Golf Club in White Sulphur Springs, West Virginia. He won his first PGA tournament in 1936 and a total of twenty-eight tour events through 1942. His humble origins, folksy, homespun humor, and early success made him a darling of the media, but a classic collapse at the 1939 U.S. Open at the Philadelphia Country Club's Spring Mill course haunted him for the rest of his life. Leading Nelson by two strokes in the final round with two holes to play, he dropped one shot with a bogey five on the seventeenth hole. With no leader board to show him the current standings, he mistakenly believed he needed a birdie four on the par five eighteenth hole for victory. What followed was a disheartening hooked drive into the rough, a topped two-wood into a fairway bunker, a duffed sand shot, an explosion into another bunker, a fifth shot onto the green, and three putts for a disastrous eight. The next day Nelson prevailed in a three-way playoff over Craig Wood and Denny Shute. Snead came close to winning the U.S. Open several more times over his long and illustrious career, but he never captured that one major trophy. He often said: "If I'd shot 69 in the last round of my Opens I'd have won nine of them." In 1942 he did manage to claim his first major title when he won the PGA Championship.

John Byron ("Lord Byron") Nelson was born February 4, 1912, in Waxahachie, Texas, just south of Fort Worth. The son of a Texas grain and feed merchant, his family lived in a house near Fort Worth's Glen Garden Country Club. As a caddie there he began a long-term rivalry with Hogan, whom he defeated for the club's caddie championship in 1927. He turned professional five years later and earned his first major title at the Masters in 1937. After an inconsistent year in 1938 his victory at the U.S. Open in 1939 sealed his status as one of the premier golfers of the pre–World War II era. He added major titles at the PGA Championship in 1940 and the Masters again in 1942 (beating Hogan in an eighteen-hole playoff).

Although he won no major titles prior to the end of World War II, "Bantam Ben" Hogan would eventually eclipse Nelson as the greatest golfer of their era. Born William Benjamin Hogan in 1912 in Dublin, Texas, he suffered early trauma at the age of nine when his father, a blacksmith, committed suicide with a handgun. After his family moved to Fort Worth, Hogan sold newspapers and began caddying at the age of twelve at the Glen Garden Country Club. As a young man he honed his skills with long hours of practice; he would sustain his habit—or obsession—with countless repetition of all his shots for the rest of his career. He turned professional in 1930 and, after struggling for much of the Depression, won seventeen tournaments between 1938 and 1942. Weighing only about 135 pounds, he was the leading money winner on the PGA tour from 1940 through 1942.

⊙ ⊙ ⊙

In 1941 prospects for golf in the United States on both private and public courses seemed promising, even as war raged in Europe and Asia and the nation moved closer to direct involvement in the conflagration. Most of the country clubs that had survived the ravages of the Depression were in sound condition, and municipal links had benefited enormously from the assistance provided by New Deal programs. Business at winter golf resorts was booming. In January of 1941 *Golfdom* reported a total of 5,209 courses (of which 3,288 were private) and 2,351,000 golfers (among whom only about 650,000 were members of country clubs) who played about 63,406,000 rounds. But given the threatening world situation, commentators anticipated troubles ahead for clubs, particularly in the areas of course maintenance and retention of membership. As early as October 1940 *Golfdom* predicted that despite these potential problems, if war came, the country would witness much more emphasis on physical fitness. That might help the sport "by accenting the physical benefits of golf more, instead of depending, as previously, principally on the social values of the game." The president of a Pacific coast club thought "it would be a good thing for the nation, as well as for golf, if the idea could be put across that inefficiency and poor physical condition are disloyal acts."

After the Japanese attack on Pearl Harbor on December 7, 1941, spurred a full mobilization for war by the United States, American golfers faced a repeat of the challenges they had encountered during the First World War of 1917–18, although on a much greater scale. Perhaps the greatest obstacle they had to overcome in 1942 was a widespread assumption among the general public that playing golf was frivolous and perhaps even unpatriotic during wartime. In response to this stigma, writers and national association officials argued that golf could contribute greatly to the nation by promoting fitness and efficiency among the workforce, and also by raising critically needed funds. In June 1942 Herb Graffis, editor of *Golfing* and *Golfdom* magazines, argued that "the only justification for golf or any other sport in these times is that of providing earned relaxation for war workers and protecting and renewing the keenness of those who are doing their full duty on the civilian front." One year later he conceded that "golf loafers are out," but he insisted that "golf as a reward and refresher for those who are doing their level patriotic damndest [*sic*] is logical, legitimate and valuable . . . on its drastically revised basis . . . as a corollary of intense war effect."

The presidents of the USGA and the PGA wholeheartedly agreed, and the golfing community was able to persuade the federal government that the sport should continue during the war, although with significant restrictions required by the emergency. In 1943 George Blossom, Jr., of the USGA proclaimed that "golf in wartime has a mission—to help keep us fit and to aid war charities. If it is patriotic to be in shape physically, mentally and spiritually, then it is patriotic to play golf." Ed Dudley of the PGA seconded this view. After reporting that golf organizations had already raised more than a million dollars for the war charities, he urged golfers to retain their club memberships and play the game as much as possible. Graffis, Blossom, Dudley, and others lobbied successfully for a qualified endorsement for golf from the Roosevelt administration. As early as late December 1941, John B. Kelley, the assistant U.S. director of civilian defense in charge of physical fitness, was supportive in a reply to a letter from Graffis. He wrote: "This is the time when golf really must score for the physical and mental conditioning of American citizens under wartime pressure. . . . Golf's strong attraction as a sport in which more than 2 ¼ million of our citizens exercise regularly in the open air qualifies the game for national service of a vital character." In April 1942 President Franklin Roosevelt gave qualified approval to golf and other recreational pastimes, within "reasonable limits." His secretary informed Dudley that the president believed "the war efforts would not be hampered but actually improved by sensible participation in healthful pursuits." Perhaps Roosevelt's love of the game as a young man prior to his paralysis made him more disposed to approve the playing of golf during the war.

As golf enthusiasts lobbied to persuade the masses in general and public officials in particular that their favorite sport could make a positive contribution to the war effort, private and public clubs and players struggled to cope with numerous challenges that interfered with their sport. As a *New York Times* Sunday magazine essay explained on June 21, 1942: "Golfers are feeling with anguish the priorities and ration cards of a war to which nothing is sacred. Balls, clubs, caddies, shoe spikes, gasoline, the grill menu, course architecture . . . have been seized by the rude hand of Mars. Golf is handicapped." The most difficult problems they faced were shortages in equipment, caddies, and gasoline. The War Production Board's ban on the manufacture of golf clubs in the spring of 1942 to conserve iron and steel did not have a drastic immediate effect on the sport, because of record supplies on hand and players' willingness to use old woods and irons. On the other hand, the prohibition of the production of golf balls to save rubber proved to be far more troublesome, as golfers agonized over balls driven into the rough or trees. Supplies of golf balls proved to be adequate for 1942, but in 1943 club officials, players committees, and professionals launched a nationwide drive to collect 12,000,000 used golf balls for reconditioning by golf ball manufacturers. Caddie shortages also plagued private clubs as older boys flocked to aircraft and other war industry factories. As younger and smaller boys showed up at courses *Golfdom* magazine urged members to "give the caddies a break!" by packing fewer clubs in a lighter bag. Transportation to both country clubs and municipal courses presented even greater obstacles because of gasoline rationing imposed by the federal government. In most cases golfers solved the problem through car pools, but some did resign their memberships in private clubs because of rules that restricted automobile pleasure driving and bus travel to places of amusement. The hardship was less acute for those who patronized more accessible city public links, but the public facilities in more remote areas experienced a sharp drop in attendance. In June 1942, early in the war, managers of the four new courses at Bethpage on Long Island, New York, reported a severe decline in players, prompting them to cut expenses, in part by closing two of the courses during the week. On June 9th of that year one player at Bethpage laughed as he told a *New York Times* reporter: "Don't ask me when I'll be back. . . . I've got a guilty conscience about driving out here today."

In the end most private and public clubs and courses survived the trials of World War II reasonably well by making the necessary adjustments to suit the trying times. Although apparently only a few country clubs took the drastic step of consolidation, many others helped their members arrange car pools, cut their budgets (in part by offering more buffet meals), opened their grounds to men and women in the armed forces, scheduled Red Cross and other meetings in their facilities, collected used golf balls, scheduled charity events, and established victory gardens to grow vegetables.

As golfers and their private and municipal clubs and courses adjusted to wartime conditions, the USGA, PGA, and regional associations drew upon their experiences during the First World War as they debated two major issues. The first was whether they should continue to hold their annual championships; the second concerned what patriotic services their sport could provide to the American war campaign. In January 1942 the USGA took immediate action by canceling its four national championships for the duration of the emergency: the Open, men's and women's amateur, and amateur public links. Its officials reasoned that such a policy was appropriate because many of the most skilled contestants would be unable to compete because of military service or other war-related work. The USGA also launched a patriotic campaign to raise funds for the Red Cross and numerous other charitable organizations. In particular, it scheduled a series of special charity competitions, known as "Hale America" tournaments, for Decoration (Memorial) Day, Independence Day, and Labor Day, which ended with a spectacular winning performance by Ben Hogan with a score of 271 for the final four rounds. It also encouraged its member clubs and associations to hold lesser events for charities, to open their links to service personnel, and to donate equipment to the armed services. In addition, to promote the sale of United States savings bonds and stamps, it amended its bylaws to permit amateurs to compete for prizes of bonds and stamps, up to a limit of one hundred dollars for each award. By the end of 1942 the USGA reported that member clubs had raised at least $309,000 for war relief and recreation funds and had sold more than $3.7 million worth of war bonds and stamps. It expanded its efforts over the next few years, especially in helping to organize tournaments for the Red Cross and the National War Fund, an umbrella agency that included all major wartime charities except the Red Cross.

The PGA also joined in the crusade to raise funds for the cause of America, but it differed from the USGA in that it continued its annual championship for professionals each year except for 1943. In 1942 it announced a large-scale program of war relief exhibitions and tournaments, with the proceeds dedicated to the U.S. Army, U.S. Navy, USO, and Red Cross. Its two feature events that year were the PGA Championship in late May (won by Sam Snead) and a match in July between a Ryder Cup team and a squad of challengers captained by Walter Hagen. (The Ryder Cup side prevailed.) Hollywood celebrities Bing Crosby and Bob Hope (both skilled golfers) also toured the nation, participating in exhibitions for charity. While Hogan, Snead, and some four hundred members of the PGA enlisted in the armed forces during the war, a few who were rejected for military service (including Byron Nelson) played in charity exhibition matches and visited army and navy camps and hospitals. Nelson reported that he and others who had medical exemptions helped to sell war bonds and provided entertainment for servicemen undergoing rehabilitation. On the home front "Lord Byron" won the 1942 Masters tournament at the Augusta National Golf Club (the only Masters held during the war). But his most astonishing achievement came as the war ended in 1945, when he won an amazing eleven consecutive PGA tournaments, including the PGA Championship. Remarkably, that year he won a grand total of eighteen PGA events, averaging 68.33 strokes over 120 rounds of tournament competition.

Golf also proved to be a popular pastime in army and navy camps and hospitals for both newly inducted soldiers and sailors and those who were recuperating from injuries sustained in battle. In many cases their play on military links created or strengthened their addiction to the sport, which carried over into the postwar golfing boom. While courses at some military bases were converted into drill fields or used for other purposes, many other facilities reported extensive participation on links patronized by both officers and enlisted men. The course at Ashford General Hospital in White Sulphur Springs, West Virginia, boasted one of the largest and most scenic layouts in the nation. There, ambulatory veterans and amputees on crutches used donated sets of clubs and balls to enjoy the forty-five holes.

Golf instruction proved to be especially therapeutic to servicemen who were blinded in combat. Prior to World War II the premier blind golfer in the United States was Clinton Russell of Duluth, Minnesota. (Blind golfers play with the assistance of coaches who help them to direct their strokes.) Russell lost his eyesight in 1924 at the age of twenty-eight when an automobile tire exploded in his face as he was changing it. He gained international notoriety in 1938 when he defeated Dr. Beach Oxenbridge of London, England, in a battle of the world's leading sightless golfers. Toward the end of the war Russell urged officials in the Veterans Administrations to implement golf therapy for the blind. The program was a great success, and one of its chief beneficiaries soon surpassed Russell to become the dominant champion of blind golfers over the next few decades. Charley Boswell of Birmingham, Alabama, lost his vision when a German artillery shell exploded nearby moments after he rescued a fellow soldier from a tank in the Battle of the Bulge in 1944. A former football star at the University of Alabama, Boswell was a talented athlete who had never played golf before his accident. Doctors persuaded him to take up the sport at a rehabilitation center in Philadelphia. In 1946 he finished second to Russell in the first blind golfers championship in the United States, and he went on to win sixteen national titles. In 1948 Russell helped to launch the first national association of blind golfers, which was succeeded by the United States Blind Golf Association, founded by Bob Allman in 1953. Both Russell and Boswell later received the Ben Hogan Award from the Golf Writers of America, which was given annually to a golfer who overcame a physical handicap and whose example inspired his community.

The surrender of Japan in August 1945 marked the end of fifteen years of sustained crises for both the United States and its golfing community. This "greatest generation" of Americans weathered both depression and war, as upscale members of country clubs and middle- and working-class patrons of public courses used their favorite pastime as a relief from the hard times of the 1930s and the wartime emergency of the first half of the 1940s. Golf helped both able-bodied civilians and disabled veterans survive the trials of the Second World War. A brighter future for the sport lay ahead in postwar America.

THE
POST–WORLD WAR II
BOOM

During the fifteen years that followed World War II, American golf celebrated its second golden age as the sport's growing popularity exceeded its progress achieved during the flush times of the 1920s. Although many commentators have attributed this boom to President Dwight D. Eisenhower's obsession with the game during the mid-1950s, in fact it began a few years before his first inauguration in 1953 and resulted from several, more influential factors. Among these were the prosperity of the period that generated a rising standard of living for blue- and white-collar workers, new rounds of suburbanization and the extension of resort and retirement communities, the promotion of golf by media celebrities (especially Bing Crosby and Bob Hope), the advent of golf cars (today called "carts"), popular heroes (especially Ben Hogan and Arnold Palmer), and the rise of television. While some of these forces (most notably the economy, residential trends, and the role of champions) had shaped golf's fortunes during earlier eras and were cyclical, others (especially the introduction of golf cars and television) were unique to this period.

Economic and business factors provided the foundation that supported golf's revival after World War II. Increases in wages and salaries substantially exceeded the rise in prices, resulting in a rising standard of living for factory workers and corporate managers. Between 1950 and 1960 the average annual wages for industrial workers increased from $3,330 to $5,545, while annual pay for retail trade employees rose from $2,711 to $3,911 and compensation for government employees grew from $3,043 to $4,628. Men and women of modest means could afford to play a round a week on municipal, daily-fee, or industrial company courses, despite rising green fees. A study that compared the costs of golf equipment (irons, woods, and balls) in 1940 and 1960 concluded that although the retail prices of these items had doubled during this twenty-year period, their actual cost in terms of hours of work required to purchase them had dropped dramatically. For example, while the price of a set of irons rose from $68 to $140 during this period, the numbers of hours of labor needed to buy them declined from 103 to 61½.

The business world continued to value golf as an important means of promoting corporate connections and especially sales to clients. Corporations often paid for country club memberships for their key managers, expanding on a practice that dated to the early decades of the twentieth century. In the words of a Dupont executive: "The tour of the links, with a financial purpose in mind, has become just another important facet of good sales technique, and is finding its way to the company expense account with the regularity of such items as 'visitor's entertainment,' 'business dinner,' and a box of fine Havanas at Christmas time." Although some country clubs objected to the more blatant cases of members using their links to seal deals, corporate golfers learned more subtle ways to use golf to strengthen business relationships and sell their products and services.

During these years new waves of suburbanization also contributed to the growth of golf, but even more important were the expansion of resort and retirement communities whose developers recognized the value of courses to attract tourists and to sell homesites to seasonal or full-time residents. In 1948 Adolph Zukor, chairman of Paramount Pictures, announced plans to develop his eight-hundred-acre estate in Rockland County, New York, as the site of five hundred residences. Feature attractions for buyers included an eighteen-hole golf course, tiled swimming pool, country lodge, formal gardens, and miles of winding paved roads. Del Webb, co-owner of the New York Yankees, became a multimillionaire promoting retirement centers in Arizona, California, and Florida. He understood that a well-designed and well-maintained links could sell building lots in desolate areas and that the profits realized by selling property in his communities would far exceed its construction costs. Prescott, Arizona, opened a championship eighteen-hole course at no cost to taxpayers by building on city land and by selling adjacent acreage to real estate subdividers. The project required the use of city water initially, but the town planned ultimately to shift to the use of purified water from the local sewage treatment plant. Future plans included the sale of land for a resort motel-hotel.

Although the mid-century golf boom was already well underway by the time Eisenhower took the oath of office as chief executive, his passion for the sport certainly helped popularize it throughout the nation. On May 31, 1953, the *New York Times* stated: "The game has been booming for years, but the chances are the golfing President has done it even more good than might normally have been expected." Two months later John Fitzpatrick of *Golf Digest* credited Eisenhower with creating a "golfing fever" in Washington, D.C., reporting that "thousands of government workers, from Vice President Nixon down to the lowliest office clerks, are rushing to learn the game." In that seat of government "equipment sales, lessons, daily fee play and applications for private club memberships" were "at an all-time high." Outside the nation's capital Eisenhower's love of the game probably inspired countless citizens to take up the pastime or to play more frequently. Just a few months after his inauguration he enthusiastically endorsed the sport in an address to the country's "golfers and fellow duffers." He proclaimed: "Golf obviously provides one of our best forms of healthful exercise accompanied by good fellowship and companionship. It is a sport in which the whole American family can participate—fathers and mothers, sons and daughters alike. It offers healthy respite from daily toil, refreshment of body and mind." He demonstrated his love for golf by playing nearly eight hundred rounds during his two terms in office, mostly at the Burning Tree Country Club in Washington, D.C., the Augusta National Golf Club in Georgia, and the Newport Golf Club in Rhode Island. He especially treasured his membership at Augusta, where he spent many hours in the company of Bob Jones and club chairman Cliff Roberts. That prestigious all-male club honored Eisenhower by building a cottage for his use and naming a pond and a tree for him. Among his predecessors in the Oval Office only President Wilson played golf more regularly. But Eisenhower was a far superior player than Wilson or William Howard Taft or Warren G. Harding. He also played regularly with golf and media stars, including Hogan, Palmer, and Hope. Although he tried to keep his scores private, he regularly played rounds in the upper 80s and low 90s and shot in the high 70s on several memorable occasions.

Eisenhower's obsession with golf did create some political controversy for him with members of both parties. His friendly rivalry on the golf links with Senator Robert A. Taft of Ohio ("Mr. Republican") caused some strain with the man whom he had defeated for the party's nomination for the presidency. Newspaper editors often poked fun at his passion for golf, and naturally Democrats were more critical than Republicans. Journalists reported that practically every day in the late afternoon Eisenhower put on his cleats and hit irons on the south lawn or practiced putting on a special green built for him near the Oval Office. The practice green was the site of a minor crisis in 1955 when gray squirrels scratched and marred its surface. The president ordered that the offenders be trapped and removed from the grounds, but Senator Richard L. Neuberger (a freshman Democrat from Oregon) protested and founded a "save the White House squirrel fund." White House officials relented and suspended the trapping of the animals. The squirrel incident produced some bad press for the president, as his aides worried that his frequent golf outings were generating a negative reaction among the American people in general, and not just the Democrats. But former president Harry Truman (who was a walker but not a golfer) came to the president's defense by stating that "to yap at him because he plays a game of golf is unfair and downright picayunish. . . . He has the same right to relax from the heavy burdens of the greatest office as any other man."

President Dwight D. Eisenhower holding a button that reads "Don't Ask What I Shot" at a golf match with Senator Robert A. Taft of Ohio at the Augusta National Golf Club, April 20, 1953. AP/WIDE WORLD PHOTOS.

After his heart attack in September 1955 Eisenhower used golf as part of his rehabilitation in 1956, and his re-election to a second term that fall proved that his favorite recreation was not a major political liability among the American people.

During the 1940s and 1950s film, radio, and television stars also helped popularize golf among the masses of Americans. Bing Crosby and Bob Hope were the two most famous celebrities who had a close connection to the Scottish sport long before Eisenhower's inauguration. Both were talented low-handicap players who competed in national and international amateur tournaments. While Crosby and Hope were never a threat on the links to the nation's leading golf amateur and professionals, they provided invaluable services to the nation and their favorite sport during and after World War II. Perhaps most notable were their fundraising campaigns for the Red Cross, war bonds, and other causes, during which they played many matches with Byron Nelson, Ben Hogan, Jimmy Demaret, Frank Stranahan, and other local and nationally known amateurs and pros. To increase the cash contributed they often agreed to auction off their clubs, bags, balls, and even clothing after the event. Both also founded celebrity tournaments that featured leading amateurs and professionals and generated funds for charities. "Crosby's Clambake," begun in 1937 at Rancho Santa Fe, California,

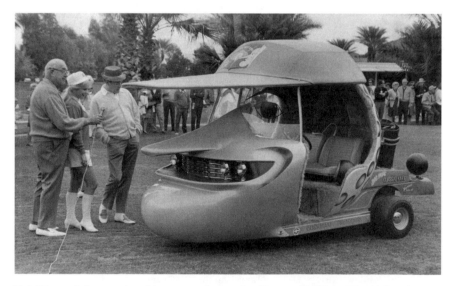

Bob Hope, right, examines his custom-designed golf cart with Harry Von Zell and Barbara Eden during the Desert Golf Classic he sponsored at Palm Springs, California, February 4, 1970. AP/WIDE WORLD PHOTOS.

and then suspended during the war, grew into a major tournament in 1947 contested over several scenic courses on the Monterey Peninsula—including Pebble Beach, Spyglass Hill, and Cypress Point. In 1965 Hope emulated his film partner and golfing rival by launching and hosting the Bob Hope Desert Classic Pro-Am in Palm Desert, California, which raised millions of dollars for the Eisenhower Medical Center in Palm Desert, California, and other charities in the region. For all their contributions to golf, both received the United States Golf Association's Bob Jones Award and were inducted into the World Golf Hall of Fame.

As Eisenhower, Crosby, Hope, and other public figures and entertainers spread the gospel of golf during the 1950s, a revolutionary innovation appeared on the links that would profoundly transform the sport for millions of players in the United States. While a few golfers tried out the first motorized golf "caddie" cars in Texas and California during the late 1940s, they arrived in rapidly increasing numbers during the 1950s. Surveys estimated there were about a thousand of them in 1953, four thousand in 1954, twelve thousand in 1957, thirty-five thousand in 1960, and forty-five thousand in 1962. Numerous manufacturers produced both electric battery and gasoline-powered models. Most were sold or leased to country clubs or semiprivate daily-fee courses for rental to players, but some were purchased by private individuals. They were a major technological advance over the hand-pulled golf bag cart, introduced during the 1940s, that was commonplace on public links during this period, saving many golfers the cost of a caddie as they walked the course. But the rapid rise of golf cars during their first decade did not come easily, for they faced widespread opposition throughout the 1950s, especially in the Northeast.

Those who were most enthusiastic about motorized golf cars pointed to their advantages for elderly or handicapped golfers, their prospects for speeding up play, and their potential for adding much-needed revenue for professionals or clubs. In August 1955 *Golf Digest* remarked: "All concerned admit that the cars are a boon to those who could not otherwise play golf because of heart conditions, or other physical impairments. The cars have also made it possible for many elderly golfers to come out of retirement and once again enjoy the thrill of hitting one stiff to the pin on No. 18." President Eisenhower's frequent use of a golf car certainly gave them a big boost, even before his first heart attack. Many commentators also overoptimistically predicted that golf cars would allow players to complete thirty-six holes per day instead of eighteen, or even solve the course shortage problem by permitting more people to play each day. Managers of country clubs also began to see the economic advantages of bringing golf cars to their courses, especially as their associations' costs escalated due to rising taxes and payrolls. At first they permitted their professionals to benefit from the income from car rentals, but eventually they decided that the clubs should reap the bulk of the expanding revenues.

Opposition to the new golf cars came from those who either worried about their practical and financial consequences or who viewed them as a violation of time-honored golfing traditions. A primary concern was their impact on fairways and areas adjacent to greens, but officials also highlighted the extra costs incurred for servicing and storing the vehicles and for constructing stronger bridges and asphalt or concrete pathways to spare fairways. Traffic congestion and accidents, which raised issues of club liability, alarmed directors. According to an October 1954 article in *Golfdom*, causes of these mishaps included "improper car design, mechanical failures, inexperience of drivers, improper operation, carelessness and 'horsing around.'" Moreover, old-timers lamented the reduction in the ranks of caddies, even as good ones were becoming more scarce. On the other hand, many private courses still required the hiring of at least one caddie per car. Many also believed that walking a golf course was an integral part of the game, and that permission to use the vehicles should be restricted to those with a valid medical certificate. Tournament officials for major competitions honored this objection by banning golf cars in their events.

By 1960 it was clear that golf cars had come to stay in the United States, although according to a March issue of *Golf Digest*, in the Northeast and a few other areas "the verdict is still pending as to whether golf cars are mechanical marvels or impractical monsters that rob the game of its tradition and health benefits." But in other regions—especially those in Florida, California, and those parts of the South and the Southwest with large retirement communities—they achieved near unanimous acceptance. Throughout the nation courses adopted reasonable rules for drivers that preserved their grounds and prevented accidents. *Golf Digest* saw a bright future for the machines in March 1960, predicting (correctly) that rental rates would decrease and that the number of both caddies and privately owned cars would drop significantly. That magazine also expected that younger players would ride cars, but that time saved on the links would be minimal because "you can't play faster than the walking foursome you will catch up with sooner or later." It also remarked that golf cars were not that destructive to courses if they were driven properly. A February 1962 article in *Golf* magazine noted that the golf car had arrived as a status symbol for the country club set. It also concluded that for many of the millions of American golfers "the golf car is the finest thing to come along since the discovery of the 19th hole." It added: "Aside from that, the golf car has exploded the once common belief that Americans played golf for exercise. It isn't the exercise they enjoy, it's the golf."

⊚ ⊚ ⊚

As the new golf cars, President Eisenhower, and Crosby and Hope all boosted golf during the 1950s, three champions merit special notice for their vital roles in promoting the game during this transitional era of the mid-twentieth century. Ben Hogan's brilliant achievements capped a career that began in the 1930s and featured heroic feats after the war. Sam Snead continued to captivate the nation's golf fans by winning dozens of tournaments, even as they shared his disappointment over several more disheartening losses in the U.S. Open. Arnold Palmer's meteoric rise to fame and fortune was just beginning as television arrived to propel his career and the sport to new heights during the 1960s and 1970s.

Hogan became a legendary figure in American golf during these years because of his character and courage in the face of adversity and because of his remarkable victories in major championships. Although he lacked an engaging personality or the interpersonal skills necessary for good relations with the media, he attained a heroic status that nearly equaled that of Bob Jones. In Demaret's words: "What set Ben apart from everybody else was his inside game—the unbelievable will to win, the quiet determination, the intense concentration." The "Hogan mystique" was a product of his performance under pressure combined with his quiet demeanor and his aversion to interviews and publicity of any kind.

Hogan had already established himself as a premier performer before World War II, but he achieved true stardom during the postwar era. After two years of military service he captured his first major title in the 1946 PGA Championship, followed by another PGA title and his first U.S. Open crown in 1948. The next two years brought Hogan both tragedy and triumph. His career (and life) nearly ended on a desert highway near the small town of Van Horn, Texas, on February 2, 1949, when a Greyhound bus changed lanes and crashed head-on into his automobile. Perhaps a second before impact Hogan threw himself in front of his wife Valerie, seated next to him. That desperate lunge protected her and probably saved his life, for the impact drove the steering column through the driver's seat. Valerie escaped serious injury but the accident left Ben with a double fracture of the pelvis, a broken collarbone, a fractured ankle, and a chipped rib. Complications from these traumas required several operations to stop blood clots from forming in his legs. Months of rehabilitation followed, but then Hogan amazed the golfing world by entering the Los Angeles Open in January 1950 and scoring a four-under-par 280 for the four rounds, good enough for a tie with Snead. Although Hogan lost the playoff, he had completed a remarkable comeback, and more spectacular performances and victories lay ahead. In June of that year he entered the U.S. Open at Merion, Pennsylvania, and reached the 72nd hole needing a par to qualify for a playoff. Despite sore legs and the fatigue of playing a double round on the final day of the event, he hit what became perhaps the most memorable shot of his life—a perfect one-iron to the green. He made the two putts for par and the next day defeated Lloyd Mangrum and George Fazio to win his second U.S. Open Championship.

Although Hogan proved that he was back and better than ever in 1951 with victories in the Masters and U.S. Open, it was his accomplishments in 1953 that elevated him to the ranks of golf's immortals. That year he was victorious at the Masters in Augusta National in Georgia, the U.S. Open at Oakmont Country Club in Pittsburgh, and the British Open in Carnoustie in Scotland. Because the PGA Championship overlapped in dates with the British Open, he did not have the opportunity to win the sport's famed modern Grand Slam of professional major titles. His triumph in Scotland was all the more impressive because it was his first (and only) attempt to win Great Britain's most prestigious event. When he and his wife returned by ship to New York in July, the city gave "Bantam Ben" (or the "wee ice mon" to the British) the same type of ticker-tape parade and hero's reception that had welcomed Bob Jones back in 1930. The notoriously publicity-shy Hogan was moved by the warmth poured out to him by the New Yorkers and other public dignitaries and sporting celebrities that day. He replied simply: "I have a tough skin, but I have a soft spot in my heart and this tops anything that ever happened to me." At a luncheon he received a telegram from President Eisenhower that praised Hogan as a "great competitor and a master of your craft but also as an envoy extraordinary in the business of building friendship for America." A few days later the people of Fort Worth, Texas, greeted the conquering hero with a red-carpet reception, downtown parade, and luncheon.

Sam Snead's peak performances also came during the postwar period, as he won fifty-one tournaments between 1945 and 1965. Highlights included eleven wins in 1950, PGA Championships in 1949 and 1951, and

Masters titles in 1949, 1952, and 1954. Perhaps his most satisfying moment came in 1946 at the first British Open held since 1939, when Snead made a last-minute decision to cross the Atlantic to compete on the historic St. Andrews links in Scotland. Tied for the lead after fifty-four holes, he struggled through the front nine with a shaky 40. But he steadied his game and finished with two pars for a final round of 75 that was good enough for a four-stroke victory. The following year he lost the U.S. Open when he missed a three-foot putt. Although he would never win his own nation's open crown, he at least had the satisfaction of claiming Britain's open title at the cradle of golf. Over his long and illustrious forty-two-year career on the regular and senior PGA tours, he compiled a remarkable record of 135 tournament titles, including 82 PGA events (nine more than Jack Nicklaus) and seven major championships. A youthful golfing prodigy of the 1930s, he outlasted Nelson and Hogan and still excelled on the links well into the age of Palmer.

The rise of Arnold Palmer, golf's newest superstar, during the late 1950s coincided with the first attempts to televise the sport across the nation, and Palmer's aggressive style of play and charismatic personality perfectly suited the new medium. Earlier in the decade, local radio and television golf shows that combined instruction and consumer information with some commentary by professionals and celebrities enjoyed a modest success with audiences. But network producers hoped to achieve high viewer ratings with broadcasts of major tournaments and also packaged (or "canned") series of edited matches presented weekly.

In August 1953, well before Palmer's debut on the PGA tour, a spectacular finishing shot at the first nationally televised tournament showcased the new medium's potential for promoting American golf. The scene was the eighteenth hole of the final round of George S. May's "World Championship" at the Tam O'Shanter Country Club, just north of Chicago. Lew Worsham needed a birdie three to tie the leader, Chandler Harper. After a long drive Worsham stroked a 120-yard wedge shot stiff to the pin. It took a large bounce and rolled into the hole for an eagle two and victory. The ABC network had provided only one camera to televise the event, but it was perfectly placed at the eighteenth green. It beamed the climactic shot live to about 646,000 homes, coast to coast, and nearly one million viewers (estimating 1.5 persons per set). It is likely that Worsham's fantastic feat played a key role in convincing television network executives that they could sell time for advertisements to sponsors for future tournaments. The following year the USGA began authorizing network telecasts of the U.S. Open.

National telecasts of premier golf championships were expensive to produce and technically challenging, and the first ones were marred by embarrassing incidents. Sportscaster Lindsey Nelson recalled that when NBC televised the 1954 U.S. Open from New Jersey, he and his partner were perched on top of the clubhouse with trees blocking their view of the eighteenth green. While they did have a monitor to see the action, strong sunshine reflecting off of it rendered it useless. To make matters worse, NBC aired a commercial at the exact moment when Ed Furgol sank a putt on the final hole to win the championship. In an era before videotape, the millions of fans who had tuned in missed the event's climax. The following year commentator Gene Sarazen climbed down from his booth to congratulate Ben Hogan after he holed out on the eighteenth green for what appeared to be his record-setting fifth title. But shortly after NBC ended its show, Jack Fleck came from behind to tie Hogan and force a playoff the next day, which Fleck won. Yet despite these mishaps, the first golf telecasts demonstrated their potential to attract large audiences, despite their costs and the logistical and technical problems of following numerous contestants and of showing the ball in flight. Television clearly was the critical factor in the PGA's decision in 1958 to change its championship's format from match play to four rounds of stroke play, which gave more players the opportunity to win on the final day and thus generated more excitement for the viewers. By 1960 it was obvious that golf and television strongly boosted each other, as the new medium showcased the game and its cast of characters while the sport provided viewers with dramatic and sometimes thrilling entertainment.

While filmed matches edited for one-hour golf shows could never match the interest and tension of a televised live event, they proved to be popular among viewers during the fall and winter months. "All-Star Golf" premiered on ABC in October 1957 and ran for twenty-six weeks on 150 stations coast to coast. The producer, Peter DeMet, offered a total purse of $80,000 and attracted such luminaries as Cary Middlecoff, Gene Sarazen, Sam Snead, Mike Souchak, Lloyd Mangrum, Julius Boros, and Jimmy Demaret. Each week viewers watched an eighteen-hole stroke-play contest between two players, with the winner earning $2,000 and the chance to compete against a new opponent. The prize money also included $500 for an eagle and $10,000 for a hole-in-one. Recording these matches proved to be a daunting technical challenge for the director and camera and sound crews, with long waits often required between shots for the professionals. But all seemed to be eager to participate, because the money at stake was generally far more than what was offered at regular tour events, even greater than the combined purses of the U.S. Open, PGA Championship, and Masters. Moreover, these series gave professional golf additional exposure during the months when most golfers in the colder climates could only dream about their favorite sport. DeMet also thought his shows would win over new fans and "keep interest alive in a great game that too often is not considered a spectator sport." He added: "Our series, we feel, is bound to change thinking in that regard and bring millions of people out to courses who never thought of watching or playing the game before." Executives of other networks noted the success of "All-Star Golf" and scheduled competitors over the next few years, including "World Championship of Golf" and "Wonderful World of Golf" on NBC.

While television networks experimented with broadcasting tournaments and all-star challenges, Arnold Palmer dreamed of becoming the world's greatest golfer. Born on September 10, 1929, in Latrobe in western Pennsylvania, he was the son of the greenkeeper and professional at the Latrobe Country Club. His father, Deacon, taught him to play the game at the age of five, and during his youth he became the star of his high school team and a junior champion in his region. A collegiate player at Wake Forest College between 1947 and 1950, he left school for three years of service in the U.S. Coast Guard. His victory in the 1954 U.S. Amateur Championship marked his arrival on the national golfing scene. The following year he turned professional and won the Canadian Open with a 265, the second-lowest score in the tournament's forty-six year history. In 1958 he achieved one of his life's goals by winning a major title—the Masters. Just short of thirty, he had become one of the world's best golfers, with a relentless, attacking, and bold approach to the game off the tees and fairways and even on the greens.

In 1960 Palmer achieved the status of a golfing superstar with two spectacular triumphs in major championships—the Masters and the U.S. Open. At Augusta in April he came to the last two holes on the final day needing a birdie to tie and two birdies to win. On the seventeenth green he sank a twenty-seven-foot putt for his birdie, and on the eighteenth his six-iron approach stopped five feet from the pin. He calmly drained the putt, took one stride, and then jumped for joy. In its April 18, 1960, issue *Sports Illustrated* called Palmer "an authentic and unforgettable hero." Two months later at Cherry Hills in Denver, he began his final round seven shots behind the leader, Mike Souchak. But after a run of six birdies on the first seven holes and one birdie on the final nine he carded a 65 for the lowest final round ever shot by the winner of the U.S. Open to that date. His four-day total of

280 was two strokes better than the runner-up, Jack Nicklaus, a twenty-year-old national amateur champion who would soon become Palmer's greatest rival. Writing for *Sports Illustrated* on June 27, 1960, Herbert Warren Wind labeled Palmer "a marvelous golfer" and "destiny's favorite."

Palmer's come-from-behind heroics in these and other tournaments gained him a huge following among spectators on the courses and television viewers at home. "Arnie's Army"—the crowds that thronged around him on the links—loved his hard-hitting ball striking and his penchant for taking chances when his errant shots landed in the rough or in the trees. He fed off the energy of his fans as they yelled "charge!" to urge him toward victory. Unlike the stoic and detached Hogan, he openly showed his emotions, from jubilation over a brilliant stroke or putt to agony over a costly blunder. A handsome man with an engaging smile, he was polite, pleasant, and articulate with golf writers and broadcasters. On January 9, 1961, *Sports Illustrated* named him its "Sportsman of the Year" for 1960, proclaiming: "With his golf credo—'Hit it hard'—that horrifies traditionalists, his boyish enthusiasm, his athletic good looks and irrepressible will to win, he has dominated the game as no one has since the heyday of Ben Hogan nearly a decade ago. Thus he has ended his sport's long wait for a fresh, vibrant personality, bringing a new age to golf: The Palmer Era." Although Jack Nicklaus, Gary Player, Lee Trevino, Tom Watson, and other stars would match or eclipse his record during the following three decades, none of them would equal his popularity with America's golfing masses.

◎ ◎ ◎

World War II had a more negative impact on private country clubs and daily-fee links than it did on municipal courses, and during the postwar period several factors spurred new growth in public golf grounds and facilities constructed by corporations for their employees. With many golfers serving in the armed forces and with travel restrictions necessitated by petroleum shortages, the total number of golf courses in the nation declined by at least five hundred during the war. Yet the National Recreation Association reported that in 1946 there were only fourteen fewer municipal golf courses in the nation than in 1938. In the fifteen years after peace in 1945 the number of golfers on public courses increased dramatically, which naturally spurred a demand for new municipal facilities. In addition to the boost given to the sport by the exposure provided to veterans in military bases and hospitals, youth, high school, and college programs also stimulated interest among young people. Moreover, as Rex McMorris, the executive vice president of the National Golf Foundation pointed out in 1954, "our rising standard of living, shorter working hours and earlier retirement ages have provided more people with the time and means to enjoy the game; and last but not least, the very nature of golf—placing no premium on age, sex, physical stamina or skill—gives it a universal appeal which has transformed it from the 'silk hat' game of the twenties to a game for everyone." On June 25, 1955, *Business Week* noted the dramatic demographic change among the country's golfers. It reported that while "golf used to be a snooty pastime, indulged in mostly by the male members of the carriage trade," its patrons now numbered an "estimated 5 million factory workers, school teachers, grocery clerks, housewives, and businessmen of all ranks." Significantly, that magazine highlighted the increasing participation of women, "small fry" (through instruction and school teams), Negroes (nearly 400,000), and "Old Folks" who were joining senior golf associations in droves.

As the postwar baby boom swelled the nation's population, the need for more housing generated new waves of suburbanization, which frequently encroached upon existing (mostly private) golf links. The loss of many golf grounds to residential development, coupled with increasing participation, put even more pressure on the existing public courses. Towns and cities tried to respond to the call for more facilities, but they fell far short of meeting the demand. According to statistics compiled by the National Golf Foundation (NGF), in 1946 there were 723 municipal golf courses in the United States (up slightly from 711 in 1941), and the number increased to 877 in 1955. The following year that organization reported the more pessimistic news that eighty-four cities with a population of at least fifty thousand had not a single public course. In 1958 the NGF noted a small decline to 855 that year (about 15 percent of the nation's total of 5,745), which still constituted a 16 percent increase from 1948. It estimated that the number of golfers in the nation had increased about 45 percent during that ten-year period, and that public links were the site of about 40 percent of all rounds played in the United States. In 1962 the 931 municipal golf links made up about 13 percent of the nation's total of 7,070 courses (including the shorter par-three layouts). These statistics suggest that the supply of municipal golf facilities during this period fell far short of the demand generated by recreational players.

City planners in the major metropolitan regions of the United States were keenly aware of the shortage of courses, and many of them supported projects to acquire land and build new grounds. The situation was particularly critical in Los Angeles. In 1948 it had only thirty golf courses (public and private) for a population of 3,690,000, compared to forty-seven courses for a population of 2,202,510 in 1930. The "City of Angels" had used golf to attract tourists and capital from other regions of the United States after World War I, but after 1945 it lagged far behind other American cities in public golfing facilities. In 1949 the Los Angeles Parks and Recreation Board began to address this problem by opening the new eighteen-hole Rancho Golf Course on the site of a defunct private course. In 1954 Los Angeles city administrators launched a "Save Our Golf Courses" program to identify and lease golf grounds that were in danger of being divided up into residential lots.

Across the continent in the New York City metropolitan area the supply of golf courses also fell far short of the demand. In August 1953 *Golf Digest* estimated that within sixty miles of Times Square there were about fifty public courses and two hundred private clubs for a total population of almost fourteen million people that included about 350,000 active golfers. Real estate developers had bought out most of the semiprivate daily-fee courses in suburban counties, except in New Jersey. By comparison, in Chicago there were 153 links (90 of which were public) for that city's six million people. In New York, patronage of the city's ten municipal courses after 1945 rebounded strongly from the war years, when the total number of rounds per year dropped about 25 percent to 445,000 in 1944. In 1948 that figure reached 685,423, despite an increase in permit fees from five to ten dollars plus a nominal green fee of twenty-five cents per round on weekdays and fifty cents on holidays and weekends. About 3,500 of Gotham's municipal employees were avid golfers during these years, including large contingents from the police, fire, sanitation, and other departments. Thanks in part to assistance provided by the Metropolitan Professional Golf Association, the New York City Police Golf Association was especially active, sponsoring monthly tournaments and competing against teams representing organizations from neighboring states.

While the number of semiprivate daily-fee courses far exceeded the total of municipal links in the United States during this period, those that were located in large metropolitan regions faced increasing financial pressures from rising real estate taxes and higher costs. In many cases their owners were tempted to sell their property to residential or commercial developers. A 1959 survey listed 2,023 semiprivate courses in the nation, compared to 871 municipal and 3,097 private links. An owner of a Chicago daily-fee facility was pessimistic about the future in an interview published in the November 1960 issue of *Golf* magazine. "Why should you continue to worry and fret to make maybe five per cent on your investment," he asked, "when you can sell out and make several hundred thousand dollars even after paying the capital gains tax?" He estimated that a new private operator of a public golf course would have to invest a minimum of $700,000 to open new grounds. He predicted that "20 years from now the only way we can survive is by expanding our facilities so that the customer will spend more time—and money—at the course. Only the state or municipalities can afford to build now for public play."

In the mid-twentieth century, playing a round on a public links in a large city could be an unnerving experience. Writing in *Golfing* magazine in June 1947, Harold D. Green depicted the frustrations facing the hordes of new golfers. He and his partner endured long waits at both the first and tenth tees, flying golf balls struck by players pressing them from behind, divot-ridden fairways, poor manners, and mind-numbing slow play. In the end they needed eight hours to complete eighteen holes "under conditions that could have been perfect but were miserable, if not actually dangerous." He lamented: "We arrived home physically worn out and mentally depressed from an excursion that should have left us invigorated and anxious to repeat." Instead, he declared: "If I never see a public course again it will be too soon." But rather than ending his essay on a note of hopelessness, he suggested some remedies: building more public golf facilities, educating the playing public in the rules and etiquette of the sport, and banning those who refuse to learn the basic techniques and manners of golf. But conditions did not improve significantly on the most crowded courses during the 1950s. An article in *Life* magazine on June 9, 1961, described tricks to try to obtain prized tee times, long waits, and crowded and dangerous conditions on municipal courses, with rude behavior commonplace. John McDermott reported: "The municipal golfer . . . is sniped at by hookers and slicers hitting from parallel fairways. He is constantly nagged at by players behind who pressure him into hurrying his shots. He falls prey to petty thieves in front of him who pocket his ball when it lands beyond sight." At the Dyker Beach course in Brooklyn, gangs of boys cut through mesh linked fences, hid in gullies, stole golf balls, and even threatened players with bows and arrows, which they carried on the pretext of hunting rats. McDermott marveled at the dedication of the municipal golfers who kept coming back, "despite the frightfully crowded course, the chiselers, the rule breakers and etiquette breachers." In fact, conditions on popular public links had not changed much since the early years of the twentieth century.

Despite these trying circumstances, out of the millions of American golfers who hacked their way across the fairways of municipal and semiprivate daily-fee courses, a dedicated and talented few competed for fame (if not fortune) at the "poor man's amateur championship"—the national Public Links tournament sponsored by the United States Golf Association. The only restriction for entry into this annual competition was that the player could not be a member of a private golf club. *Golf Digest* reported in July 1952 that all the contestants were from "the great democracy of golf"— people who were "the real fanatics among this pay-as-you-play clan." That journal explained: "They're the kind who play twilight golf, or get night jobs so they can play during the day. On weekends they're out at 6:00 A.M. in order to beat the crowd and get in their 36. They carefully plan their vacations, and save their money, so they can make the annual pilgrimage to the scene of the big event. If the job interferes with these plans, they quit it—and get a new one when they get back." Between 1949 and 1951 the three "Publinx" winners of the grinding eight rounds of match play included a policeman, a truck driver for a liquor distributor, and a college student at UCLA.

During the postwar period, employees of many American business corporations had a more attractive alternative to playing on crowded public links, as their companies actively promoted golf for their white- and blue-collar workers by lobbying for golf courses in regions where they built offices and factories, by constructing industrial courses, and by sponsoring recreational golf leagues. Industrial golf programs were generally part of a larger company benefit that also allowed wives and children to enjoy swimming pools and playgrounds. John Budd, golf professional at the En-Joie Golf Club of the Endicott-Johnson Company in Endicott, New York, explained: "Big and medium sized corporations are recognizing that money expended in this type of recreation program is good business. The workers are better satisfied, enjoy better health and are happy because of leisure time well spent." By the mid-1950s at least seventy-six American companies had constructed golf facilities. In addition to those at several IBM locations (Endicott, Poughkeepsie, and Sands Point, New York) and at Endicott-Johnson, there were notable courses at DuPont (Wilmington, Delaware), Hershey (Pennsylvania), Bethlehem Steel (Pennsylvania), Firestone Rubber (Akron, Ohio), United Shoe (Beverly, Massachusetts), National Cash Register (Dayton, Ohio), and General Electric (Rexford, New York; and Erie, Pennsylvania). In cases where it was not practicable or cost-effective for companies to build extensive golf grounds, they often supported the sport by organizing or sponsoring employee golf leagues, where workers played on semiprivate or municipal links. In 1955 the U.S. Commerce Department reported that golf ranked third (behind softball and bowling) among recreational outlets for industrial workers; two years later it trailed only bowling. In 1958 more than four hundred golfers from ten states competed in Illinois in the Midwestern Industrial tournament, and the National Industrial Recreation Association estimated that more than 22,500 businesses sponsored some form of golf activity.

The flush times of the postwar period gave an enormous boost to American golf, as President Eisenhower, Hollywood celebrities, and star professionals attracted enormous attention from the media. Modern technology enabled countless golfers to speed across fairways on golf cars, while the miracle of television beamed exciting matches into living rooms during every season of the year. Although the number of new public courses did not match the increased demand, business corporations made up part of the shortfall by providing their workers with fairways and greens to enjoy during their leisure hours. The primary beneficiaries were white, middle- and upper-class males, but enthusiasm for golf also spread to minorities and females. At the middle of the twentieth century, African Americans and women struggled to achieve admission to the golfing fraternity of the United States.

AFRICAN AMERICANS
AT MID-CENTURY

Early on the morning of December 7, 1955, Dr. George C. Simkins Jr., an African American dentist from Greensboro, North Carolina, gathered with five of his friends for a regular Wednesday round of golf. Normally the group played public courses open to black golfers, but on this occasion they resolved to visit Gillespie Park, a municipal facility that operated as a private club for white residents who leased the grounds from the town for one dollar. Lease agreements such as the one in Greensboro were common in those southern cities that sought to circumvent court orders that outlawed all forms of discrimination in public recreation. When Simkins and his five black companions arrived at the Gillespie Park golf shop, the attendant told them they could not play because they were not members of the club. Simkins and his friends then left their green fees on the counter and teed off on the first hole. On the fifth hole the head pro, Ernie Edwards, caught up with them and threatened to have them arrested if they did not leave the grounds. When Edwards asked Simkins why he was on the course, he replied: "We're out here for a cause—the cause of democracy. We're taxpayers. This is a city golf course funded by our taxes and we should be allowed to play it." The Simkins party ignored Edwards's curses and warnings and finished nine holes. That evening a black police officer arrested the men and took them to the county jail. The "Greensboro Six" were soon out on bail, having just launched a long battle to desegregate all public golf courses in Greensboro.

Nearly four years earlier, in late January 1952, former heavyweight champion boxer Joe Louis, African American professional golfers Charles Sifford, Bill Spiller, and Teddy Rhodes, and three black amateurs teed off in the qualifying round of a Professional Golfers' Association (PGA)–sponsored tournament in Phoenix, Arizona. Organizers of the Phoenix event had granted the group permission to play only after Louis and his friends had applied extreme public pressure to open the competition to black contestants. Grudgingly, the officials scheduled Louis and the others in two groups in the first early morning tee times to get them on the course before most of the gallery gathered. In his autobiography, *Just Let Me Play*, Sifford recalled the shocking and unsettling greeting that awaited them on the first green. As he walked to the pin to pull the flagstick out "something seemed funny" as he glanced down at the hole. He wrote: "Somebody had been there before us. The cup was full of human shit, and from the looks and smell of it, it hadn't been there too long before we got there that the cup had been filled. Obviously, someone associated with Phoenix's fanciest country club had known who would be the first to reach the green—the black guys."

These incidents illustrate two of the greatest challenges that faced African American golfers in the post–World War II era: the struggle to desegregate municipal golf courses in the South and the Southwest and the battle to provide black professionals a fair chance to compete in tournaments sponsored by the PGA. From the late 1940s to the mid-1960s there was bitter strife and ultimate triumph in the civil rights movement regarding school integration, voting rights, access to public accommodation, and other causes. In the world of sports, Jackie Robinson broke the racial barrier in baseball, and desegregation followed in football and basketball. Opposition to desegregation was more intense in those individual games in which country clubs exerted enormous influence on national amateur and professional associations. In golf, the crusade for equal opportunity on the links mirrored the more highly publicized campaigns for desegregation of the schools, buses, lunch counters, hotels, voting booths, and courtrooms of America.

During the pre–World War II period, African Americans renewed their long struggle for equal opportunity in golf. Despite the hardships of the Depression, they significantly increased their presence on American golf courses during the 1930s. In reporting on the United Golfers Association's "Negro Open" of 1938, *Time* magazine noted in its issue of September 12th that of a total black population of twelve million in the United States, about fifty thousand played golf. It stated that "Northern Negroes" knew nothing of the game until they became prosperous enough to enjoy it as a pastime. But the situation was different in the South, where country clubs hired black caddies, and "many moppets learn the fundamentals of golf along with their ABCs." In April of that year *Golfing* magazine underscored the role of black caddies in southern tournaments. That journal also highlighted "the several communities of colored people" who were virtually dependent upon golf for their living, especially Taylorville, near Pinehurst, which was "named for a former slave who caddied ably almost to his 80th year, then continued until his death as head man for the Pinehurst caddie colony."

During the Depression years, middle- and upper-class African Americans founded new private golf clubs and supported golf at black colleges. The fourteen new golf clubs joined perhaps a half dozen organized in the 1920s that were still operating. Two of the most prominent and active were the Royal Golf Club and the Wake Robin Golf Club, both of Washington, D.C. The Royal Golf Club, originally named the Capital City Golf Club, was launched in 1933. With demand by black golfers overwhelming the nine-hole Lincoln Memorial municipal course, its officers lobbied intensively with federal administrators for the construction of a second public golf course for the black community in the nation's capital. Their efforts finally bore fruit in June 1939 with the opening of the John Langston Golf Course, with the work funded by the Civilian Conservation Corps and the Works Projects Administration. Still, the members of the Royal Golf Club were disappointed that the new course only had nine holes and black golfers remained barred from the city's other five courses. In 1936, thirteen women (most of whom were wives of members of the Royal Golf Club) organized the Wake Robin Golf Club. Their aims were "to perpetuate golf among Negro Women, to make potential players into champions and to make a permanent place for Negro Women in the world of golf." On the club's fiftieth anniversary one commentator emphasized the boldness of their action: "Under a system of racism, in an atmosphere of sexism, black women playing golf was not a light matter. It was a political act." Although these ladies met with some resistance from the some of the members of the all-male Royal Golf Club, their example stimulated action among black women interested in organizing golf clubs in Chicago, Baltimore, Atlantic City, Philadelphia, and New York. These female clubs arranged social events, supported charities, and raised funds to pay for travel expenses for members to compete in tournaments. As the African American elite adopted golf, it also became a favorite pastime at black colleges. The Southern Intercollegiate Athletic Conference (SIAC) promoted competitive golf among teams from Morehouse, Tuskegee, and other colleges. Tuskegee was the first black college to construct a nine-hole golf course, a 3,400–yard, par-35 facility. The SIAC sponsored its first intercollegiate golf tournament for black colleges in 1938.

The national open championships for African American golfers sponsored by the United Golfers Association (UGA) showcased the talent of the most skilled black players and generated more interest in the sport within black communities of all regions. Women earned the right to compete in their own amateur division. Male winners of this event during this period included Robert "Pat" Ball, John Dendy, and Howard Wheeler. Ball began his career as a caddie for Bob Jones at the East Lake Country Club in Atlanta, then moved to Chicago to pursue greater opportunities in the world of golf. Ball became a grocer and distinguished himself not only through his victories in black competition, but also through his triumphs in white regional tournaments in the Midwest after he was able to gain admission to those events. In 1934 Ball became the UGA's first three-time champion. Dendy, a locker boy at North Carolina's fashionable Asheville Country Club, took the title in 1936 and 1937. *Time* magazine's account of the UGA's 1938 "Negro Open" praised Wheeler's performance, although its account of his success was laden with racist language. Its story described how the gallery of three hundred watched the "lanky, wooly-topped" Wheeler "shuffle along the fairways in a Stepin Fetchit gait, plop down on the greens while waiting his turn to putt." Wheeler won the event and the two-hundred-dollar prize "on a tough, hilly course he had never seen before." His score of 284 set a new record for the Negro Championship and was just three shots higher than the all-time U.S. Open record set by Ralph Guldahl.

On the eve of World War II, several black golf clubs spearheaded efforts to desegregate white-only municipal golf courses in Kansas City, Missouri, and Washington, D.C. In 1938 in Kansas City, four members of the Heart of America Golf Club filed a lawsuit against the city for the right to play on the segregated public courses in Swope Park. (They were barred from one course and were limited to Mondays and Tuesdays on the other.) In Washington, D.C., during the summer of 1941, several black golfers planned to play rounds on the segregated East Potomac Park Golf Course. Ultimate responsibility for policy at Washington's public parks rested with the secretary of the interior, Harold Ickes. When he was informed of the golfers' intentions, Ickes concluded: "I can see no reason why Negroes should not be permitted to play on the golf course." He wrote in his diary: "They are taxpayers, they are citizens, and they have the right to play on public courses on the same basis as whites. To be sure, we have maintained a golf course for Negroes in Washington, but the cold fact is that we haven't kept it up and it is not surprising that Negroes do not care to play on it." In early July three activists, protected by six U.S. Park Service police officers, attempted to play at the segregated East Potomac Park Golf Course. They apparently completed their round despite a hostile crowd of whites who jeered at them and threatened them with assault. But Ickes could not provide adequate protection for all black golfers, and those who attempted to play at segregated local municipal courses did so at considerable personal risk. The ladies of the Wake Robin Golf Club also applied for and received permission to hold their annual tournament in the East Potomac course, but they later withdrew their request after intense white opposition.

African Americans were active agents in the post–World War II golf boom in the United States, as the desegregation of the armed forces and the civil rights movement spurred increased participation in the sport among black servicemen and civilians. During and after the war, black soldiers and sailors enjoyed more access to courses on military bases, while black middle-class citizens joined a growing number of private (although still segregated) clubs. African American celebrities such as Joe Louis, Sugar Ray Robinson, Jackie Robinson, Billy Eckstine, and many other stars took up the Scottish game and popularized it in black communities. African American newspapers devoted more coverage to black clubs, tournaments, and leading players, countering the image perpetuated in the white media that black participation in golf was limited to caddying and other servile duties.

After 1940 the African American elite and upper middle class founded several dozen new golf clubs that joined the black associations organized during the 1920s and 1930s that survived the Depression. The list includes those launched in Los Angeles, Miami, Houston, Detroit, Pittsburgh, Cleveland, Dayton, Gary, Indianapolis, Chicago, St. Louis, Minneapolis, and Atlanta. In most cases these associations could not afford to maintain their links in first-class condition, but in the North, Midwest, and West members had access to municipal grounds that were often superior. That was not the case where segregation ruled on public courses in the South and Southwest, but on their own turf the black bourgeoisie entertained themselves with social events and club tournaments, often inviting black celebrities from the worlds of sports, music, and theater to join in the fun. On one level, the black golf club enabled African American businessmen and professionals to imitate their upscale white counterparts as they displayed their elevated status in their own communities. But on another level, they promoted participation in the sport among black men and women of more modest means—especially caddies who qualified for instructional positions. Members of these clubs also contributed greatly to the crusade to desegregate municipal golf courses and to integrate professional tournaments.

African American stars who became addicted to golf spurred interest in the sport among the black masses and contributed mightily to the integration battles on all fronts. Joe Louis first tried the sport in 1936, one year prior to winning the heavyweight boxing title. He soon became obsessed with the game, taking lessons and playing so frequently that his managers feared that his golfing was detracting from his boxing training. In August 1941 he sponsored the Joe Louis Open in Detroit, an event interrupted by the war but which resumed in 1945 and continued annually through 1951. After the war he competed as an amateur in numerous black tournaments, and he even won a few titles. As heavyweight champion from 1937 to 1949 Louis energetically promoted golf among other black celebrities and the black masses, and he laid the groundwork for his later campaign to integrate the PGA. Billy Eckstine did not have the star power of Joe Louis, but he was a popular jazz vocalist and bandleader in the 1940s and 1950s who shared Louis's passion for golf. Perhaps his greatest contribution to the sport was his patronage of the young Charles Sifford.

◎ ◎ ◎

During the post–World War II period, African American golfers generally had access to municipal links in the Northeast, Midwest, and West, although a few semiprivate, daily-fee courses excluded them. However, black players in the border states or the South faced major obstacles before they could even tee off on the first hole of a public course. In those regions racial segregation dictated that blacks were excluded entirely from public courses, restricted to inferior separate links, or permitted to play on a very limited basis (often one day a week) on "white only" grounds. But the late 1940s and early 1950s witnessed a series of legal challenges to racial segregation in public education and recreation that had profound consequences for the desegregation of municipal golf courses. More specifically, these cases raised questions about the definition and validity of the "separate but equal" doctrine established by the Supreme Court in 1896 in *Plessy v. Ferguson*. The *Brown v. Board of Education* ruling in 1954 marked a turning point for this type of litigation, because even though that landmark case ordered only public school desegregation, the Supreme Court and lower courts soon applied its principles to public recreation in general and municipal golf courses in particular. But these judicial decrees did not necessarily result in the immediate integration of these facilities, because their implementation depended upon compliance by local officials, who in some cities faced open resistance by white residents. It is also true that, quite apart from judicial rulings, long-term historical trends were contributing to increasing racial integration in American society. These included rising income and leisure time among the black middle class, growing international pressure for equal rights during the height of the cold war, and more media coverage of civil rights demonstrations. Thus the actions of the Supreme Court and federal and state courts were not necessarily the decisive factors in the desegregation of municipal golf courses.

During the 1940s and early 1950s black golfers filed lawsuits in Baltimore, Miami, Houston, and Nashville that sought to desegregate municipal golf courses. In these cases, adjudicated under the "separate but equal" doctrine, the plaintiffs argued that the facilities provided for African American players were either nonexistent or not truly equal to those available to their white counterparts. In each case a federal judge agreed, but still instructed the municipality to provide equal opportunity for the golfers while maintaining the traditional policy of segregation. For example, in Nashville, the town's three municipal links were reserved for whites only. In the case of *Hayes v. Crutcher* (1952) a federal district judge declared, in denying the plaintiffs summary judgment, that while the general policy of segregation was consistent with "the general principles of natural law," Nashville was required "to afford equal facilities, apportioned to the need, to the segregated groups, either part-time use of present facilities or full-time use of separate facilities, or such other arrangement for equal and fair opportunities as conditions may require." Subsequently, in 1954 Nashville permitted black golfers to use the Shelby Park Golf Course exclusively on Wednesdays and on alternate Saturdays and Sundays, pending the completion of a new municipal course for black players. After that segregated course was opened, Nashville officials took action to once again ban blacks from the Shelby Park links. But in 1956 a different federal district judge set aside all previous orders in that case and ordered a full desegregation of all Nashville municipal golf courses.

Less than one year after the *Brown* decision, the U.S. Court of Appeals for the Fourth Circuit applied its principles to a case that involved public beaches and bathhouses in Maryland in or near Baltimore. In *Dawson v. Mayor and City Council of Baltimore City* (1955) that court referred explicitly to the *Brown* decision in rejecting arguments that supported the separate but equal policy. "It is now obvious," the per curiam opinion stated, "that segregation cannot be justified as a means to preserve the public peace merely because the tangible facilities furnished to one race are equal to those furnished to the other." It concluded that "racial segregation in recreational activities can no longer be sustained as a proper exercise of the police power of the State; for if that power cannot be invoked to sustain racial segregation in the schools, where attendance is compulsory and racial friction may be apprehended from the enforced commingling of the races, it cannot be sustained with respect to public beach and bathhouse facilities, the use of which is entirely optional." The court declared that segregation in these public facilities was unconstitutional, and the U.S. Supreme Court summarily affirmed the decision.

The *Brown* and *Dawson* decisions opened the door for a series of federal rulings that outlawed racial discrimination on municipal golf courses in Atlanta and several other southern cities. In Atlanta in 1951 Dr. Hamilton M. Holmes, Sr., his sons Oliver Wendell Holmes and Alfred ("Tup") Holmes, and Charles T. Bell resolved to challenge their city's policy of racial segregation on its seven public courses. All were members of the community's African American elite and its black-owned Lincoln Country Club. Dis-

African American golfers integrate the North Fulton public golf course in Atlanta, Ga., December 24, 1955. Left to right, C. T. Bell, Alfred "Tup" Holmes, and Oliver Holmes. Copyright Bettmann/CORBIS.

satisfied with the poor condition of its nine-hole layout and frustrated with their board of directors' unwillingness to invest in improvements, the four men hatched a scheme to invade the restricted Bobby Jones Golf Course, situated in the affluent northwest section of the city. "Tup" Holmes, a black union steward at Lockheed Aircraft and a former amateur golf champion, was the radical rabble-rouser of his family. While playing for the Tuskegee Institute team in 1939, he had been a victim of racism when the NCAA barred him from its annual golf tournament. The Holmes group sent a blond-haired and light-skinned African American friend to the Jones course. While he was able to register and play a few holes, later that day the head professional barred "Tup" Holmes and Bell from the grounds.

The Holmes group then took two years to prepare a lawsuit that sought the full desegregation of Atlanta's public golf courses and parks. In the case of *Holmes v. City of Atlanta* (1954), a federal district court decided in favor of the plaintiffs, but postponed implementation of its decree to allow the city "a reasonable opportunity to promptly prepare and put into effect regulations for the use of the municipal golf facilities which, while preserving segregation, will be in full and fair accord with its principles." In his opinion the judge noted that the *Brown* ruling rejected the doctrine of separate but equal "only as it applied to public education." In June of the following year the U.S. Court of Appeals for the Fifth Circuit affirmed that judgment, once again applying the doctrine of separate but equal. But in November the U.S. Supreme Court vacated that ruling and remanded the case to the district court with brief directions to enter a decree for the petitioners in conformity with its *Dawson* decision on the same day. On December 22nd a federal district judge ordered the city of Atlanta to permit Negroes to use its municipal golf courses "immediately." Governor Marvin Griffin objected, proclaiming: "Co-mingling of the races in Georgia state parks and recreation areas would not be tolerated." But Mayor William B. Hartsfield weighed the options of selling the city's courses to individuals or closing down all the links and decided to comply with the court order. He stated: "Should we close our courses it would deprive nearly 70,000 white players [of their golf] and nearly 100 city employees of their jobs and their rights in order to deny a few Negro players the use of the golf links."

As federal courts ordered the desegregation of municipal golf courses during the 1950s, town officials in several southern cities implemented a variety of plans designed to evade or delay compliance. Their strategies ranged from leasing or selling the grounds to private clubs to outright closure to repeated petitions for more time to implement integration of their links. Greensboro,

North Carolina, tried the first approach when that city leased its municipal course to the Gillespie Park Golf Club (a nonprofit corporation) in 1949. As recounted above, Dr. George Simkins, a prominent local dentist, community activist, and head of the local chapter of the National Association for the Advancement of Colored People, challenged the segregationist policy of that club in 1955 when he and several of his friends played nine holes on the links and were arrested for criminal trespass. The following year, while their trespass case was still in process, Simkins and his friends filed a federal lawsuit against the City of Greensboro, charging it with racial discrimination in attempting to exclude them from its public links (*Simkins v. City of Greensboro*, 1957). The district judge ruled in favor of the plaintiffs. After the U.S. Court of Appeals for the Fourth Circuit affirmed this ruling and after an arsonist had burned the clubhouse to the ground, apparently to prevent blacks from using the facilities, the Greensboro City Council voted unanimously to close the golf course. After a long legal battle, Simkins and his fellow golfers were convicted of criminal trespass, but North Carolina's governor eventually commuted their thirty-day prison sentences. During these years Tallahassee, Fort Lauderdale, Jacksonville, and several other Florida cities also attempted to circumvent court desegregation orders by leasing or selling municipal grounds to private groups.

Perhaps the most notorious case of a closing of a municipal golf course in response to a desegregation order occurred in Birmingham, Alabama, which was then a hotbed of civil rights agitation. In October of 1961 a federal district court judge ruled that racial segregation in public facilities was unconstitutional. Safety commissioner T. Eugene "Bull" Connor then closed all the city's parks, football stadiums, swimming pools, and golf links, with the intention of offering them for sale to private bodies. They remained closed until June 29, 1963, when the town's new mayor began implementing a plan to comply with demands of civil rights protesters. On June 21, 1963 the *New York Times* explained that "there reportedly had been some grumbling among white golfers who could not afford a private club at the city's failure to reopen the public courses." However, there were no public facilities at any of the three integrated courses and the players were required to furnish their own caddies. A third tactic a few southern cities employed in response to court orders for desegregation was to seek extended delays in implementing integration. Obstructionists in Memphis blocked the integration of the city's public recreation facilities for several years in the early 1960s until the Supreme Court rejected its claims for more time to implement court orders.

The passage of the Civil Rights Act of 1964 marked a landmark in federal legislation mandating integration in many areas of American life, including public accommodations and such public facilities as municipal parks, golf courses, and swimming pools. After its enactment, southern cities began complying with its provisions by integrating their city golf courses. An example is Jackson, Mississippi, where in early July eleven black players teed off on the Jackson Municipal Golf Course with the apparent consent of the city. Thus, after decades of struggle, African American golfers had finally won the right to play on public grounds. The victories won in the federal courts during the 1950s and 1960s earned black golfers more than just the right to play on public grounds. They also signaled greater progress in the quest for more respect and fair treatment for African Americans.

⊙ ⊙ ⊙

While the desegregation of municipal golf courses in the United States marked a major milestone on the road to equal opportunity for recreational African American golfers, for the handful of talented black professionals one huge hurdle remained. The PGA had barred black players from its organization informally since its founding in 1916, and it codified that restriction in 1943 through an amendment to its constitution that limited its membership to "professional golfers of the Caucasian race, residing in North or South America." The most talented black golfers who wished to compete for prize money during this era could enter only three tournaments that were racially integrated: the Los Angeles Open, the Canadian Open, and the Tam O'Shanter Open in suburban Chicago. Their other (and main) option was to play in events sponsored by the UGA, but even the most successful on that circuit could barely earn enough to cover expenses and perhaps scratch out a modest living for themselves and their families. Beginning in the late 1940s a few of them challenged the PGA, demanding the right to play against the best golfers in the world. Although they won limited access to several tournaments during the 1950s, the PGA did not repeal its "Caucasian clause" until 1961, and even after that date black professionals still faced major obstacles before they finally achieved equal treatment.

Each summer during the postwar period the UGA organized a full schedule of tournaments that culminated with its annual national championship for amateurs (both men and women) and professionals. Although most of the entrants were African American, the UGA did not discriminate against white players, and a few of them crossed the color line and teed off in their events. The national championships became gala social occasions for many among the black elite and for such celebrities as Joe Louis, who won the amateur title in 1951. They also showcased the skill of the stars of the world of African American golf even as they prepared them for the few interracial competitions that they were able to enter. The UGA thus became roughly the equivalent of the Negro Leagues in baseball. It produced players who earned public acclaim and demonstrated that they could compete against whites. But unlike the case of baseball, which became racially integrated during the late 1940s and 1950s, professional golf remained mostly white before and after the PGA dropped its "Caucasian clause." Thus the UGA did not meet the same fate as the Negro Leagues, which became defunct after the integration of major league baseball.

Among the stellar performers in UGA tournaments, the most talented were Howard "Butch" Wheeler, Bill Spiller, Ted Rhodes, and Charlie Sifford. All four overcame enormous obstacles to reach the upper echelon of black golf in the United States, but among them only Sifford was able to experience some success and recognition for his performance on the PGA regular and senior tours after 1961. Born in Atlanta in 1911, Wheeler learned to play golf as a caddy at several country clubs and eventually became caddiemaster at the East Lake Country Club. Known as a long driver with an unorthodox cross-handed grip, he turned professional in 1931, won several UGA-sponsored events, and captured his first national UGA title in 1933. His second UGA crown in 1938 earned him recognition in *Time* magazine, which reported that "with this accomplishment Howard Wheeler took his place alongside Bobby Jones, Charley Yates and others who have made Atlanta a starred spot on the golfing map." He would go on to win four more UGA Championships, the last one coming at the age of forty-seven in 1958.

While Wheeler did not choose to challenge the racism of the PGA, Spiller, Rhodes, and Sifford were pioneers in the campaign to end the "Caucasian clause." Spiller was born in 1913 in Tishomingo, Oklahoma, and moved to Tulsa at the age of nine to live with his father. There he was a star athlete in track and basketball in high school, and after graduation he earned a degree in education and sociology at Wiley College, an all-black institution in Marshall, Texas. Trained and certified to be a teacher, he turned down a sixty-dollar-a-month position in 1938 and journeyed to Los Angeles to live with his mother. He found work as a redcap at a railroad station, where one of his fellow employees challenged him to a game of golf in December 1942. Spiller had only hit a few golf balls as a youth, but as a twenty-nine-year-old novice he soon became addicted to the sport, and within four years he had won all the black tournaments in southern California. In 1947 he turned professional and traveled to the east to tour the UGA circuit. He experienced mixed results in tournaments and in gambling on private rounds, but on one occasion he hustled Joe Louis out of $7,000 in an all-day marathon match. (He used the earnings to buy a small house.) During this period his most notable achievement was a score of 68 to tie Ben Hogan for second place after the first round of the Los Angeles Open at the Riviera Country Club in 1948. (He ultimately finished twenty strokes behind Hogan, who won the event.) Spiller's rise to prominence was unusual in that, unlike Rhodes, Sifford, and most of the other African American golfers, he had not learned the sport as a caddie. He was also much more militant in his outspoken protests and actions against racism in golf, perhaps because of his bitter experiences with prejudice as a child as well as his college education that made him more sensitive to insults.

During these postwar years Rhodes became a legendary character among African American golfers, ruling as the premier black golfer until Sifford surpassed him during the late 1950s. Born in 1913 in Nashville, Tennessee, he began caddying at twelve at the Belle Meade and Richland Country Clubs. As a youth he could play occasional rounds as a caddie on those private grounds, but as an adult he was barred from the segregated public courses in Nashville. After service in the navy during World War II he returned to Nashville and improved his game on military courses nearby. During the late 1940s Rhodes also benefited enormously from the patronage and generosity of Louis, who hired him to be his personal instructor and who provided financial support that enabled Rhodes to take lessons in California and to play on the UGA tour. Rhodes reeled off six consecutive victories during one thirteen-month period in 1946–47; the last one came at the Joe Louis Open on the Donald Ross–designed Rackham Golf Course in Detroit. Over his career he won more than 150 tournaments, including UGA national titles in 1949, 1950, 1951, and 1957.

Sifford was born in 1922—nine years after both Spiller and Rhodes. While his long career spanned the two eras of segregated and integrated professional golf, by the 1960s he was too old to reap the full benefits of widening opportunities for black golfers. A native of Charlotte, North Carolina, he started caddying at ten at the Carolina Country Club. Within a few years he was earning almost as much money working after school as his father brought home doing backbreaking work at a local fertilizer plant. When he was in the eleventh grade, club members began complaining that the organization's management was being too lenient in granting Sifford playing privileges on the course. At about that time a nasty racial incident forced Sifford to move to Philadelphia to live with an uncle, where he honed his skills on the public Cobbs Creek course while working full-time at the National Biscuit Company. After military service during World War II (where he served in Okinawa and played on an army golf team) he decided on a career as a professional golfer. After struggling for a few years Sifford landed a prized position working for Billy Eckstine as a valet and golf instructor and playing partner. In his autobiography Sifford remembered the camaraderie and democratic character of that phase of his golfing life. He wrote: "You can put a black man, a rich man, a Japanese guy, and a poor white man together on a golf course, and they're all going to have a good time. . . . Golf is such an incredible equalizer. . . . We may have different skill levels, but we all struggle with the game equally. When we're together on the course, we're all at the mercy of the winds and the grass and our own frailties, and none of this stuff between people—the racial tensions, the upper/lower class boundaries, the political or religious differences—makes a damn bit of difference." He also recorded his growing resolve to pursue his personal sporting American dream. He kept hearing a voice in his head that asked: "Why can't I play professional golf with the best players in the world? . . . Why, in this supposedly free country of ours, am I being denied the right to try to prove myself against the best? More important, why can't I have the chance to go after some of that money that Ben Hogan and Sam Snead and Lew Worsham are making?"

Spiller and Rhodes spearheaded the first assault on the PGA's "Caucasian clause" in January 1948 after their strong performances in the Los Angeles Open qualified them for the following week's Richmond tournament near Oakland, California. After they played two practice rounds, a PGA official informed them they were being excluded from the event because they were not PGA members. Infuriated, Spiller and Rhodes then released their story to an ABC sportscaster and contacted an attorney, Jonathan Rowell, who agreed to represent the two men plus a third black golfer, Madison Gunther, who had also been barred from the Richmond competition. Rowell then filed lawsuits against the PGA seeking $100,000 for each man for denying them the equal opportunity to practice their profession, and against the Richmond Country Club seeking $5,000 for each man for damages (loss of a possible $2,000 prize, plus a humiliation award.) Editorial reaction around the nation to this challenge was mixed. On January 28th the weekly periodical *Golf World* labeled the legal action "a mistake," stating: "If the

PGA should insist on accepting entries of Negroes, against the wishes of the private clubs, the PGA might well find its winter tour disintegrating. And then who would be 'deprived of the opportunity to make a living?'" On the other hand, the January 18th *New York Times* strongly criticized the PGA for its exclusion of the black golfers, calling its policy "neither sportsmanlike nor American," while also noting that Jackie Robinson and other Negroes attended and competed for California universities.

This 1948 episode generated valuable publicity for the cause of integration of professional golf, but it yielded few or no practical results for Spiller, Rhodes, and other black golfers. About six weeks after the Richmond tournament, Rowell negotiated a deal with a lawyer representing the PGA in which the golfers dropped their lawsuits in exchange for a promise that the PGA would revise its racially restrictive policy. Over the next few years the PGA took no such action but was able to dodge the issue by labeling its PGA co-sponsored events as "open invitationals," thus giving private country clubs the right to exclude African American golfers or anyone else from their events. Spiller was disappointed at this outcome, but he later remarked that the action "did what I went to do in the first place: make the public aware of the situation." He concluded: "I always said our salvation would be public opinion, because most people are primarily good people."

Four years later the issue of racial discrimination in professional golf became headline news when Louis, Spiller, and another African American, Eural Clark, applied for entry into a tournament in San Diego in January 1952. At first the sponsors welcomed the three (probably in part because of the star power of Louis), but later they cancelled the invitations. Louis then blasted PGA president Horton Smith, calling his battle with his organization the "biggest fight" of his life and proclaiming: "I want the people to know what the PGA is. . . . We've got another Hitler to get by." He also called Walter Winchell, who then told his national radio audience that if Joe Louis could carry a gun in the U.S. Army he could carry a golf club in San Diego. Smith then traveled to San Diego to try to defuse the situation, claiming that he favored "evolution" rather than "revolution" on racial matters. He also expressed a hope that the PGA would follow the policy of the United States Golf Association, which allowed blacks to enter its national championship provided the host club accepted their entries. Smith then negotiated an agreement that permitted Louis to compete in San Diego as an invited amateur, but which still barred Spiller and Clark. Concerning future policy, Smith gained approval for a new plan that would allow a small number of black golfers to enter PGA tournaments provided local sponsors and the host club of an event approved their applications. This scheme also recommended the creation of a screening committee composed of leading black golfers that would nominate qualified players for PGA tournaments. While the idea of a screening committee was roundly criticized in the black press and does not appear to have been implemented, Smith's actions did open the door for a half-dozen black amateur and professional golfers to compete in the following week's Phoenix Open, as well as in several other events later that year. Spiller, Rhodes, and a few other black golfers wound up playing in ten PGA tournaments in 1952 and fifteen in 1953. The San Diego incident generated criticism of the PGA from the Congress of Industrial Organizations and several newspapers across the nation.

For the remainder of the 1950s black golfers were second-class citizens in the world of golf, struggling to enter a few PGA tournaments each year. As Spiller and Rhodes faded from the scene due to their advancing age and deteriorating health, Sifford emerged as the premier African American player. While he dominated the UGA national championships (winning titles every year from 1952 through 1956 and also in 1960), his goal was to compete on equal terms with whites. A victory in the 1957 Long Beach Open (not a PGA event) earned him some celebrity, but it was not until 1959 that he achieved a major breakthrough that gained him acceptance by the PGA as an "approved player" and easier entry to events outside the South and the Southwest. He attributed his improved prospects in part to the support of Jackie Robinson, who had learned to play golf in the 1940s and who had closely monitored Sifford's career. In a series of newspaper columns in the *New York Post*, Robinson attacked racism in golf, and he asked why Sifford had not been invited to either the Bing Crosby tournament at Pebble Beach or the Palm Spring Desert Golf Classic. In 1960 he wrote: "Golf is the one major sport in America today in which rank and open racial prejudice is allowed to reign supreme. Though often called the sport of gentlemen, all too often golf courses, clubs, and tournaments apply the ungentlemanly and un-American yardstick of race and color in determining who may or may not compete."

By 1960 Sifford had finally earned partial acceptance into the PGA as an "approved player," but the "Caucasian clause" still barred him from full membership. The final assault on that racial restriction came in 1960 and 1961, when Sifford and Spiller enlisted the support of Stanley Mosk, the attorney general of California, who urged the PGA to drop the clause from its constitution. When that body refused to do so at its annual meeting in November of 1960, Mosk informed the PGA that because of its practice of racial discrimination it would no longer be permitted to hold its tournaments in California. Mosk also urged other attorneys general to take similar action against PGA events in their states. After Mosk's challenge the PGA voted to move its 1962 championship out of Los Angeles. The pressure applied by Mosk and the National Association for the Advancement of Colored People in 1961 resulted in the PGA's unanimous vote in November to delete the clause from its constitution. The co-sponsors of the resolution were delegations from Georgia and Alabama, New York State, and Southern California. It also eliminated the restriction on members who resided outside North and South America. Lou Strong, its president reported: "The action was a realization of changing conditions in the world situation. This was a constructive measure, coinciding with decisions set forth by the United States government."

The abolition of the "Caucasian clause" did not eliminate all the barriers that faced Sifford and other black golfers after 1961, because each player had to serve a five-year apprenticeship during which he had to compete in at least twenty-five tournaments per year. Further trials lay ahead for Sifford and younger African American golfers, but they benefited enormously from the trailblazing efforts of Wheeler, Spiller, Rhodes, and other black golfers during the "Jim Crow" era of the sport. But by the early 1960s at least the masses of African American players could tee off on municipal courses, and the most talented had more of a chance to test their skills against Arnold Palmer, Jack Nicklaus, Gary Player, and other star white golfers.

WOMEN AT
MID-CENTURY

In October 1964 the editors of *Golf* magazine published an article that they knew would enrage many of their female readers. In "I Say, Ban Women Golfers!" Oscar Fraley lamented the passing of the male-dominated golf club. He asked:

> "Men, remember when it used to be Our Club? . . . When they didn't even have a washroom for women, and those who were brave enough to invade our courses had to change their spikes in the car? . . . Look at the scene today. . . . Women are everywhere—in the card room, in the lounge, and even in our old barber shop, which a pair of suspicious looking Frenchmen now run as a 'Beauty Salon.' Back in those wonderful days when the club was strictly a place where men played golf, we didn't have swimming pools (and the wading pool for the kiddies, of course), tennis courts, bridge rooms, steam baths and 'Bingo every Tuesday.' And it didn't take us four to five hours to negotiate the course behind a creeping female foursome!"

In the December issue of *Golf* the women retaliated with a barrage of blistering replies that excoriated Fraley for his blatant male chauvinism. Writing from Nashville, Tennessee, Stella Morris placed the struggle of female golfers in the context of the women's rights movement. She explained: "Women have had to fight for the right to vote, the right to hold jobs, the right to bathe in reasonable clothing, the right to smoke, make dates, choose their own husbands, own property, hold public and business office. You name it. Men have been so scared of being replaced by women for so long that they can't even take the wonderful calming game of golf in peace . . . they've got to worry about the female invasion. Girls, don't you worry. We've been strong for centuries and we have always won." One month later the periodical printed a full rebuttal to Fraley by Phyllis Battelle in which she acknowledged that "everybody dislikes women golfers, except club pros, golf equipment salesmen, and occasionally, their own children."

But she countered Fraley's attack point by point, arguing that female players were not slower on the links than many men, displayed better manners on the course, and, perhaps most importantly, were essential to the financial health of the clubs.

While probably many male golfers shared Fraley's views, they could do little or nothing to stop the tidal wave of girls and women who swept onto America's courses during the post–World War II golf boom. In July 1962 *Golf* magazine reported a gain of 67 percent since 1948 in the number of females playing golf, estimating that more than 883,500 of them above the age of eighteen completed fifteen or more rounds in 1961. It added that the women's rate of participation was accelerating faster than that of the men, although there was still only one woman for every three or four men on the nation's courses. Golf professional Roland Hill attributed the growth in women's golf in the 1950s to "better equipped and better organized homes, golf instruction of girls at most of the leading colleges and universities, evening sessions at golf ranges, improved economic conditions, less strain in the management of infants and a more independent and vigorous spirit of young women." During that decade the vast majority of middle- and upper-class women stayed at home to manage their households and raise their children, and thus they had more opportunities to play golf than did working women. Denied access to political and economic power, they were more willing to assert themselves in social settings. Thus while the growing female presence was unmistakable on both public and private courses, the revolution was most apparent at country clubs. As one manager of a sub-urban association explained: "You don't have a man's club anymore. What you have is a family social center." Although many clubs still restricted women's play on weekend mornings, in many other ways they catered to female demands for more services and amenities.

Perhaps the greatest positive contribution of women to country club life was economic, both through higher family membership fees and other financial contributions to clubs and especially through lessons and their patronage of the golf professional's shop. As one club official explained: "This transition to a family-type operation has saved the necks of a lot of clubs. A good many men have groused about it, but, with costs going up all the time, it's hard to keep going with golf alone, and the biggest part of it just on weekends." Even Fraley conceded that for the golf professional, "the lady of the house is from heaven." Jim MacLaughlin, head pro of the Miami Shores Country Club in Florida, reported that women purchased far more golf clubs and clothing than did the men. He added that they were perhaps twenty times as likely to take lessons, because they had more leisure time and were intense about improving their game. On this point Battelle agreed with Fraley, stating, "It is women who keep the golf courses financially healthy." As proof she listed high markups for clothing, "family memberships at ungodly prices," fundraising for swimming pools, and the purchase of golf clubs for themselves and their men.

The invasion of the ladies onto private links during this era posed a series of problems for golf professionals at country clubs, who realized that if they wished to keep their positions (or at least their sanity) they had to be sensitive to women's demands. This was especially true regarding disputes over rules, giving lessons, and arranging foursomes. According to Fraley, the women knew the rules "a lot better than the men," but that was often bad news for club members and professionals. He explained: "Most of the time when men play it's a casual, sporting affair of give and take. But when the ladies go at it, bub, it's a federal case if one of them so much as slightly warps Rule 96, Section 8." Teaching women the fundamentals of the sport could also be challenging, especially for females who lacked both the athletic ability and strength to become good players. Professionals also had to be aware of the pitfalls in arranging foursomes for females, who were often perturbed about pairings with ladies they disliked.

In the post–World War II golf boom, as in its post–World War I counterpart of the 1920s, there were many wives of golf addicts who shunned the links and who became increasingly resentful of their spouses' long weekend absences from their homes and families. In July 1963 *Golf* magazine published an article titled "Ten Ways to Keep a Golf Widow Happy" that summarized suggestions from a panel of marriage counselors. The essay began with a review of the factors behind the marital tensions and the women's tactics in expressing their displeasure with their husbands. Two of the most common reactions were withholding sex and serving canned or cold dinners. The number one remedy proposed by the therapists was persuading the wife to take up the sport herself. If that approach failed, the counselors suggested a variety of strategies, including the time-honored giving of candy, switching and staggering tee times, encouraging her to start a new hobby (like painting or pottery), helping more with childcare on weekends so she could have more time for herself, and planning family vacations.

⊙ ⊙ ⊙

As increasing numbers of girls and women crowded America's public and private golf courses after World War II, a few who were most skilled struggled to earn a living as the first female professional golfers in the United States. Betty Hicks, Mildred "Babe" Didrikson Zaharias, Patty Berg, and a few other brave souls launched the Ladies Professional Golf Association (LPGA) in 1949. But for that fledgling organization to have any chance of success, it needed a true superstar who could attract media attention and keep the women golfers in the public eye. Fortunately for the LGPA, such a superstar appeared in the colorful character of the "Babe."

"Babe" Didrikson Zaharias holds a unique place in the history of women in American sports in general and golf in particular. Her legendary status encompasses not just the medals, trophies, and earnings she amassed throughout her brilliant multisport career, but also the image she projected for her adoring public. A natural athlete, she achieved championship performances in a variety of individual and team sports, but especially in golf. When in her twenties she realized that American sports fans were turned off by her masculine image as a "Texas tomboy" or a "muscle moll," she reinvented herself as a ladylike, feminine married woman with proper clothes, makeup, manners, housewife skills, and an adoring husband to match. As her leading biographer, Susan Cayleff, summarized her "two personas": "Battered by the press for her boy-girl image, Babe abandoned her androgyny to present herself publicly as 'feminine.' Intimates reveal little congruence between the at-home Babe—in shorts, no makeup, proudly strutting her athleticism—and the public Babe—softer spoken, counseling conventionality, and primed for the pages of *Good Housekeeping*."

Babe's legend began with her stunning achievements as a youth in Texas, where she excelled in basketball, track and field, baseball, and any other athletic endeavor that caught her fancy. Although as a celebrity she gave her birth year as 1913, 1914, or 1915, her baptismal certificate lists the actual date as June 26, 1911. Her parents, Ole and Hannah Didriksen (Babe later changed the spelling of her last name), were Norwegian immigrants who settled in Port Arthur in east Texas in 1908 and moved inland in 1914 to Beaumont after a hurricane ravaged the Port Arthur region. Ole and Hannah were working-class people who struggled to support seven children. Babe had a combative and active girlhood, filled with rough contests with her siblings and especially with neighborhood boys. In 1933 she told a reporter that as a junior high school student "the girls did not play games that interested me. I preferred baseball, football, foot-racing and jumping with the boys, to hop-scotch and jacks and dolls, which were about the only things girls did. . . . I guess the habit of playing with boys made me too rough for the girls' games. Anyway, I found them too tame." By the time she was a senior in high school she had set her personal lifetime goal to be "the greatest athlete that ever lived."

As Babe approached the end of her teenage years, her performances in basketball and track and field propelled her into the national sports lime-light. In 1930 and 1931 she earned all-American basketball honors and won championships and set records in Amateur Athletic Union (AAU)-sponsored meets in the 80–meter hurdles, broad jump, baseball throw, and javelin throw. Her most spectacular performance came at the 1932 national AAU championships at Evansville, Illinois, which also served as the tryouts for the 1932 Olympic Games. Competing as a one-woman team representing the Employers Casualty Insurance Company of Dallas, Texas, Babe entered six of the ten events. She won six of them, setting national or world records in the shot put, baseball throw, javelin throw, and 80–meter hurdles. She also took the gold medal in the broad jump, tied for first in the high jump, and claimed the team championship for Employers Casualty. In the 1932 summer Olympics in Los Angeles, AAU regulations limited Babe to three events: the javelin throw, 80–meter hurdles, and high jump. Her javelin throw earned her a gold medal and a new Olympic and world record. Next she won her second gold and set another Olympic and world record in the hurdles in a controversial photo finish against a U.S. teammate, Evelyn Hall. Babe also tied for first place in the high jump, but judges placed her second when they ruled she had employed an illegal head-first technique. The press reaction to her performance was explosive, as headlines lauded her as the "Amazing Amazon," the "Terrific Tomboy," the "Texas Tornado," and the "World-Beating Girl Viking of Texas."

After her Olympic triumphs Didrikson tried to cash in on her fame through endorsements, stage appearances, stunts, and bookings with sports teams, until she finally resolved to concentrate on golf. Although she later claimed that she took up the sport in 1932, in fact she played at least a few rounds as a teenager on the municipal course in Beaumont and was a member of her high school girls' golf team. After moving to Santa Monica, California, in 1933 she took lessons from Stan Kertes, who recalled that she would practice up to fifteen hours per day, hitting fifteen hundred balls each session until her hands started to bleed. Shortly thereafter she met Gene Sarazen, who invited her to accompany him on a golf tour that gave her invaluable instruction, experience, and a good income from exhibition fees. She also signed a lucrative contract from the P. Goldsmith Sons sporting goods company. But just as she was beginning her quest for golf immortal-ity, the United States Golf Association dealt her a severe blow by banning her from amateur tournaments for three years. That action limited her to a few open events each year plus exhibitions.

Nineteen thirty-five marked a turning point in Didrikson's life because that was the year she decided to remake her image. She was aware that newspaper reports stressed her masculine demeanor, and she understood that she could use the press to present her as more feminine. To soften her image that fall Didrikson consulted a Texas friend, Bertha Bowen, who took her shopping to buy new clothes, recommended a new hairstyle, advised her on makeup, and even tried unsuccessfully to get the Babe to play golf wearing a girdle. Sportswriters soon noticed and approved of Didrikson's makeover. In her autobiography, she remembered: "Some writers have said that around this time a big change took place in me. Their idea is that I used to be all tomboy, with none of the usual girls' interest, and then all of a sudden I switched over to being feminine." She dismissed such characterizations as "tomboy talk" and denied any such transformation. She stated, "I'm still the same Babe. It's just as you get older, you're not as rambunctious as you used to be. You mellow down a little bit." But here surely Didrikson was being disingenuous, minimizing her conscious effort to please the sporting press and public.

Didrikson's marriage to wrestler and sports promoter George Zaharias in 1938 further enhanced her new image as a heterosexual, traditional American woman. The two met as competitors in January in the 1938 Los Angeles Open, and it was love at first sight. They married in December, and the press devoted extensive coverage to their whirlwind romance and the new Mrs. Zaharias's domestic duties of shopping, cooking, and sewing. George soon took over the management of Babe's exhibition schedule and his financial success as a sports promoter enabled Babe to give up her professional career and apply for reinstatement as an amateur. But the USGA required a three-year waiting period, so during the early 1940s Babe busied herself with celebrity exhibitions and wartime charity events with such stars as Bing Crosby and Bob Hope. She loved clowning with Hope, who would tell the gallery: "There's one thing wrong about Babe and myself. I hit the ball like a girl and she hits it like a man."

In January 1943 the USGA reinstated Babe as an amateur, but because of wartime disruptions she had to wait until 1945 to resume a full schedule of tournaments. In 1946 she set her sights on two goals: capturing her first U.S. Women's Amateur Championship and establishing the longest winning streak in the history of women's golf. Beginning in August she ran off thirteen victories in a row (although she later claimed seventeen), with the fourth being the one she most coveted: the U.S. Women's Amateur title. The streak ended in 1947, and later that year George persuaded her to travel to Scotland in June to try to become the first American woman to win the British Ladies Amateur Championship. Although Babe was reluctant to go without her husband, she finally agreed to make the journey because she wanted to follow in the footsteps of Walter Hagen, Bob Jones, Gene Sarazen, and Sam Snead, who had secured their places among golf's immortals through victories in British national championships. Although

Patty Berg (left) and Mildred Didrikson Zaharias (Babe Zaharias), June 19, 1944, Women's Western Open golf tournament. AP/WIDE WORLD PHOTOS.

she had some difficulty with the changeable weather and a bruised left thumb, she dazzled the British press and public with her powerful game and wisecracking with the huge crowds that turned out to watch her play. After her victory in the final round, the fans gave her a long ovation, and the English and American newspapers and magazines praised her to the skies. In a June 13th editorial titled "The Incomparable Babe," the *New York Times* noted a special national quality in her achievement. It remarked: "In her own way she is more American than many representatives we have sent abroad. There is in her an abounding vitality, a directness, an ability to concentrate on a goal and then achieve it that we like to think is typical of us as a nation." After her triumph in Scotland Babe had finally won the two national amateur titles most dear to her, and in August 1947 she announced her decision to turn professional for the second time. She then hired sports agent Fred Corcoran, who promptly negotiated a lifetime contract for her with the Wilson Sporting Goods Company.

During the late 1940s Babe Didrikson Zaharias joined the small company of women golfers struggling to support themselves as professionals. Back in 1943 George S. May, a Chicago sports entrepreneur, sponsored the All-American Open, which featured the first golf tournament that awarded cash prizes to women. (Earlier events had offered war bonds or merchandise to female winners.) May's Open continued for a decade, generating revenue for his privately owned Tam O'Shanter club and providing an early showcase for women's professional golf. May's inaugural Open inspired Hope Seignious, Betty Hicks, and Ellen Griffen to found the Women's Professional Golf Association (WPGA) in 1943. Incorporated in 1944, it met stiff resistance from amateur organizations that did not approve of women professionals and therefore pressured country clubs to refuse to host WPGA events.

After the war the WPGA continued to limp along with minimal financial backing, and while it did inaugurate the U.S. Women's Open in 1946 and conducted countless clinics, it was barely breathing by 1949. In January of that year Patty Berg, Babe and George Zaharias, and Corcoran met in Miami to discuss launching a new women's professional golf association. They knew they could count on the crucial support of L. B. Icely, president of the Wilson Company, who pledged corporate financial backing as a strategy to market golfing equipment to women. The group then hired Corcoran to be its tour director. Corcoran tried to persuade Seignious to give up her charter for the WPGA, and when she refused, Corcoran's attorney suggested that the upstart organization bypass the WPGA and simply name itself the Ladies Professional Golf Association (LPGA). The six founding members of 1949 grew to thirteen by August of 1950, when the LPGA filed its official articles of incorporation. Patty Berg became its first president, serving from 1949 through 1952. Corcoran later wrote that the creation of the LPGA "touched off a national storm of indifference," but he did string together a tour of fourteen tournaments. Yet the total prize money offered was only $50,000 and he had to recruit amateurs to round out the fields of these events. Help arrived later in 1950 from more corporate sponsorship, this time from Alvin Handmacher, head of the Weathervane Company, manufacturer of women's sportswear. Corcoran suggested a novel idea, a transcontinental series of four thirty-six-hole Weathervane tournaments, with the final held in New York. Handmacher pledged $15,000 in prize money, with $5,000 to the champion. Corcoran then hired Helen Lengfeld to manage the events.

During the early 1950s the pioneers of the LPGA faced financial hardships, a grueling coast-to-coast schedule, and trying playing conditions. In 1953 Betty Hicks recalled that she won $3,750 in prize money, but her expenses totaled $3,335. She also put forty thousand miles on her car and walked a thousand miles on courses. Travel between events could be daunting as a caravan of cars filled with the women and their equipment journeyed down hundreds of miles of highways. Upon reaching their destination the players often found the courses in poor shape. Lacking enough marshals and volunteers, they were expected to set the hole locations, mark boundaries, set up the tees, and even make rules decisions. Unruly galleries sometimes disrupted play or made hitting balls dangerous. In 1953 dissatisfaction among the players over money and the lack of tournaments led to a revolt among the players, which resulted in a change in tour management. Handmacher's Weathervane Company withdrew its support and the three major golf manufacturers (Wilson, MacGregor, and Spalding) collectively stopped subsidizing Corcoran's salary. Babe and George Zaharias, Betty Hicks, and a few other players and administrators then tried to lead the LPGA until Corcoran returned for a second tour of duty in 1958.

Babe Didrikson Zaharias was the undisputed star and by far the main attraction of the LPGA during its early years. She frequently demanded and received appearance money from sponsors of tournaments, and from time to time she would remind her fellow competitors how dependent they all were on her exalted reputation. She succeeded Berg as president of the organization in 1953, and on one occasion she called a membership meeting and lectured them on her special status. She announced: "Let me tell you girls something: you know when there's a star, like in show business, the star has her name in lights in the marquee! Right? And the star gets the money because the people come to see the star, right? Well, *I'm* the star and all of you are in the chorus. *I* get the money and if it weren't for me, half of our tournaments wouldn't even be." She could be just as intimidating in the locker rooms and on the fairways. Betty Dodd, perhaps her closest friend and confidant, acknowledged that Babe "made it very, very hard on a lot of these women golfers because she'd walk right up and say, 'What are you girls practicing for? You can't win this tournament.'" She backed up her talk with her play, dominating the LPGA tour during her final eight years as a pro, winning thirty-one tournaments, including U.S. Women's Open titles in 1948, 1950, and 1954. From 1948 through 1951 she was the leading money winner among the women, victorious in eighteen of the thirty-nine tour events during that period. Perhaps her most memorable triumph came in the 1954 U.S. Women's Open Championship when she finished twelve strokes ahead of the runner-up one year after surgery for colon cancer.

Babe's cancer returned in 1955, and when she died in September of 1956 at age forty-five, she left a sporting and cultural legacy unmatched by any other American female athlete of the twentieth century. The Associated Press voted her Woman Athlete of the Year six times and honored her in 1950 as the Female Athlete of the Half Century. Patty Berg, perhaps her greatest rival, summed up her contribution to her sport: "Babe changed the game of golf for women—not only by bringing along the LPGA, but by her kind of golf. She came along with that great power game and it led to lower scores and more excitement. She even changed the swing. It used to be built on the Scottish method and we hit waist high, more flat. Babe would swing high and hard. And she brought all that humor and showmanship to the game. She humanized it. . . . Our sport grew because of Babe, because she had so much flair and color. . . . Her tremendous enthusiasm for golf and life was contagious—even the galleries felt good when Babe was around." On the day after she died, President Dwight D. Eisenhower praised her as a woman who had earned the admiration of the American people both for her sports achievements and for her three-year battle against cancer. On September 28th the *New York Times* celebrated her as "this greatest woman athlete of our time" and highlighted her humble origins and will to win. It declared that her legacy lay not just in the record books, but also "in the inspiring story of a warm human being who had to do it the hard way and who did it magnificently." It added: "She had no silver spoon with which to start, and her royal road to triumph was more than usually rocky."

During this era Berg, Louise Suggs, and Betsy Rawls were also popular professional golfers who took turns sharing second billing to the Babe on the LPGA circuit. Unlike Didrikson, Berg came from an affluent country club family. Her father was a grain merchant in Minneapolis and a member of the upscale Interlachen Golf Club, where Patty learned the sport. As a girl she shared the Babe's love of rough sports with local boys, playing quarterback on her neighborhood's football team, the 50th Street Tigers. In 1986 she recalled that "a woman athlete in my younger days had to deal with the tomboy image a little more than nowadays, but I never got ragged for being an athlete." A sensation as an amateur during the 1930s, she turned professional in 1940 at the age of twenty-two, signing an endorsement contract with the Wilson Company. During World War II she recovered from a broken knee suffered in a traffic accident and joined the Marine Corps, serving as a recruiting officer. After the war in 1946 she won the inaugural WPGA-sponsored U.S. Women's Open, served four years as LPGA president, and captured dozens of tour events during the 1950s. A fierce competitor, she could more than hold her own against the Babe's game and gamesmanship. In interviews after Zaharias died, Berg had nothing but kind words to say about her.

Suggs did not share Berg's admiration for Zaharias, perhaps because of the Babe's treatment of her and perhaps because her own impressive accomplishments followed in the wake of the Babe's more celebrated victories. Suggs learned to play golf on a public course built by her father, a former baseball player turned golf professional, in Lithia Springs, near Atlanta, Georgia. After winning several major amateur titles during the war years, during the late 1940s she succeeded Zaharias as the U.S. Women's Amateur champion in 1947 and the British Women's Amateur champion in 1948. After turning pro in 1948 she signed an endorsement contract with MacGregor and won U.S. Women's Open crowns in 1949 and 1952. Suggs nearly matched Zaharias in skill, but she was resentful of the Babe's special treatment by the LPGA. The two were also polar opposites in personality. More serious and nearly colorless compared to the flamboyant Babe, Suggs was uncomfortable with the Babe's demands and antics. As she remarked: "Either it went her way, or she was difficult." As Fred Corcoran remembered, "Babe could do anything—play the mouth organ, dance, kid around with the press. Louise was always in her shadow. I'd set up a tournament and try to promote them with flashy little gimmicks. You know, I'd bring Humphrey Bogart out to kiss the winner of the tournament. . . . Babe loved it, but Suggs? Once she won, and instead of standing there to be kissed, she screamed and ran into the locker room."

During the 1950s Betsy Rawls vied with the Babe, Berg, and Suggs for top honors on the LPGA tour. She took up golf at the rather advanced age of

seventeen when her father gave her some lessons in their home town of Bur-
net, Texas. She benefited enormously from the instruction of the legendary
Harvey Penick at the Austin Country Club when she was a college student
at the University of Texas (where she earned Phi Beta Kappa honors as a
physics major). In 1986 she commented on the "problem of women athletes
being taken as tomboys, as being too masculine." But she further declared
that "when I started out I can't recall there being any kind of stigma attached
to woman athletes in Texas, at least not to women golfers. You see, golfers
weren't that way, much. Most of them I ran into were at country clubs and
from the upper classes, so to speak, and knew how to behave." Rawls turned
pro in 1950 after just a few years as an amateur, signed on with the Wilson
Company, won the 1951 U.S. Women's Open Championship, and added
three more national open titles in 1953, 1957, and 1960. She recalled the
resentment when the Babe demanded special treatment, but she also had
fond memories of the good times she spent with her. She recalled: "I loved
the Babe. She was good to play with, fun to be around. She was very witty
and kept the gallery laughing all the time. Wisecracks all the way around.
Very uninhibited. She was a little crude, and some things she said shocked
me a little because I was just the opposite, but the gallery loved her. There
will never be another like her."

⊚ ⊚ ⊚

While white women became a major force in private golf clubs
and leading female players founded the LPGA, African American women
struggled to gain respect within the black golfing world and equal opportunity in national golf organizations that were still restricted to whites. The
first challenge was to overcome sexism and gain acceptance for black women
in the United Golfers' Association (UGA). The next goal was to battle
racism and integrate the USGA and the LPGA. Pioneering players from
all-women's black golf clubs led both crusades during the mid-1900s.

During this period the two most prominent organizations of African
American women golfers were the Wake Robin Golf Club of Washington,
D.C., and the Chicago Women's Golf Club (CWGC). In 1939 Anna Mae
Robinson and Ella M. Williams of the CWGC journeyed to the annual
meeting of the UGA in Los Angeles to request membership in that all-male
association. Although the ladies met a frosty reception from some of the
delegates, they did gain admittance, and the following year the Chicago
women hosted the annual UGA tournament. In 1941 Paris Brown, president of the Wake Robin Club, was elected vice president of the UGA. But

after World War II, black women were barred from the 1947 Joe Louis tournament and several other events sponsored by the UGA. In 1949 the vice president of the UGA responded to complaints of female players by stating: "While the UGA could not compel club members to open their tournaments to women golfers, the UGA could urge them to lift all restrictions against the girls." As black women fought to gain full acceptance in the UGA, that organization recognized their contribution by electing Brown as its tournament director, a position she held until 1964. During her term of office Brown was renowned for her professionalism, efficiency, impartiality, hostility to gambling, and tireless efforts to promote golf among young African Americans.

To gain admission into the segregated world of female amateur and professional golf at the national level, black women needed talented players who could withstand the pressure of interracial competition. Ann Gregory and Althea Gibson broke the initial racial barriers in the 1950s and 1960s and blazed the trail for minority women golfers who followed them. Born in Aberdeen, Mississippi, in 1912, Gregory moved north to Gary, Indiana, in 1930. A good athlete and accomplished tennis player, she married an avid golfer but did not take up the game herself until her husband was drafted into military service during World War II. After the war she performed well in local and regional tournaments, and in 1950 she captured the first of her four UGA women's national championships. Over the next few decades Gregory became the premier black female golfer in the nation, choosing not to turn professional and winning perhaps one hundred amateur contests. She also played her part in the campaign to desegregate municipal golf courses in the early 1960s when she defied the managers of the Gleason Park public golf course in Gary, Indiana, and played a round on an eighteen hole course that was off limits to blacks. Her bold action moved the officials to drop their racial restrictions on the longer course.

Gregory next set her sights on national competition against the best of her white counterparts. That required admission into USGA-sponsored championships, including the U.S. Women's Amateur. Gregory joined the CWGC in 1952, which then applied for affiliated membership in the USGA so that she could play in its events. After the USGA admitted the CWGC as its first black member club, Gregory entered the 1956 U.S. Women's Amateur Championship, held in mid-September at the Meridian Hills Country Club in Indianapolis. As the first black woman ever to compete in that event, her first-round match against Carolyn Cudone received national publicity. Gregory began well and led Cudone by two holes after the first nine, but she faltered down the stretch and lost the match, 2 and 1. An ugly racial incident marred her appearance in the 1959 Women's Amateur Championship at the Congressional Country Club in Bethesda, Maryland. On the eve of the championship the host club barred Gregory from the players' banquet. Despite this snub, Gregory won her first two matches, including a second-round triumph over the Georgia state champion. Although she lost in the third round, she had maintained her dignity and her composure. That event was doubly troubling for her because members of the UGA had criticized Gregory for choosing to play in the USGA event instead of the UGA's national tournament held the same week in neighboring Washington, D.C.

Althea Gibson could not match Gregory's golf skills, but her fame as a world champion tennis player and her overall athletic ability earned her the distinction of being the first African American golfer to gain admission into the LPGA. Born on August 25, 1927, in Silver, South Carolina, she grew up in Harlem in New York City, where she learned to play tennis. During the late 1950s she reached the peak of women's tennis with national singles titles in France (1956), in Wimbledon in England (1957 and 1958), and in the United States (1957 and 1958). With no professional opportunity open to female tennis players, she turned to golf in 1960. She played in her first LPGA event in 1964, and over the next few years she struggled to compete against the elite white women pro golfers. During that decade she also had to cope with racial discrimination in some southern cities, enduring the indignity of having to change her shoes in her car when she was barred from the clubhouse at tournament sites. At other events she was banned entirely from playing. In response, Leonard Wirtz, director of the LPGA, threatened certain sponsors that he would cancel golf events if they protested the participation of African American women. Overall Gibson achieved only modest success on the pro golf tour, but she did open doors for Renee Powell, Barbara Douglas, and other black women who followed her.

Despite their differences in talent, race, and social class, Gibson, Gregory, Didrikson, Berg, Suggs, Rawls, and countless American female amateur and professional golfers who played on private and public courses during the mid-1900s had much in common. They had demonstrated convincingly that they were enthusiastic about the game and were determined to gain respect and a fair chance to demonstrate their talent on the links. They played an enormously important role in the postwar golf boom, and they would help lay the foundation for new waves of the sport's growth for the remainder of the twentieth century. But they had not broken down all the barriers of gender discrimination, for daunting challenges still lay ahead.

10

From Palmer to Woods

On Wednesday afternoon, April 10, 1996, Arnold Palmer and Jack Nicklaus played a practice round in preparation for the Masters Tournament at the Augusta National Golf Club. Thirty-two years had passed since Palmer's fourth and final Masters victory; a decade earlier, at the age of forty-six, Nicklaus had earned his sixth green jacket. Joining these two legends of American (and world) golf on the first tee was a twenty-year-old Stanford sophomore, Eldrick "Tiger" Woods. Although the young man did not play especially well that day, Nicklaus and Palmer were impressed with his game and predicted great performances from Woods in the future. "Arnold and I both agreed," said Nicklaus, "you probably could take Arnold's Masters and my Masters and add them together, and this kid should win more than that." He continued: "This kid is the most fundamentally sound golfer that I've ever seen at almost any age. And he is a nice kid. He's got great composure. He handles himself very, very well. Hits the ball nine million miles." Surely Nicklaus was engaging in some hyperbole both in estimating the distance of his drives and in his prospects for winning eleven Masters titles. But he and Palmer did see something special in Woods, even though that year he failed to make the cut over the next two days. That spring and summer, Woods won the NCAA individual men's championship and his record third consecutive U.S. Amateur title. After turning professional in late August he won two tournaments before the end of the year. The following April he began to fulfill Nicklaus's prophecy when at twenty-one he became the youngest Masters champion with the lowest score in tournament history and a record twelve-shot margin of victory.

During the final four decades of the twentieth century, professional golf strengthened its standing as one of the most popular sports in the United States. Building on the post–World War II boom of the 1950s, it benefited enormously from the star power of its premier champions, expanded coverage from print journalists and especially television networks, skyrocketing funding from corporate sponsors and advertisers, and skillful management by administrators of the Tournament Players Division of the Professional Golfers' Association, renamed the PGA Tour in 1975. While writers labeled the first part of this era the "Age of Arnold Palmer," Nicklaus, Gary Player, Lee Trevino, Tom Watson, and other professionals also thrilled the golfing public with their heroic performances on the nation's fairways and greens. Most African American players continued to patronize the United Golfers Association (UGA) tournaments, but a few of the most talented finally gained the opportunity to compete in PGA-sanctioned events, including the Masters. As the century drew to a close, Tiger Woods took center stage, as the multiracial boy wonder matured into a golfing phenomenon who reinvigorated and revolutionized the sport. Golf's superstars and journeymen players all reaped the rewards generated by the modern PGA Tour, and when they passed the age of fifty they had a second chance for glory on the Senior Tour (renamed the Champions Tour in 2003).

The new era of professional golf that began in the late 1950s also profoundly influenced career choices of talented younger players. In the past, Francis Ouimet, Bob Jones, and several others chose to retain their amateur standing with the USGA while supporting themselves with income earned in business, finance, or the professions. On the other hand, Walter Hagen, Ben Hogan, Sam Snead, Byron Nelson, and many others elected to play for pay early in their careers. But the new order of tournament prize money and lucrative endorsement deals generated monetary incentives that proved irresistible to virtually all the newcomers, whether they came from privileged circumstances (such as Frank Stranahan) or humble origins (Ken Venturi). The model of gentlemen's amateur golf championed by the USGA since the 1890s now seemed a quaint relic of the past as Palmer and his pursuers chased fame and fortune on fairways and greens.

The creation of the modern PGA tour during the late 1960s marked a key point in the development of professional golf as a multimillion-dollar business in the United States. It was born out of a long-standing controversy within the PGA between club and tournament professionals. Most of the 6,300 members of the PGA were employed at country clubs or public courses and were chiefly concerned with instruction, renting carts, scheduling events, and selling merchandise and equipment at their shops. One or two hundred of them were skilled enough to compete in national tournaments, and they resented restrictions imposed on them by the PGA. In particular, many demanded their own commissioner to replace the PGA's

Tournament Committee, control over the negotiation of television contracts and the scheduling of tournaments, and a looser affiliation with the parent organization. In his autobiography *A Golfer's Life*, Palmer conceded that "as crass as it sounds, the issue was really money—more precisely television money." In Nicklaus's words in his own life story, "the bottom line was money. In a nutshell, as the rewards of the tour grew, the players saw less and less reason why noncompetitors should profit from it." But Palmer also insisted that he and his peers were increasingly annoyed and frustrated over numerous PGA regulations, including one that barred a tour rookie from accepting any tournament prize money for the first six months of his career, and another that mandated a five-year waiting period before a player was eligible to participate in the PGA Championship.

The criticism of the PGA by prominent touring professionals intensified during the mid-1960s and escalated into outright rebellion in August of 1968. They resolved to take action after they learned that the PGA had negotiated contracts for the television rights to the World Series of Golf and Shell's Wonderful World of Golf without consulting the players, and that it had decided to put all the proceeds into its general fund. A dissident group then announced the formation of a new organization—the American Professional Golfers (APG). Palmer supported the APG (which some PGA officials and supporters derisively called the "Arnold Palmer Golfers"), but he kept a low profile and eventually worked to negotiate a settlement with the PGA. The APG's leadership committee featured such stars as Jack Nicklaus, Gardner Dickinson, Frank Beard, Doug Ford, Billy Casper, and Jerry Barber. Dickinson explained that "what we want is the right to cast the deciding vote over such matters as where, how, and under what conditions we will play." Although Warren Orlick, treasurer of the PGA, insisted that the quarrel had "nothing to do with money," in fact hundreds of thousands of dollars of television contracts were at stake. The PGA went to court to obtain a temporary restraining order blocking the APG from signing contracts with sponsors for future tournaments.

The standoff between the two warring parties lasted through the annual meeting of the PGA in November, but in mid-December attorneys representing both sides reached an agreement. The "Declaration of Principles" created a new Tournament Players Division (TPD) within the PGA (later renamed the PGA Tour) and a ten-member tournament policy board composed of three PGA officials, four players, and three prominent business leaders. That committee established all policy concerning PGA competitions, including schedules, purses, television commitments, disciplinary actions, and all other matters pertaining to the tour. One month later the policy board announced the appointment of Joseph C. Dey, Jr., executive director of the USGA, as the new commissioner of the TPD. Dey served until 1974, when he was replaced by Deane R. Beman, whose term ended in 1994. Under Dey and Beman tournament purses and revenues skyrocketed from the hundreds of thousands to the hundreds of millions of dollars as golf reached new heights of popularity. Meanwhile the PGA concentrated on its rank-and-file membership, helping club professionals serve their members and turn a profit at their home shops.

One of the highlights of Beman's first decade as commissioner of the PGA Tour was the creation of the Senior PGA Tour in 1980. It grew out of the popularity of Liberty Mutual's "Legends of Golf" television series, which debuted in 1978. On January 16, 1980, a group of aging former champions that included Sam Snead, Julius Boros, Dan Sikes, Bob Goalby, Gardner Dickinson, and Don January met with Beman and persuaded him to back the idea of founding a senior tour for men over the age of fifty. The gathering also agreed to recruit star performers to help sell the concept to the public and especially to potential sponsors and television networks. The support of Palmer turned out to be critical, for he was not only famous but also well-connected with the corporate world. The new senior tour also gained more exposure and credibility after Palmer won both the 1980 PGA Seniors' Championship and also the 1981 Senior U.S. Open title (after the USGA had lowered the age restriction from fifty-five to fifty for that event). The Senior PGA Tour flourished partly because of Palmer's heroic exploits, but also because Gary Player, Chi Chi Rodriguez, Raymond Floyd, Billy Casper, Trevino, Nicklaus, and other big names of the golf world turned fifty during the 1980s and 1990s. It became perhaps the most successful venture in all of American professional sports during the 1980s, growing from a modest experiment of two co-sponsored events with prize money of $250,000 in 1980 to thirty tournaments with purses totaling more than $52 million at its twenty-fifth anniversary.

Although the PGA Tour enjoyed spectacular growth under Beman's leadership, during the early 1980s Beman survived a challenge from Nicklaus, Palmer, Watson, and a few other premier players over his policies. In their view, Beman placed the interests of all the touring professionals ahead of those of the elite contestants. In part he did this by selling tournament naming rights to corporate sponsors. In a few cases companies then dropped endorsement deals with individual professionals in favor of signing deals directly with the PGA Tour. Nicklaus wrote that Beman "saw generating cash and other benefits for the players *collectively* not only as his principal mission but as the best way of establishing and sustaining his power base." Nicklaus applauded Beman's efforts "to increase purses, lock in solid sponsors and cut rich television deals," with the resulting funds "dispersed strictly according to player ability." But he and the other star performers strongly objected to his other revenue-generating projects, in particular the construction of PGA Tour courses and the signing of PGA Tour endorsement deals. In the end Beman refused to follow the suggestions of Palmer and Nicklaus, partly because he had the solid backing of the Tour's rank-and-file members. Nicklaus concluded that "if push came to shove, the collective as represented by the commissioner would easily defeat the 'names' as represented by Palmer, Watson, Nicklaus, etc." Beman prevailed in his showdown with the tour superstars and later concluded in an interview with Howard Sounes: "They're not interested in the PGA Tour and golf, they're interested in what's best for *them*."

Although Arnold Palmer did not win the most major championships during the 1960s and 1970s, he was the era's dominant personality because of his charismatic qualities and his extensive business interests that generated enormous income and influence far beyond his earnings and record on the links. After winning the Masters in 1958 and both the Masters and the U.S. Open in 1960, he set his sights on the British Open. In 1961 he carried off the Claret Jug, emblematic of the championship of that venerable tournament. 1962 proved to be another magical year for Palmer as he captured a third Masters title and a second British Open crown. His fourth Masters green jacket in 1964 raised his lifetime total of major championships to seven. He would never win another, but his remarkable run of stirring victories over a six-year span secured his place in sports history for all time. On April 13th, 1964, after Palmer's final Masters triumph, a *New York Times* columnist proclaimed: "Palmer is a hero to all, the darling of an era in which television has put golf into millions of homes. The man in the street finds a sense of identification with him . . . he discovers a little of himself in this athlete of athletes. . . . He has also captivated the public perhaps as no other athlete since Babe Ruth or Jack Dempsey. He is golf's finest showpiece." While golf fans most remember Palmer for his thrilling come-from-behind victories, he also suffered several agonizing defeats. Perhaps the most memorable came in 1966, when he blew a seven-shot lead with nine holes to play in the final round of the U.S. Open, then lost the playoff to Billy Casper. But win or lose, Palmer touched the hearts of his adoring legions. On July 8, 1966, a writer for the *Wall Street Journal* explained: "His intense competitiveness, daring style of play, expressive features and what has been called an 'All-American' appearance have captivated galleries. He is that rare champion whom spectators root for like an underdog." Adoring fans in "Arnie's Army" cheered him on at tournaments (and often were rude or hostile to other contestants) because they felt personally connected with his performance. In the words of one psychologist: "He looks and acts like a regular guy, and at the same time he does the kind of things others wish they could do. His expressiveness makes his spectators feel they are part of his game; he looks as though he needs their help, and they respond."

In the late 1950s Palmer joined into a partnership with Mark McCormack, a lawyer from Cleveland, Ohio, and founder of International Management Group (IMG). Together the two men took the field of sports marketing to a new level of profitability as they parlayed Palmer's success on the links into a business empire that included golf equipment manufacturing, golf franchises, sportswear licenses, golf books and pamphlets, and television and radio shows and exhibitions. Other interests included a dry cleaning franchise business and insurance. One business executive whose company had a licensing contract with Palmer described his magic: "When you buy the Palmer name you buy quality, goodness, honesty and sincerity. . . . People love him; they want to do things for him." Later Palmer would add a lucrative corporation that designed golf courses. His success on the Senior PGA Tour kept his name in the public eye so that decades after his last major title he was still reaping millions from endorsement and course construction deals.

Jack Nicklaus was Palmer's main rival, and he would ultimately eclipse Palmer to become the greatest golfer of the era. But despite his enormous talent, early in his career he was plagued by a negative public image. Born on January 21, 1940, in Columbus, Ohio, the son of a middle-class pharmacist, he was a talented all-around athlete who had spectacular success as a young golfer in local and state tournaments. National amateur champion in 1959 and 1961, he was runner-up to Palmer in the 1960 U.S. Open at Denver. In 1962 Nicklaus earned the ire of Arnie's Army when he defeated its idol in a playoff for the U.S. Open title at the Oakmont Country Club, close to Palmer's home town of Latrobe, Pennsylvania. In January 1964 a journalist for *Golf* magazine remarked on Nicklaus's "frozen face and lumbering stride," his "state prison stare," and his irritating slow and deliberate style of play. Nicklaus also suffered from a weight problem. As a student at Ohio State he was known as "Blob-O" or "Whaleman"; as a professional he was "Ohio Fats," "Baby Beef, or "Fat Jack." In his autobiography Nicklaus acknowledged his image problem as a young golfer. A fierce competitor, he aimed to defeat Palmer, and he explained that if that meant "also toppling a legend and throwing half the population into deep depression, well, so long as it was done fairly and squarely, fine and dandy." But as he reflected back on his early battles with Palmer, Nicklaus realized that "I was in the entertainment business as much as the golf-playing business." He conceded: "Sure, I was overweight and crew-cut, and sure, I dressed like a guy painting a porch, and sure, I had a squeaky voice and didn't laugh and joke a lot in public, and sure, I often lacked tact and diplomacy in my public utterances." But he also believed that golf fans would have forgiven all those failings if he had downplayed his will to win—"including, particularly, trying to knock the game's best-loved idol off his throne." By the end of the 1960s the golfing community had finally accepted Nicklaus as a great champion and genuine hero who had become more warm and relaxed. In an interview in *Golf Digest* in July 1971 Nicklaus attributed his increased popularity to

Arnold Palmer (left) congratulating Jack Nicklaus after the conclusion of the 1962 U.S. Open at Oakmont Country Club, Oakmont, Pa. Nicklaus was the winner. GETTY IMAGES. Photographer: John Dominis.

greater maturity, weight loss, longer hair, and more stylish clothing. Now he was beloved as the "Golden Bear."

A powerful driver and accurate iron player with a deft touch on the greens, Nicklaus had a flair for the dramatic and a capacity to intimidate and demoralize opponents. Between the 1960s and 1980s he earned a reputation as the sport's best golfer, capturing eighteen major titles. These included six Masters (1963, 1965, 1966, 1972, 1975, 1986); four U.S. Opens (1962, 1967, 1972, 1980); three British Opens (1966, 1970, 1978); and five PGAs (1963, 1971, 1973, 1975, 1980). His record for peak performance over a long career separates him from all previous legendary golfers. With the exception of the British Open, he won each major championship in three different decades. Perhaps equally remarkable were his nineteen second-place finishes in major competitions. His willingness to travel also made him a beloved sportsman around the world, especially in the British Isles, South Africa, and Australia.

When Nicklaus decided to turn professional in late 1961, Palmer introduced him to McCormack, who became his business manager for the next nine years. With the rise of Gary Player (another IMG client), the big three all benefited from McCormack's management, especially through lucrative personal appearances, exhibitions, and endorsements. But by the end of the decade Nicklaus had become disenchanted with his connection to McCormack and IMG. In July 1970, after the death of his father, Nicklaus parted company with IMG and formed Golden Bear, Inc., a conglomerate that specialized in advertisement, golf equipment and clothing, golf course design, real estate, leasing, travel, media, and other businesses. As the empires founded by Palmer and Nicklaus competed with each other for clients during and after the 1970s, especially in the field of golf course design, each man also launched a signature annual golf tournament. Nicklaus took the lead in that enterprise with the inaugural Memorial Tournament in May 1976 at the Muirfield Village Golf Club in Dublin, Ohio, close to his native city of Columbus. Three years later, Palmer welcomed an offer to move the ailing Florida Citrus Open to his Bay Hill club near Orlando, Florida, where it was renamed the "Arnold Palmer Invitational" in 2007.

While Palmer and Nicklaus collaborated in their campaigns to reform the PGA to suit their financial and business interests, they were fierce competitors for product endorsements and especially golf course design projects. Over the decades, both experienced several real estate failures, but in the long run Palmer proved to be more successful as a golf entrepreneur. In the late 1990s, as Palmer approached the age of seventy, he still ranked near the top of the list of highest-paid sportsmen in the world, earning approximately $18 million in 1998–99. By contrast, during that same decade Nicklaus's Golden Bear Golf went through a financial collapse that its namesake was fortunate to survive. Then, three decades after he left IMG, Nicklaus asked Mark McCormack to again manage his business interests. In the field of golf course design, Palmer delegated much of the work to staff architects—especially longtime collaborator Ed Seay, while Nicklaus applied a more "hands-on" approach to his projects. Arnold Palmer Course Design in Florida constructed more facilities than Nicklaus's Golden Bear Golf, but Nicklaus charged a higher commission—as much as $2.5 million per course. In 2001 the Golf Research Group ranked Nicklaus's "Signature" courses superior to those designed by Palmer's company. In 2001 the two men codesigned the King and Bear course at World Village at St. Augustine, Florida, a course that reflected each man's principles of course layout.

Nicklaus also made a major contribution to international golf through his proposal for a change in the format for the Ryder Cup competition, which traditionally had matched golfers from the United States against those from Britain and, after 1973, Ireland. Between 1927 and 1977 the U.S. team won nineteen of the twenty-three matches (one ended in a tie). During the 1977 match in England Nicklaus asked Lord Derby, the president of the British PGA, to consider making the event more competitive by broadening the membership of the British side to include leading European players. Although the British officials were at first reluctant to part with tradition, the following year they agreed that for the 1979 contest a few Europeans would join the British and Irish contestants, and that their side would be renamed "Europe." As a result, the balance has tipped toward the European side, especially since 1995. Between 1979 and 2006 the European team won seven of the fourteen events, with one tie. Since 1995 the Europeans have dominated the Americans, wining five of the last six matches. Most of the Ryder Cup challenges have exhibited the good sportsmanship that was always a hallmark of the series. The notable exception occurred in 1999 at The Country Club in Brookline, Massachusetts, when a cheering and unruly crowd of players and spectators rushed onto the seventeenth green after Justin Leonard sank a forty-five-foot uphill putt. The fans' action delayed Jose Maria Olazabal's attempt to keep their match tied by holing a twenty-foot putt. When he missed, Leonard was guaranteed at least a halve for the match, which sealed the victory for the American team. Olazabal did salvage a halve after he won the meaningless eighteenth hole. Leonard's long putt provided the U.S. team with a narrow victory by 14.5 to 13.5 points, but the gallery's behavior and the ensuing patriotic display earned the Americans a good deal of ill will from their European opponents and their supporters across the Atlantic.

During the 1960s a young South African joined Palmer and Nicklaus as one of the "big three" golfers in the world. Gary Player was born on November 1, 1935, in Johannesburg and took up golf at the relatively advanced age of fifteen. Like Ben Hogan, he was small for a champion golfer (five foot seven inches tall and about 155 pounds), but he was fanatical about physical fitness, diet, and relentless practice. He always dressed in black because he believed that color better absorbed energy from the sun. He was a brilliant bunker specialist, but it was his powers of concentration and sheer will that made him such a successful competitor. He won his first major championship at the British Open in 1959, and he also captured the Claret Jug in 1968 and 1974. His first Masters title in 1961 (and the first won by a foreigner) came as a result of Palmer's stunning double bogey at the final hole. Player also earned two more green jackets at Augusta in 1974 and 1978. Victories at the PGA in 1962 and 1972 and at the U.S. Open in 1965 elevated him to international fame. Over a twenty-year period he won nine major titles, becoming one of only five men to win each of the four modern major tournaments—the career Grand Slam. The others are Sarazen, Hogan, Nicklaus, and Woods.

Palmer, Nicklaus, and Player were the most talented golfers of this era, but beginning in the late 1960s they shared the limelight with a wisecracking newcomer from a poor Mexican American family in Texas. Born on December 1, 1939, Lee Trevino spent his childhood on the outskirts of north Dallas, where he lived across the street from the Glen Lakes Country Club. He learned to play golf as a caddie and as a helper at a local driving range. A tour of duty in the Marine Corps gave him the opportunity to play regularly, and after his discharge he improved his game at local competitions on public links. His skill landed him a job as a professional at the Horizon Country Club in El Paso. His meteoric rise to fame and fortune began in 1967 when he qualified for the U.S. Open at Baltusrol in New Jersey and finished fifth. Named Rookie of the Year on the PGA Tour for 1967 by *Golf Digest*, he soon reached golf stardom when he won the U.S. Open in 1968 with a record-tying score of 275 at the Oak Hill Country Club in Rochester, New York.

Trevino was hugely popular with golf galleries and television viewers because of his American Dream story and his ebullient personality, and his star power provided a major boost to the PGA Tour during his prime.

Nicknamed "Super Mex," he was not ashamed of his humble origins. As he told one interviewer: "We *were* poor. We couldn't even afford Mexican food sometimes, so I learned to like bologna and crackers at an early age." During the 1970s he was second only to Palmer as a crowd favorite. In September 1971 Al Barkow of *Golf Magazine* thought that Palmer was the average golfer's ideal, but Trevino was "the people's pro—pure." He explained: "Right down from his foreign name to his over-size cap to the sometimes raunchy joke lines to his wide open stance and awkward-looking swing that is straight out of the public golf course, Lee Trevino is the stuff of the American proletariat." In March 1971 Nick Seitz of *Golf Digest* described Trevino as "the garrulous madcap with loud red socks and a pitcher of tequila nearby, the young hustler from the legendary muni courses of Texas, where everything is bigger than reality, cockily grateful for all the fame and fortune that have befallen him." In February 1978 *Golf Magazine* published a feature story on Trevino's collection of cars and his eight-thousand-square-foot mansion in New Mexico. He told the writer than even with all his wealth, "the fans still see me as an underdog, an underdog who made it." He continued: "In their minds I'm still the guy who had nothing. It doesn't matter how much money I've got—to them I'm a poor slob who had the guts to prove himself and pulled it off." Perhaps because of his humble beginnings and Mexican heritage, he never felt comfortable at Augusta National (he skipped the tournament several times and on other occasions changed his shoes in the parking lot), and he never played well at the Masters. But before graduating to the Senior Tour in 1990 he won six major titles, including two each at the U.S. Open (1968, 1971), the British Open (1971, 1972), and the PGA Championship (1974, 1984).

As they battled among themselves for top golfing honors in the United States and abroad, Palmer, Nicklaus, Player, and Trevino competed against dozens of talented American and foreign pros who ranked just below them in skill and in their capacity to perform under extreme pressure. Tom Watson, Billy Casper, Hale Irwin, Tom Weiskopf, Raymond Floyd, Hubert Green, Lanny Wadkins, Nick Faldo, Nick Price, Greg Norman, Seve Ballesteros, and Bernhard Langer were the best of this supporting cast. Among this group Watson merits special attention, especially because of his success in several classic duels with Nicklaus. Born on September 4, 1949, in Kansas City, Missouri, Watson earned a degree in psychology from Stanford University and turned pro in 1971. In 1977 he edged Nicklaus in both the Masters and the British Open, and in 1982 at the U.S. Open his spectacular chip-in on the seventeenth hole at Pebble Beach deprived Nicklaus of yet another major title. A man of medium build (five feet nine inches tall and about 160 pounds), Watson was a strong driver and a very accurate iron player, but he was best known for his short game and especially his superb putting. Before he joined the Senior Tour in 1999 he won eight major championships: two Masters (1977, 1981), one U.S. Open (1982), and five British Opens (1975, 1977, 1980, 1982, 1983).

All the men cited above and dozens of other world-ranking golfers benefited enormously from the exposure provided by television, as did champions of earlier eras (including Byron Nelson, Gene Sarazen, and Jimmy Demaret), who achieved greater recognition as hosts of taped series than they had enjoyed as stars of pretube times. In March 1966 *Golf* magazine proclaimed that golf heroes had become the "new matinee idols," citing a survey that proved they were better known among the general public than the stars of football, baseball, basketball, and hockey. Televised golf tournaments were still in their infancy during the 1960s, but new technology and production techniques enabled viewers to follow more contestants on more holes. As directors gained more experience, they provided audiences with more drama as they cut from player to player during deciding holes of tournaments. Events sponsored by film and television celebrities sometimes achieved higher ratings than regular PGA Tour events or even major championships. Joining Bob Hope and Bing Crosby as hosts were Jackie Gleason, Danny Thomas, Sammy Davis, Jr., Andy Williams, Dean Martin, and Glen Campbell, among others. According to the January 1974 issue of *Golf Digest*, sponsorship of a golf tournament had become "the ultimate status symbol," superseding "railroad cars, yachts, Rembrandts and chorus girls." As more and more American families purchased color televisions during this era, golf telecasts gained more viewers, especially when tournaments featured celebrated contestants. Although television coverage and ratings for golf did dip down toward the end of the 1970s, both rebounded as new stars emerged. The widespread adoption of cable television gave all sports and especially golf an enormous boost during the 1990s. The advent of the Golf Channel in 1995 (with Palmer as a co-founder) and the rise of Tiger Woods heralded a new and extremely profitable age for professional golf.

⊙ ⊙ ⊙

While white professional golfers competed for fame and fortune on the PGA Tour during the final decades of the twentieth century, their black counterparts demanded fair treatment, equal opportunity, and respect. The majority of them struggled to earn their expenses and save a few dollars on the United Golfers' Association (UGA) circuit, but after the PGA rescinded its "Caucasian clause" several African American players qualified for PGA events. An aging Charlie Sifford pioneered the way, but Lee Elder, Calvin Peete, Jim Dent, Jim Thorpe, Pete Brown, and others reaped the rewards made possible by the campaign of Sifford and others who had forced the PGA to end its discriminatory racial policies. Elder's invitation to the 1975 Masters at Augusta National marked a major milestone in the desegregation of professional golf. Fifteen years later the PGA forced private clubs to end exclusionary admission practices if they wished to host its tournaments. At the end of the century the rise of Tiger Woods focused renewed attention on the issues of race and class in American golf.

During the 1960s the most skilled black golfers continued to scratch out a subsistence living competing for small purses at UGA-sponsored tournaments. While most of the white players grew up with access to exclusive country clubs and first-class instruction, all the black contestants were former caddies who were self-taught. Most of the UGA events were held at municipal courses that were far inferior to the impeccably groomed country club courses of the PGA Tour, which featured lush, well-watered fairways, thick rough, strategically placed deep bunkers, and slick, contoured greens. By contrast, black pros played on easier layouts with wide fairways, virtually nonexistent rough, fewer bunkers, and larger and slower greens. As a result, African Americans faced more challenging conditions when they did gain the chance to play against white pros on tougher courses. In addition, to gain a coveted PGA touring player's card, an applicant had to find a sponsor, provide proof of adequate savings, and survive in a highly competitive PGA qualifying school.

The African American presence on the PGA Tour peaked during the 1970s, declined in the 1980s, and appeared to vanish in the early 1990s, prior to the arrival of Tiger Woods. Between 1969 and 1980 there were at least ten black members on the PGA Tour each year. (In 1974 there were ten black players among the 318 members of the Tournament Players Division of the PGA.) Not counting Woods, there have been twenty-six blacks certified as PGA Tour members. (Labeling Woods as an African American is problematical, as will be discussed below.) But in 1985 Adrian Stills was the last African American to qualify for the PGA Tour before Woods joined in 1997 (by virtue of his earnings and victories after he turned pro in the fall of 1996). One of the reasons for the decline of the black golf touring professional lies in the diminishing number of caddies at many private clubs (due to the rise of golf carts), and thus fewer chances for minority youth to gain early exposure to golf. Another factor is the widening gap in opportunities to play and learn the game between urban and suburban youth, despite recent golf programs that target minority youngsters.

Charlie Sifford's long career spanned the eras of segregation and integration in professional golf. In 1964 he finally realized his goal of earning a Class A PGA membership, but by that time he was forty-two years old and past his prime as a tournament competitor. Yet he still distinguished himself by finishing in the top sixty money winners every year between 1960 and 1974 and by victories in the Puerto Rican Open in 1964, the Hartford Open in 1967, and the Los Angeles Open in 1969. His total earnings on the PGA Tour for his entire career were $341,345, but after he turned fifty he won another $800,000 on the Senior Tour, capturing the PGA Seniors Championship in 1975 and the Suntree Classic in 1980. But despite Sifford's achievements, he was bitter about the abuse he experienced and the racism that denied him the opportunity to compete for fame and fortune when he was a young man. And while some hailed him as the "Jackie Robinson of golf," he rejected that distinction because he could not see any brighter prospects for the next generation of black golfers. As he explained in his autobiography, *Just Let Me Play*: "If I was the Jackie Robinson of Golf, I sure didn't do a very good job of it. . . . Jackie was followed by hundreds of great, black ballplayers who have transformed their sport. . . . But there are hardly any black kids coming up through the ranks of golf today."

Sifford was especially angry at Clifford Roberts, chairman of the Masters Tournament, for his refusal to invite him to play in the prestigious annual event. In his autobiography he criticized the Masters as "the worst redneck tournament in the country, run by people who openly discriminate against blacks." He added that "for a black man, the Masters golf tournament was and maybe still is a symbol for where he really stands in American society." Sifford acknowledged that the Masters Tournament Committee had a complicated set of qualification rules for entry, but he also knew that it could issue special invitations if it wished, as it frequently did for prominent foreign golfers. In 1968 the committee responded to Sifford's attacks by stating: "Every USA golfer, regardless of his racial background, has an opportunity to qualify for a Masters Tournament invitation and we doubt that anyone seriously expects us to change these Qualification Regulations in order to accommodate one person." But the pressure applied by Sifford and others did appear to have some impact on the Tournament Committee, because in 1971 it passed a new rule that guaranteed an invitation to any golfer who won a PGA Tour event in the twelve-month period preceding

Charlie Sifford celebrates holing the putt that tied him for the lead
after seventy-two holes at the Los Angeles Open, January 13, 1969.
He won the playoff for the championship with a birdie three on
the first extra hole. AP/WIDE WORLD PHOTOS.

the Masters. But the new provision was not retroactive and came too late
to benefit Sifford.

The African American golfer who would finally integrate the Masters
Tournament was Robert Lee Elder. Born on July 14, 1934, in Dallas, Texas,
he was the son of a coal truck driver. A caddie as a young boy, he moved
to Los Angeles after his father was killed while serving in the army during

World War II. After dropping out of Manual Arts High School after two years, he concentrated on his golf game, worked for professional Lloyd Mangrum for three years, then joined the army. He became captain of the Sixth Army golf team and finished second in the 1959 Inter-Service Championships behind Phil Rodgers. After his discharge in 1960 he secured a golf instructional position at the Langston Golf Course in Washington, D.C., became a protégé of Ted Rhodes, and joined the UGA tour, winning four national titles between 1963 and 1967. He earned his PGA touring card in 1967, and the following summer he enthralled a national television audience when he lost a dramatic sudden-death playoff on the fifth extra hole to Nicklaus in the American Golf Classic at the Firestone Country Club. Over the next few years Elder became well-known among the American golfing public through his acceptance of Gary Player's invitation to oppose apartheid by playing in South Africa. In 1972 he won the Nigerian Open and at home ranked thirty-second on the list of players' tour earnings.

Elder's rising profile renewed the pressure on Roberts and the Masters Tournament Committee to invite an African American to compete in their prestigious event. In March 1973 eighteen members of the U.S. House of Representatives sent a letter to Roberts urging him to invite Elder to that year's event. Roberts rejected their request, explaining that to give Elder an invitation without his meeting the standards "would be practicing discrimination in reverse." Elder finally secured the victory that gained him the coveted Masters invitation in April of 1974 at the Monsanto Open in Pensacola, Florida, just a few weeks after that year's Masters Tournament. That triumph was laden with irony, because five years earlier he had vowed never to return to Pensacola because of racial epithets directed at him by spectators. He told the press that "I'm tired of being called 'nigger' or 'black boy.' It's just come to a head. . . . It's very difficult for a Negro to play on the tour. . . . It's very hard to concentrate when you hear some of the comments." But in 1974 he changed his mind after some coaxing from the tournament sponsors. His historic win in Pensacola also proved to be highly dramatic, as he sank an eighteen-foot birdie putt on the fourth playoff hole. Roberts then congratulated Elder, invited him to Augusta to play a few practice rounds on the course, and gave him a warm welcome when Elder arrived at Augusta for the 1975 Masters Tournament. Although Elder failed to make the cut that year, he would play in five more Masters, with his best finish a tie for seventeenth in 1979. That year he became the first black golfer on the American Ryder Cup Team.

Lee Elder, the first African American golfer to qualify for the Masters Tournament, leaves the clubhouse to practice at the Augusta National Golf Club, April 7, 1975. AP/WIDE WORLD PHOTOS.

Calvin Peete's journey to stardom as a black golfer on the PGA Tour was even more improbable than those of Sifford and Elder, since he did not pick up a club until he was twenty-three years old. He was also handicapped by a crooked left arm caused by a shattered elbow he suffered in an accident when he was twelve. Born on July 18, 1943, in Detroit, Michigan, he spent his childhood in Florida, where his father was a farm laborer. After dropping out of high school, he earned a living selling goods to migrating farm workers as they traveled north to harvest seasonal crops. During a trip to Rochester, New York, he became fascinated with golf, and within eighteen months he was breaking par—without ever taking a lesson. Inspired by Elder's success, through sheer determination and hard practice he earned a PGA touring card in 1975 at age thirty-two, on his third attempt. In 1978 he won his first PGA tournament, the Greater Milwaukee Open, and in 1982 he captured four titles and earned more than $317,000. Through 1984 his total prize money approached $1.25 million. Peete was selected to be a member of the 1983 Ryder Cup team after he obtained a required high school diploma by passing the equivalency examination. A twelve-time champion on the PGA Tour, as he approached fifty he lamented the diminishing number of black professional golfers. In 1990 only he and Jim Thorpe (age forty-two) remained active on the regular PGA Tour, while five continued to compete on the Senior tour (Sifford, Elder, Jim Dent, Charles Owen, and Rafe Botts). In an attempt to reverse that trend he founded the Calvin Peete Foundation to promote golf among minority youth in urban areas.

In 1990 the PGA faced a new racial controversy, but this time it did not involve the eligibility of African Americans to join the organization and compete in its tournaments. Instead, the issue concerned policies of racial discrimination at private clubs that hosted PGA Championships or tour events. The firestorm began following comments made by Hall W. Thompson, founder of the Shoal Creek Country Club in Birmingham, Alabama, the site of the PGA Championship scheduled for early August. On June 20th Thompson told a reporter from the *Birmingham Post-Herald* that although Shoal Creek had women, Jews, Italians, and Lebanese as members, "we don't discriminate in every other area except the blacks." He added: "The country club is our home and we pick and choose who we want." Although he also stated that members could bring blacks as guests if they wished, he admitted that "that's just not done in Birmingham."

When Thompson spoke those words, he probably had no idea they would initiate a national debate over exclusionary policies at country and golf clubs across the United States. Certainly it was common knowledge at the time that many private clubs did not admit Jews or Catholics and that most barred African Americans. But the question raised by the Shoal Creek incident was whether it was appropriate for national associations such as the PGA or the USGA to support discriminatory practices by providing the resources and prestige their events brought to the clubs that hosted their events. Reaction came swiftly from the black community both in Birmingham and across the nation. Dr. Benjamin Hooks, executive director of the National Association for the Advancement of Colored People (NAACP), condemned racial discrimination as "repugnant, immoral, and un-American," while the Rev. Joseph Lowery, president of the Southern Christian Leadership Conference (SCLC) organized a protest demonstration in Birmingham. While the African American response was not surprising, more telling from an economic standpoint was the reaction of the business community. At least six corporations (American Honda, IBM, Anheuser-Busch, Toyota, Sharp Electronics, and Lincoln-Mercury) announced they were withdrawing their advertisements from the telecasts of the event by ABC and ESPN. Advertisers also pondered whether they should continue to fund the bulk of the $50 million in prize money on the PGA Tour. One media expert explained: "People are going to do a lot more research of any sponsorship in the future to make sure they don't get into this kind of situation where they compromise their good will with the public. That is marketing suicide."

In order to salvage the upcoming championship, the interested parties reached an understanding that resolved the Shoal Creek affair and also spurred more general policy changes on the national level. On July 31st the PGA, the Shoal Creek Country Club, and the SCLC reached a compromise agreement whereby the club pledged to accept black members and the civil rights organization promised to call off its picketing of the championship. In particular, the Shoal Creek Board of Governors extended an honorary membership to Louis J. Willie, age sixty-six, an African American who was president of a Birmingham insurance company. Willie was granted full privileges, but he was reluctant to accept because he had last played golf on a segregated public course in Birmingham decades earlier. He finally consented because he thought that action was best for the community. Shortly thereafter the PGA addressed the issue more broadly. On August 3rd its PGA Tour board announced a new policy that none of its yearly tournaments would be held at a club that denied membership on grounds of race, religion, or sex. In particular, the new rules stated that PGA officials would investigate whether private clubs that sought to sponsor events on the regular, senior, or "satellite" Ben Hogan tours had taken "appropriate action" to encourage minority membership. In November the USGA followed suit when its executive committee adopted a policy stating that host clubs for its championships could not discriminate against members of minority groups or women.

In the short run, the Shoal Creek controversy did compel many of the nation's most exclusive country clubs to open their doors to a few "token" minority members, but several refused to comply. Among those that invited at least one minority member was the Augusta National Golf Club, which selected Ron Townsend, president of the Gannett Television Group. The Baltusrol Golf Club of New Jersey, which hosted the 1993 U.S. Open, also promised to enroll blacks. But eleven private clubs chose to maintain their exclusionary admission policies and thus dropped out of consideration for hosting future PGA or USGA events. Among this group were the Cypress Point Club (one of several courses used for the annual Pebble Beach Pro-Am in California), the Golf Club of Louisiana, and the Merion and Aronimink Golf Clubs of Pennsylvania. In the long run, the Shoal Creek affair did force all the nation's country clubs to review their admission policies, whether or not they were candidates for hosting national, regional, or state tournaments. Very few substantially increased their minority memberships.

The Shoal Creek incident also had a significant impact on the administration of the USGA. In 1992 that organization appointed John Merchant as the first African American to serve on its executive committee. Merchant was also the first black to join the Country Club of Fairfield, Connecticut. As a member of the USGA's executive committee, he founded an annual golf symposium, which brought golf executives, industry officials, and representative of the black community together to promote golf as a more inclusive sport in the United States. That gathering led to the formation of the National Minority Golf Foundation (NMGF). In 1996 the USGA voted to fund the NMGF for three years. In addition, in 1992 African American Leroy Richie was named general counsel for the USGA.

As the racial ramifications of the Shoal Creek affair reverberated throughout the American golfing fraternity during the early 1990s, sportswriters were raving about a precocious teenager who seemed destined to be golf's next superstar. Tiger Woods was born on December 30, 1975, in Cypress, California, the son of Earl and Kultida Woods. His father was a retired Green Beret lieutenant colonel in the U.S. Army who met his mother in 1967 when she was a secretary in the U.S. Army office in Bangkok, Thailand. When Tiger was an infant, Earl dragged his high chair into the garage so that his boy could watch his father drive golf balls into a net. At eleven months the baby was imitating his dad by swatting balls with a sawed-off club. At age two he appeared on the Mike Douglas television show, competing against Bob Hope in a putting contest. The following year he scored a 48 for nine holes on a regulation length navy golf course, and at five he was a guest on another television program, "That's Incredible." With his father as his first instructor and then with the support of a professional coach and psychologist, Tiger won a series of state and national championships as a boy and adolescent, often defeating opponents who were many years older. In 1991, at fifteen, he became the youngest player ever to win the U.S. Junior Amateur Championship. He defended his title successfully over the next two years, and from 1994 through 1996 he added three consecutive U.S. Amateur crowns. A highlight of his final Amateur Championship was a thirty-five-foot birdie putt over an undulating green on the thirty-fifth hole of the championship final. He sank the putt to extend the match, which he won on the second extra hole.

After Woods turned professional in the fall of 1996 he dramatically transformed golf in the United States and across the world. Over the next ten years his spectacular achievements went a long way toward fulfilling the remarkable prophecy that his father proclaimed in an interview with *Sports Illustrated* in December 1996. Earl Woods predicted: "Tiger will do more than any other man in history to change the course of humanity . . . he's qualified through his ethnicity to accomplish miracles. He's the bridge between the East and West. There is no limit because he has the guidance. I don't know exactly which form this will take. But he is the Chosen One. He'll have the power to impact nations. Not people. Nations. The world is just getting the taste of his power." Before he reached his thirty-third birthday Woods had won fourteen major championships (Masters 1997, 2001, 2002, 2005; U.S. Open 2000, 2002, 2008; British Open 2000, 2005, 2006; PGA 1999, 2000, 2006, 2007). His victory at the Masters in 2001 earned him the "Tiger Slam"—the distinction of being the only player ever to hold all four major professional titles at the same time (though not in the same calendar year). During his first decade as a pro he also earned hundreds of millions of dollars in endorsement income, exhibition fees, prize money, and investments. His enormous popularity boosted television ratings, PGA Tour purses, and sales of golf equipment and clothing. His fame helped to popularize golf among youngsters, and especially among minorities in the United States. His world travels promoted the game in Europe and especially in Asia and Africa.

Although Woods's impact on golf at home and abroad has been enormous, it was in the realm of race relations that he began to realize his father's dreams of serving humanity. From the time he was a boy the media described him as an African American, but as he grew to maturity he rejected that label because of his mixed ancestry through his Thai mother and his multiracial father. Kultida Woods was descended from Thai, Chinese, and Dutch stock, while Earl had forebears who were African American, Chinese, Native American Indian, and Caucasian. As a result Tiger invented a name for himself—"Cablinasian"—which reflected his heritage of Caucasian, black, Indian, and Asian cultures. In the United States the black community hailed him as the latest and perhaps the greatest African American sports hero (surpassing Muhammad Ali and Michael Jordan), while in Asia the Chinese and Thai populations claimed him as one of their own. Although his father took the view that in American society anyone with any African American ancestry was treated as black, Tiger became a role model for an American society that was becoming more multiracial and multicultural in the 1990s and early years of the twenty-first century. And while some criticized Woods for his loyalty to his corporate sponsors and his unwillingness to speak out on political and social issues, he did contribute generously to charitable and youth causes through his Tiger Woods Foundation and his Tiger Woods Learning Center.

During the 1990s the PGA Tour enjoyed unprecedented heights of prosperity, thanks in part to successful marketing of its regular events, a new international competition, and the phenomenon of Tiger Woods. In 1994, under the leadership of newly installed commissioner Tim Finchem, the PGA Tour created the Presidents Cup. Modeled after the older Ryder Cup (run by the PGA of America), the Presidents Cup is a biennial competition between teams from the United States and the rest of world, excluding Europe (which provides the opposition in the Ryder Cup). The American side won five of the first seven events, with one tie. More importantly, during this era the PGA Tour provided enormous riches for its contestants as purses skyrocketed from $1.335 million in 1960 to $131.7 million in 1999 to nearly $250 million in 2005. During this period the average first-place check grew from $5,862 in 1960 to $603,735 in 1999 to $946,314 in 2005. Leading money winners were Arnold Palmer in 1960 ($75,262) and Tiger Woods in 1999 and 2005 ($6,616,585 and $10,628,024).

As modern-era professional golfers chased these dollars, their social class origins, preparation, and corporate images differed substantially from many of their predecessors. Palmer, Nicklaus, Watson, Woods, and most of their peers grew up in middle- or upper-class households with access to country clubs, won junior championships, and benefited from some college competition. Gone but not forgotten were the colorful characters and heroes of earlier eras who came out of caddy shacks and municipal courses and turned professional with only a grade school or perhaps a high school education. Francis Ouimet, Walter Hagen, Gene Sarazen, Byron Nelson, Ben Hogan, and Sam Snead rose from humble beginnings to the pinnacle of American golf, but since 1960 only Lee Trevino lived a comparable American Dream life. Among Hispanics and African Americans, Chi Chi Rodriguez, Charles Sifford, Lee Elder, Calvin Peete, and a few others overcame poverty to win tournaments and earn substantial prize money, but successful minority pros were also becoming a vanishing breed with the demise of caddying opportunities that provided boys of all races with golfing apprenticeships in the precart days. Moreover, unlike some of the old-timers, Woods and his peers generally tempered their public comments, always mindful of not offending their television and corporate sponsors. Amateurism, exemplified by Bob Jones, was also a relic of the past, and traditionalists lamented the passing of the old order. In the March 1972 *Golf Digest*, Herbert Warren Wind had warned: "The more that golf becomes a branch of the entertainment world and a means to an end rather than an end in itself, the more it is bound to surrender that rare and special flavor that the world of sports possesses when it is at its best." But the PGA Tour was now big business, and there was no turning back the clock.

THE LPGA, GENDER,
AND COUNTRY CLUBS

On Saturday, April 12, 2003, a small band of feminists held a protest rally on a muddy and weedy patch of ground about a half-mile from the main gates of the Augusta National Golf Club. The organizer of the demonstration and the main speaker was Martha Burk, chair of the National Council of Women's Organizations (NCWO). She and her supporters were demanding that the all-male Augusta club open its membership to women. After Augusta's chairman William W. "Hootie" Johnson rejected her proposal, the club obtained a court order that limited the number of demonstrators and moved them far away from the entrance to the club. Although press reports minimized the size of the crowd, Burk claimed a turnout of 128, but her forces were far outnumbered by reporters, sheriffs, police officers, and counterdemonstrators, including a group labeled People Against Ridiculous Protests, one delegate from the Ku Klux Klan, and an Elvis impersonator. The event lasted less than one hour, and virtually all the spectators who attended the third round of the Masters that day did not hear Burk's condemnation of gender discrimination at Augusta National.

Three years later, in early June 2006, an estimated five thousand spectators flocked to the Canoe Brook Country Club in Summit, New Jersey. The attraction was the teenage phenom Michelle Wie, who was trying to become the first woman to qualify for the U.S. Open. Only sixteen years old, six feet tall, attractive, and capable of booming long drives, Wie was a media darling whose popularity approached that achieved by the young Tiger Woods. As a girl she had won the U.S. Women's Amateur Public Links Championship, but she had never finished first in a professional tournament. She aimed to prove that she could compete successfully against the best male and female golfers in the world. While some of her peers of both sexes viewed her attempt to play in men's tournaments as pointless, others wished her well. Jack Nicklaus called her effort "fantastic" and added: "I think its wonderful for the game of golf. It brings a whole new element that you've never heard before." But Wie faded with three straight bogeys on the back nine of the second round of the thirty-six-hole qualifier and failed to secure one of the coveted places in the U.S. Open at Winged Foot later that month.

These two episodes illustrate contrasting dimensions of women's golf in the United States in the early twenty-first century. As American women were demanding equal access and fair treatment at private country clubs and on public courses, female professional golfers showcased their skills on television and in front of appreciative galleries. On a variety of fronts the gender gap in American golf was closing.

In the 1960s, as men's professional golf skyrocketed in popularity during the age of Palmer, Nicklaus, and Player, their female counterparts struggled to occupy a minimal space on the landscape of American sports. Four decades later, with the assistance of a few stars, a talented supporting cast, corporate sponsors, advertisers, and broadcast and cable television networks, the LPGA tour had established itself as a respectable and thriving sports and entertainment institution. But the journey was fraught with turmoil and controversy as the LPGA labored to persuade the American public that its members were skilled athletes who could provide quality entertainment to the nation's sports fans. Along the way they had to contend with issues concerning the players' femininity and sexual orientation, the influx of foreign (especially Korean) contestants, and competition against men. By the early 2000s the LPGA tour still trailed the PGA's regular and senior tours in popularity, but its television ratings and especially its purses had increased dramatically since its formative years.

To boost their public image, in 1961 the LPGA hired Leonard Wirtz to be its tournament director and recruiter of sponsors. He took over a tour that had only about twenty-two players competing in twenty-four events for total prize money that was less than $200,000. He recalled that during the early sixties, "if we had 1,000–2,000 people to watch 30 women, it was a good crowd. Later it grew to 10,000–20,000, but early on we had to play small towns to get any attention. It was difficult to get courses. We couldn't afford to rent them, so we had the [country club] members playing on the same course after the women had teed off." Through some aggressive marketing and some early television coverage of women's matches on "Shell's Wonderful World of Golf," the LPGA Championship, and the U.S. Women's Open, Wirtz raised the profile of women's golf. When he left office eight years later the ladies tour had fifty women, twenty-eight tournaments, and about $700,000 in purses.

While Wirtz labored to schedule tournaments and recruit corporate and local sponsors and television networks, the players barnstormed across the nation in a caravan of cars, campers, and trailers, stopping mainly in small cities and towns that welcomed them as a means of boosting community pride. In addition to competing in tournaments, the women also managed these events, including setting up the courses, making pairings, recording the statistics, arranging social events, paying bills, and distributing earnings. Conditions were often challenging if not downright dangerous. At the 1967 Babe Zaharias Open in Beaumont, Texas, heavy rains at first made the course unplayable, then brought out a plague of water moccasins that unnerved the golfers. At a Florida tournament a sniper hiding in nearby bushes terrorized players. But a spirit of camaraderie sustained them, even though most earned barely enough to cover their expenses. Although the average total purse for an event was only about $7,500, the low cost of food and motel rooms enabled a player to survive comfortably on $150 to $200 a week.

During the 1960s two superstars, Mary Kathryn "Mickey" Wright and Kathrynne Ann "Kathy" Whitworth, dominated the LPGA tour and boosted the popularity of women's golf in the United States. Neither had the charismatic personality of Babe Didrikson Zaharias who preceded them or the popular appeal of Nancy Lopez who followed them in the late 1970s, but they drew large crowds and shared the limelight. Born on February 14, 1935, in San Diego, California, Wright first played golf at the age of ten and soon became a teenage prodigy. A highlight of her short amateur career was an appearance in the 1954 U.S. Women's Open, when she was paired with Zaharias for the final two rounds of Babe's last championship. While the young Wright was appalled at Babe's vulgar language and public antics, she respected her contribution to the women's tour. But she also recognized that Babe "was the complete opposite of me. She loved being in a crowd, which brought out her exhibitionist tendencies." Wright turned professional in 1955 and went on to win eighty-two tournaments (all but one prior to 1970) including four U.S. Women's Open titles (1958, 1959, 1961, 1964) and four LPGA Championships (1958, 1960, 1961, 1963). During her prime in the 1960s she also served two years as LPGA president and felt intense pressure from the press and sponsors to compete and win tournaments even as she shouldered the responsibilities of her office. But although her contemporaries viewed her as a legend and as the greatest golfer on the

LPGA tour, her natural modesty and shyness prevented her from matching Arnold Palmer's impact on American golf.

The same statement may be made about Whitworth, who was Wright's greatest rival during the 1960s. Born on September 27, 1939, in Monohans, Texas, she started playing golf at fifteen. She turned professional in 1959, but her breakthrough came three years later when she won her first LPGA title. Over her thirty-two-year career, her eighty-eight victories eclipsed both Wright and Sam Snead in setting a record for tour wins in men's and women's professional golf. In 1981 she became the first woman to surpass $1 million in career earnings. A three-time winner of the LPGA Championship (1967, 1971, 1975), she was never able to win the U.S. Women's Open. A loyal and influential member of the LPGA for decades, she served as its president for four years. Still active and highly competitive during the 1980s, she reaped some of the rewards of the improved conditions on the women's tour brought on in part by the rise of Nancy Lopez. But her reluctance to promote herself during her youth had limited the growth of

Mickey Wright during the 1958 Women's Open Championship at Forest Lake Country Club, Bloomfield Hills, Mich. She was the winner of the event. Copyright Unknown/ Courtesy USGA Archives.

Kathy Whitworth during the 1968 U.S. Women's Open Championship at Moselem Springs Golf Club, Fleetwood, Pa. Photo is by
E. Schneider. Copyright Unknown/Courtesy USGA Archives.

the LPGA. She admitted: "Had someone else been winning besides myself
who had more charisma, we might have grown faster in that earlier era."

Despite the achievements of Wright and Whitworth, the LPGA fell on
hard times during the early 1970s. Bud Erickson succeeded Wirtz as the
LPGA's executive director, but during his term the women's tour lost key
television sponsorship from Sears, Roebuck, and the number of tournaments declined to twenty-one in 1970 and 1971. But in 1972 Colgate Pal-

molive rescued the LPGA with an ambitious plan to combine sponsorship and advertising in women's golf tournaments with the purchase of several midsize sporting goods manufacturing companies. Colgate's actions proved beneficial both to itself and the LPGA as it aimed to increase women's interest and participation in golf and also use female stars to sell its golf equipment and household products. Colgate's timely assistance helped the LPGA improve its balance sheet, but it faced a costly new challenge in 1972 when it began a long legal battle against a young professional, Jane Blalock. It expelled Blalock for one year for improperly improving her lie on greens when replacing her ball, but Blalock countered with a lawsuit that challenged the right of the LPGA to discipline her. In 1973 the court ruled in Blalock's favor on antitrust grounds, and the LPGA's unsuccessful appeal threatened to bankrupt the organization.

By the middle of 1975 the officers of the LPGA decided they were willing to relinquish much of their power to a new leader who would be more aggressive in marketing their tour and who would completely reorganize the LPGA's political structure. They replaced Erickson with Ray Volpe, who was chosen because of his experience in marketing the National Hockey League. As commissioner of the LPGA Volpe created a new executive board of directors composed of himself, four players, and five members representing the corporate world or other golfing institutions. He also established a seven-person players council (whose power was strictly advisory) and an expanded management staff. In addition, he moved the LPGA's headquarters from Atlanta to New York City, which was essential to his plan to change the nature of the women's tournaments from small city affairs promoted by local interests to national events covered by the mass media and subsidized by corporate America. During Volpe's reign the LPGA tour experienced a new wave of growth, achieved through expanded network television coverage and the meteoric rise of Nancy Lopez in 1977 and 1978. In 1979 the tour held thirty-eight tournaments worth nearly $4.5 million in prize money.

Nancy Lopez's debut in 1977 and her sensational record in 1978 provided an enormous boost to the LPGA tour and had an impact that some writers compared to that of Arnold Palmer on the men's tour nearly two decades earlier. Her personal background and talents ideally qualified her to be the next great woman golfer. Attractive, photogenic, personable, and highly skilled and bold in her game, she lived an American Dream saga comparable to that of another Hispanic star—Lee Trevino. Born January 6, 1957, in Torrance, California, she was the daughter of a Mexican American body shop owner, a three-handicap golfer who played on public courses. Raised in Roswell, New Mexico, she first played golf at the age of eight and won state and national girls championships. As an amateur she tied for second in the 1975 U.S. Women's Open, and the following year she won the national women's intercollegiate golf championship as a freshman at the University of Tulsa. After turning professional in 1977 she repeated her runner-up performance in the U.S. Women's Open. In her breakout year of 1978 she set an LPGA record by winning five consecutive tournaments, then added four more titles before the end of that season. In 1979 Lopez's phenomenal success and the ensuing media infatuation with her created some bitterness and jealousy among her competitors, but Volpe and her defenders pointed to her positive impact on the women's tour as a whole, as manifested in larger galleries and purses. Still a leading player in the 1980s, she competed on the tour until the late 1990s, with some time off to raise a family. LPGA champion in 1978, 1985, and 1989, like Whitworth she was never able to win the U.S. Women's Open.

The 1970s also witnessed the rebirth of feminism in the United States, which had some profound effects on women in high school and college athletics through Title IX of the Educational Amendments Act of 1972. The Title IX program guaranteed equal funding for both sexes in high school and college sports, resulting in many more college golf scholarships for women. (Lopez was one of the early beneficiaries of Title IX, as she received the first women's golf scholarship at the University of Tulsa.) The women's sports revolution in general and Title IX in particular boosted golf for girls, who gained greater opportunities to compete in junior tournaments and later in college matches and championship events. Since the 1970s golf scholarships have provided critical financial support and invaluable training and tournament experience to women who aspired to play the LPGA tour. In May 2006 Ron Sirak, executive editor of *Golf World*, told a *New Yorker* reporter: "These kids are the first generation of Title IX babies. Their mothers were the first beneficiaries of that legislation . . . and they grew up in families where it was O.K. to play games. It wasn't like that in my generation, where athletic girls were viewed as sort of odd." But it is also telling that among the most successful young female American golfers (Wie, Natalie Gulbis, Paula Creamer, and Morgan Pressel), only Gulbis played college golf.

Volpe resigned as LPGA commissioner in 1982, and his successor, John Laupheimer, faced an upstart competitor for corporate sponsors and television rights in the newly founded men's Senior PGA Tour. Although the LPGA regularly surpassed the Senior Tour in tournament ticket sales and matched its television ratings, in 1988 the Senior Tour netted $7 million more in corporate support than the women's tour. It also topped the ladies in overall television exposure both on broadcast networks and especially on cable with ESPN. While many of the leading women professionals found it hard to accept that fans would prefer to watch aging fifty- and sixty-year-old players than much younger accomplished female golfers, in fact such idols as Palmer, Player, Trevino, and others remained hugely popular among viewers. But despite the envy and resentment over the challenge of the Senior Tour and the reality that the LPGA still lagged far behind the regular PGA Tour, during this decade the women's tour still posted solid gains. In 1989 the LPGA held thirty-six tournaments worth $13 million (compared to about $40 million on the regular PGA Tour).

Throughout the post–World War II period the management and players of the LPGA faced an issue that had plagued all forms of women's athletics since the nineteenth century. They called it the "image problem"—the public perception that females who engaged in serious sports competition were tomboys who were too masculine in behavior and unattractive in appearance. Their reaction was to urge players to dress and act in a traditional, ladylike manner. In a 1961 meeting an anonymous player stated: "The prototype image in the public's mind of a female athlete is not a pretty one, which holds true for any women's sport. . . . This element is being shattered by our dressing better and appearing as feminine as possible at all times." Mickey Wright recalled: "Unfortunately, at that time it was not acceptable for a woman to be an athlete. We all felt that when we were in public, we had to be 'on' like being on stage, and we had to watch our speech, our mannerisms, and everything we did. Not that anyone needed to, but when you are told that any woman who plays sports is nothing but an Amazon; then you have to try to counteract it." Kathy Whitworth shared the same experience: "When I turned professional, women playing sports were not looked on as ladylike. My family backed me because they thought I should express my talent, and they felt it was possible to be a lady and still play golf. The stigma was there, but we were a strong group; so we survived." During his term as tour director Wirtz worked to soften the image of the ladies even as he promoted them as superb players. He explained: "I didn't sell the women solely on sex, more as feminine athletes, which is how they are attractive. They are also the best women golfers in the world, and I always tried to sell that." But some had their doubts about this marketing strategy. Betsy Rawls remarked: "Some women are never going to look feminine and they look better in trousers. You could have put everyone in frilly clothes and had them all dolled up, but it wouldn't have brought crowds in greater numbers."

During the 1970s the LPGA endorsed an advertising campaign that featured both the talent of the players and the physical attributes of a few of the more glamorous women. Californian Laura Baugh and Australian Jan Stephenson garnered much of the media attention through interviews and especially in fashion and golf magazines. In October 1973 *Golf Magazine* introduced Baugh by proclaiming: "The ladies' tour finally has a genuine, dimpled glamour girl who can really play the game." It quoted a Philadelphia reporter: "Most newsmen have described more lunar eclipses than they have good-lookin' women pro golfers. A girl with Laura Baugh's looks and swing on the tour is about as rare as a barracuda in Pennsylvania." A few years later Stephenson created even more of a sensation when she posed for a revealing cover illustration for *Sport* magazine and even considered a nude display for *Playboy*. In 1986 a poster of her lying naked in a bathtub filled with golf balls became a classic collector's piece. But unlike Baugh, Stephenson also excelled on the golf course, winning sixteen tournaments (including the LPGA Championship in 1982 and the U.S. Women's Open in 1983) and more than $3 million in prize money over her career. During Volpe's term as LPGA commissioner he and his marketing consultant, Tony Andrea, fully endorsed using sex as a tool to attract spectators, viewers, and sponsors. For Andrea, sexual appeal was "part of the LPGA forever." He explained: "I think we can sell the Tour without sex, but the appeal of good-looking women should not be ignored. It's part of the overall marketing and selling of the sport." As a result, in 1981 the LPGA's *Fairway Magazine* featured a photo fashion section that portrayed Stephenson and several other women in suggestive, alluring poses. But not all the LPGA membership supported this promotional strategy. Blalock blasted the *Fairway* pictorial as "quasi-pornography." She asked: "Is our organization so unaware of the real glamour and attraction staring it in the face that it must resort to such trash?" Whitworth acknowledged that "the Tour needs to market a product," but she added: "I didn't join the Tour to be in a chorus line, to be an entertainer. . . . We're stuck with golf. Golf is it. We're not actors or actresses. You get the feeling that it's not good enough." Little has changed over the past few decades, as the attractiveness of the players continues to be an important element of the LPGA tour. At least that is the view of a middle-aged Stephenson. In November 2003 *Golf Magazine* reported that although she regretted sitting for her early photos that produced her "sex kitten image," she admitted that the LPGA still had to "promote sex appeal" because "the people who watch are primarily male, and they won't keep watching if the girls aren't beautiful."

As the LPGA's management tried to project an image of the players as feminine, ladylike, highly skilled athletes, they also had to contend with rumors of lesbianism that had swirled around the women's tour for decades. While undoubtedly there were gay women on the tour, they were unwilling to publicly declare their sexual preference, in part because they did not wish to create controversy for the LPGA and in part because they did not want to sacrifice corporate sponsorships for themselves. For some the strain of secrecy and public denial was hard to bear. As one anonymous lesbian golfer confessed: "There are times when all I want to do is just shock someone. Supposing we all came out. Would that shock people, open their eyes, and make them look? Of course it wouldn't. It's not worth it, and you would blow your career." An incident occurred at the LPGA Championship in May 1995 that brought the issue of the sexual orientation of some of the players out into public view. Valerie Helmbreck, a reporter from the *Wilmington News Journal* (Maryland), printed an inflammatory quote from CBS golf commentator Ben Wright. An English-born resident of the United States, Wright remarked: "Let's face some facts here. Lesbians in the sport hurt women's golf. When it gets to the corporate level, that's not going to fly. They're going to a butch game and that furthers the bad image of the game." He added that lesbianism "is not reticent. It's paraded. There's a defiance in them the last decade." When CBS officials demanded an explanation, Wright denied making the statements. But after Helmbreck stuck with her story, leaders of gay and lesbian groups were outraged. Ellen Carton, executive director of the Gay and Lesbian Alliance Against Defamation, retorted: "Wright seems to be living in another age—the Stone Age. Without American lesbian athletes, world class women's sports would not exist." Charles S. Mechem, Jr., the LPGA's commissioner, engaged in some damage control, declaring that the organization's "major problem and its biggest challenge by far is not the personal lifestyle of its players." He explained: "Our problem is quite simply that we are a women's sports organization," adding that the LPGA showcased women who were "achieving at a level equal to men." He lamented to the gathered news reporters: "As we sit here . . . the best of the best in women's golf are playing the game with cosmic skill. But we aren't out there watching. . . . We're in here dealing with this absurd and ugly charge that lesbianism is stunting the growth of the LPGA Tour." CBS decided to retain Wright for the remainder of the championship, but the network removed him from its golf telecasts in 1996. One indirect result of the Wright affair was the decision of Muffin Spencer-Devlin to become the first LPGA player to publicly announce that she was gay. She had kept her sexual orientation private over an eighteen-year career, but at the age of forty-two she decided that the time was right for her to come out of the closet. In a March 1996 interview with *Sports Illustrated* she refused to generalize about the degree of lesbianism on the LPGA tour other than to state that gay women were only a minority in the organization. She also reported that she was in no danger of losing her endorsement contracts with a food supplement company and Callaway Golf.

In the long run the most important features of the LPGA tour at the turn of the twenty-first century were not its marketing strategy or the sexual orientation of its players, but rather its solid growth and especially its increasingly international character. In 1999 it scheduled forty-three tournaments for total prize money of $36 million—a gain of 176 percent over the decade. Moreover, the number of television events more than doubled during the 1990s, from fourteen to thirty-three. European, Latin American, and Asian women increasingly won LPGA tournaments and major championships, with Annika Sorenstam of Sweden, Lorena Ochoa of Mexico, Karrie Webb of Australia, and Se Ri Pak of South Korea leading the parade of international stars. In recognition of the growing importance of European female golfers competing in the United States, American golf club manufacturer Karsten Solheim (founder of Ping) proposed the creation of a biennial challenge between teams of professional women golfers representing Europe and the United States. Modeled after the men's Ryder Cup, the inaugural Solheim Cup match was held in Florida in 1990. Through 2007 the U.S. side was victorious in seven out of the ten competitions.

Annika Sorenstam led the invasion of foreigners, and by the early 2000s she had established herself as the premier female golfer in the world and one of the best of all time. Born on October 9, 1970, in Bro, Sweden, she attended the University of Arizona, where she won the 1991 NCAA individual championship. After turning professional in 1993 she rose quickly to the upper echelon of women golfers, winning the U.S. Women's Open in 1995 and 1996. She also won three consecutive LPGA Championships in 2003, 2004, and 2005, and she captured the Women's British Open in 2003 and a third U.S. Women's Open crown in 2006. She stirred up some controversy over gender relations in 2003 when she elected to compete against men in a PGA Tour event, the Bank of America Colonial tournament in Fort Worth, Texas. With no more female golf worlds to conquer,

Sorenstam felt fully qualified to test her skills against some of the elite male players on the planet. Feminists applauded her decision, but the reaction among male participants was decidedly mixed. PGA Tour member Rocco Mediate admitted that he wanted her to finish last, "not because of anything against her but because I don't want any of my friends to deal with questions about 'losing to a girl.'" In the end Sorenstam played respectably, and although she failed to make the cut, she did finish ahead of eleven men. As recounted earlier, the teenage sensation Michelle Wie followed Sorenstam's example and attempted to qualify for the U.S. Open and also gained sponsors' exemptions that permitted her to enter a few PGA Tour events.

The most significant development in the LPGA since the late 1990s has been the stunning success of South Korean golfers. In 1998 there were only two Korean-born players on the tour; five years later there were eighteen. The most prominent was Se Ri Pak, who won the U.S. Women's Open in 1998, the Women's British Open in 2001, and the LPGA Championship in 1998, 2002, and 2006. The record of the South Koreans in the first half of 2006 was a striking indicator of the depth of their talent: eight of the first seventeen LPGA tournaments that year were won by eight different South Korean women, all of whom were under the age of thirty. Some resented the influx of the South Koreans. In 2003 Stephenson, herself an Australian, told *Golf Magazine* that "the Asians are killing our tour. Absolutely killing it. Their lack of emotion, their refusal to speak English when they can speak English. They rarely speak." To address these issues the LPGA hired language and cultural consultants to serve as liaisons between the tour and its South Korean contingent, teaching them English and helping them adjust to media expectations and other demands of the tour.

◎ ◎ ◎

While the best female golfers in the world contested for fame and fortune on the LPGA tour, women who aspired only to play recreational rounds struggled to gain fair treatment at private and public courses. The controversy over their exclusion from such all-male organizations as the Augusta National Golf Club attracted much media coverage, but far more significant were women's campaigns for respect and equal rights at country clubs and semiprivate daily-fee and municipal grounds. These included earlier starting times on weekends, facilities equal to those provided men, and a stronger voice in the direction of club life. By the early twenty-first century, women golfers had gained much ground, but full equality on the links and in the clubhouses still eluded them.

The incident that sparked a media frenzy began innocently enough in April 2002, when Martha Burk read a column in *USA Today* about the exclusion of women at the Augusta National Golf Club. Two months later, in a short private letter to the club's chairman, William W. "Hootie" Johnson, she urged the club to review its membership policies and "open its membership to women now, so that this is not an issue when the tournament is staged next year." In early July Johnson's brief reply declared that Augusta National was a private club whose members did not discuss its membership and practices with outsiders. He also dismissed Burk's letter as "both offensive and coercive" and rejected any further communication with her. Surprisingly, Johnson also sent the media a three-page press release in which he complained that "Augusta National is being threatened with a public campaign designed to use economic pressure to achieve a goal of NCWO." He explained: "We expect such a campaign would attempt to depict the members of our club as insensitive bigots and coerce the sponsors of the Masters to disassociate themselves under threat—real or implied—of boycotts and other economic pressures. . . . We will not be bullied, threatened, or intimidated. . . . We do not intend to become a trophy in their display case. There may well come a day when women will be invited to join our membership but that timetable will be ours and not at the point of a bayonet."

Burk was astounded at Johnson's intense reaction to her proposal and became even more determined to apply pressure on the Augusta National club to open its doors to women. When asked why she singled out that organization for special attention (there were about two dozen all-male golf clubs in the nation), she answered that it was because it hosted "one of the most prestigious tournaments in the world." She added: "We think they should be in the forefront of having nondiscriminatory membership practices." For Burk, golf and especially access to private country clubs were important elements of American business culture. She insisted that successful professional and business women could never rise to the highest ranks in their careers if they were banned from private associations where male movers and shakers exchanged information and sealed deals. For her, the Augusta episode's greater cultural meaning concerned how and why women were "still systematically barred from the highest echelons of power—in government, social and religious organizations, and most importantly, in corporate America." She concluded: "Far from being about a few rich females gaining admittance to one club, the gates of Augusta National Golf Club became symbolic of all the ways women are still kept out of power where it counts, and how and why we must change the system to break in."

Over the remainder of 2002 Burk and her allies lobbied the major national golf organizations (the PGA, USGA, and PGA and LPGA tours), a few members of Augusta National, and several corporate executives, urging them all to support the admission of women at Augusta National. The feminist forces considered their case to be analogous to the Shoal Creek campaign a dozen years earlier, when the issue was racial discrimination against African Americans. But many did not view the gender and racial issues as identical, and this time the golf groups refused to publicly endorse a campaign to end discrimination against women at private clubs. Burk's forces were also upset with Tiger Woods's lack of enthusiasm for their cause. Referring to private clubs, he remarked: "They're entitled to set up their own rules the way they want them. It would be nice to see everyone have an equal chance to participate, if they wanted to, but there's nothing you can do about it." Burk also demanded that the Masters' corporate sponsors (Citigroup, IBM, Coca-Cola, and General Motors/Cadillac) cancel their television advertisements, but Johnson pre-empted her by releasing those companies from their commitments to CBS television. That network then refused Burk's request that it drop the Masters from its schedule. It telecast it in 2003 and 2004 without sponsors, but resumed running advertisements in 2005.

While Burk singled out Augusta National because of its sponsorship of the prestigious Masters tournament, about two dozen other golf clubs barred women from their membership rolls. Some, like Augusta National, permitted females to play as guests of members. Others, like the Burning Tree Club in Bethesda, Maryland, banned women entirely at all times from its course, clubhouse, and even its galleries (the only exception occurred at Christmastime, when the ladies could purchase gifts for their men at the pro shop). In between these two extremes was the Pine Valley Golf Club in southern New Jersey, which has been rated the best course in the nation by *Golf Digest*. There a woman accompanied by a member could tee off after 3:00 P.M. These organizations defended their policies on the grounds that as private clubs they enjoyed the right of freedom of association guaranteed by the First Amendment of the U.S. Constitution. (Some states required that all-male clubs could not hold any public functions or events or benefit from tax abatements.) Moreover, they argued that as they engaged in their favorite pastime they were not practicing any form of discrimination that was harmful to anyone. Finally, they simply preferred the male camaraderie and bonding provided by these clubs, which permitted them a refuge from the demands imposed on them by the women in their lives. "Hootie" Johnson expressed this view in his quaint comment: "We love our women, we just don't want any fussin' with 'em."

While the exclusion of females at two dozen golf organizations irritated feminists, they were far more annoyed by the discrimination against women at the nation's 4,500 private country clubs. In the vast majority of them, women could not vote, sit on the board of directors, hold an equity interest in the club, or eat in men's grills. Since husbands generally held the primary membership rights in these organizations, divorced and other single women and widows who remarried generally either lost their membership privileges entirely or were retained on the rolls with only limited rights. Clubs also frequently denied full privileges to the partners of gay and lesbian members. For business and professional women who held full-time positions, the primary battleground over fair treatment at these clubs concerned tee times on weekend mornings. They demanded access to their courses at those prime time slots because of their work schedules, but also because they wanted the same opportunity to entertain their clients as men enjoyed. While most male members naturally defended the policies that gave them nearly complete control of their organizations, many of the wives of regular members (labeled "WORMS" by some wags) acquiesced to their second-class status because they did not wish to be viewed as troublemakers. In some states country club women gained additional rights as a result of laws that barred discrimination at private associations that held liquor licenses, conducted public events, or benefited from federal tax laws or property tax abatements. A few clubs attempted to solve the problem of tee times by permitting either spouse to be designated as the "primary member" and thus gain the coveted preferred starting slot.

While female golfers at exclusive country clubs frequently had to contend with discriminatory policies and practices, their counterparts on public courses fared somewhat better, although some also struggled to gain equal respect and treatment from men. While only a few courses hired women as head professionals, the majority welcomed female players. But at several municipal facilities men's clubs monopolized the weekend morning tee times, prompting lawsuits that demanded equal access to those preferred slots and tournaments for women. Moreover, at many public facilities tee placements and hole design were not woman-friendly, and most did not have "port-a-potties" at remote holes. Some women also reported more subtle forms of intimidation, such as discourteous starters and course rangers who were more likely to harass them than men for their alleged slow play.

By the beginning of the twenty-first century American women had earned a prominent place in the golfing community. At first their role was limited to a subordinate membership in exclusive family-oriented country clubs, but as early as the 1890s a few hardy athletic females competed in the first amateur state, regional, and national tournaments. Before long they were challenging their sisters in Great Britain for individual and team championships, and in the 1940s a few pioneers launched the first women's professional tour. Although it took decades for the LPGA to gain acceptance and popularity among the sporting public, the heroic exploits of such stars as Babe Didrikson Zaharias, Mickey Wright, Kathy Whitworth, Nancy Lopez, and Annika Sorenstam gave the women's tour real credibility as it shared the limelight with both the regular and senior PGA tours. On the country club front women had no success in gaining admission to the most exclusive all-male associations, but they did win some major concessions in membership privileges and tee times at private organizations. But more than a century after women had helped to create golf in America they had still not achieved full equality in the clubhouses or on the fairways and greens.

12

GOLF AND
AMERICAN DEMOCRACY

On June 19, 1997, the *Christian Science Monitor* reported that at the Tenison Park public golf course in Dallas, Texas, "anyone with $13 and a bag of sticks can play, and just about every type of person does." It explained: "Indeed, the emerging melting pot of players at many municipal courses across the nation defies the stereotype that golf is a game played only by rich white men in plaid pants. Not only do public courses nurture the sport's soaring popularity among women, minorities, and blue-collar workers, observers say, but they also force Americans from all walks of life to spend five hours together playing a game that punishes arrogance." Jere Mills, golf superintendent of the Dallas Parks and Recreation Department, estimated that about 25 percent of Tenison's golfers were female, and about 20 percent were minorities. The newspaper also cited golf industry accounts that a boom in course construction and the spectacular early success of Tiger Woods "have helped fuel the transformation of this game from an exclusive sport to a more democratic pastime."

Nine years later two high-end clubs debuted in Hudson County, New Jersey, providing emphatic proof that golf for the very rich was still alive and thriving in the nation's metropolitan areas, and especially around New York City. In the summer of 2006 the Liberty National Golf Club of Jersey City and the Bayonne Golf Club celebrated their grand openings on sites bordering the western bank of the Hudson River, just a few miles from lower Manhattan. The Liberty National course sits atop an old abandoned tank farm and a former army blacktop and truck driving training facility. The Bayonne layout, designed as a British links course, lies above a municipal landfill with toxic wastes buried deep below. The prospective patrons for both new facilities were not the blue-collar residents of Hudson County, but rather the well-heeled corporate executives and professionals of Wall Street. Initiation fees of $400,000 for Liberty National and $150,000 at

Bayonne excluded virtually all the local population, while helicopter and ferry services provided quick and convenient transportation for members who worked in New York City. Meanwhile, one hundred miles to the east at Southampton, Long Island, the Bridge golf club charged $600,000 in membership fees but featured a casual dress code that permitted backward baseball caps, jeans, and even tattoos and face piercings.

The patrons of the Tenison Park public course in Dallas and the members of the upscale country clubs outside New York City inhabit opposite poles in the world of American golf, but they also constitute only a small part of the nation's golfing fraternity. The momentum of the golf boom of the 1950s lasted through the mid-1970s, followed by a slowdown in the rate of growth through most of the 1980s caused by unfavorable economic conditions and increasing costs of land, construction, and maintenance. A 1983 statistical study found that more than 14 million Americans were active golfers on the nation's thirteen thousand courses, and another 3.5 million played an occasional round. The north-central and northeastern regions of the United States contained the largest number of facilities, but the southern Sun Belt and Southwest were gaining ground, mainly due to the increasing number of resort and retirement golf developments and communities. The 1990s and early 2000s brought yet another growth spurt in course construction, with developers adding more than three thousand new facilities. The number of new grounds built reached 524 in 2000, but the decrease to 200 in 2001 signaled another downturn in golf just prior to the terrorist attacks of September 11th. At the end of 2004 the nation counted 15,807 public and private courses. But this expanded supply exceeded the demand because the total number of golfers declined from about thirty million in 2000 to about twenty-six million in 2006. More significantly, the number of active participants (defined as those who play at least twenty-five times a year) fell from 6.9 million in 2000 to 4.6 million in 2005. During this period about three million people quit the game each year, slightly more than the annual number of new recruits. Economic and social factors that contributed to this decline in the relative popularity of golf since 2000 include a weakening national economy, the waning popularity of outdoor recreational activities, and family obligations that limit time available for a sport that requires four to five hours to complete a round. Thus while the popularity of Tiger Woods, the success of PGA Tour events and the Golf Channel on network and cable television, and the devotion of millions of weekend golfers point to the continuing prominence of the sport in the United States, early in the twenty-first century managers of country clubs and owners of daily-fee facilities had good reason to be concerned about the short-term prospects of the game.

Many factors contributed to the surging popularity of golf on private, municipal, and daily-fee facilities after 1960, and all reflected trends clearly apparent in the immediate post–World War II period. Suburbanization and increased leisure time and disposal income for both white- and blue-collar workers made the sport more accessible, affordable, and feasible for the masses. Telecasts of major and lesser tournaments showcased the exploits of Arnold Palmer, Jack Nicklaus, Gary Player, Lee Trevino, and other rising stars. Media coverage of presidential duffers kept the game in the public eye, even though the chief executives who succeeded Eisenhower tried to keep a lower profile when they escaped the burdens of office on the links. An increasing number of women, adolescents, and children from a widening range of social classes took up the game, as did senior citizens, who benefited from the motorized golf carts and the availability of par-three and shorter regulation courses. Participation rates also showed sizeable gains among players from a variety of ethnic and racial groups—especially Hispanics, Asians, and African Americans. Blind and other disabled golfers joined in the rage for golf, as national associations and courses adjusted rules and made accommodations for them.

While golf's brightest stars and film and television celebrities propelled the sport to new heights of popularity after 1960, presidents John Kennedy, Lyndon Johnson, and Richard Nixon shied away from the public endorsement of the game exhibited by Eisenhower. Those three chief executives were well aware of the criticism of Eisenhower's golf obsession and they all carefully weighed the political consequences of media accounts of their time on the links. Open and enthusiastic presidential support for golf returned with Gerald Ford's short stay in office during the mid-1970s. More recently, presidents George H. W. Bush, Bill Clinton, and George W. Bush have been active players who did not try to conceal their love of the game from the American public.

John Kennedy was the most talented of all the presidential golfers, but he and his staff did all they could to keep his passion for the game a secret from the masses. That was particularly true during the 1960 presidential campaign against Nixon, as Kennedy's political strategists tried to highlight his youth and energy and play down his patrician, privileged, country club background. When Lyndon Johnson took the oath of office after Kennedy's assassination, the nation gained yet another golfing president, but this time it was a man with little skill and a propensity for taking innumerable mulligans. Johnson was a poor player who did not care about his performance on the links, but he did see the value of golf outings to seal political deals. In many ways Richard Nixon's experiences as a golfer reflected his record in public office. Although he had little natural athletic ability, he worked hard to reach a respectable level of proficiency. But he also had a tendency to bend the rules to save strokes and report a final score much lower than his true total. Cheating at golf had only trivial personal consequences, but his deviant behavior in office forced him to resign the presidency in disgrace. Up to his final downfall Nixon understood that golf could be both an asset and a liability in his political career. Despite his insecurities and his controversial policies and actions as president, Nixon did make a modest contribution to popularizing golf among the American masses. In an October 1994 retrospective commentary in *Golf Magazine*, James Dodson wrote: "Nixon—with his britches worn Gomer Pyle-high and his Ban-Lon shirt often chastely buttoned to the top—demonstrated that anybody could participate in the sport . . . it was the bumblingly awkward and somehow more poignantly human Nixon who proved beyond the doubt of a five o'clock shadow that golf was a game intended for the multitudes." In Sam Snead's view, Nixon "might have understood the appeal of the game as well as any President who played," especially in the way golf "beats up your emotions and all, and like a lot of people who play the game he really *wanted* to be good." Snead added that even in his bending of the rules "Nixon could relate to the ordinary player." He remembered: "Hell, I even once caught him cheatin' a little bit—movin' the ball, you know, from some trouble when he didn't think nobody could see him. All hackers do that." Dodson concluded that at least in his passionate but often inept pursuit of excellence on the golf course, "Nixon was one of us."

When Gerald Ford took the oath of office as chief executive after Nixon's resignation in August 1974, the nation gained yet another golfing chief executive. But this time it was a man who was not shy about playing the sport in public, even if sometimes his performance resulted in some embarrassing incidents. As Arnold Palmer explained, Ford "had no hang-ups about being seen on a golf course. He adored golf and didn't care a bit who knew it." Unlike Nixon, Ford was a gifted athlete who had been a star center and linebacker and the most valuable player on the University of Michigan's football team during the mid-1930s. He also differed from both Nixon and Johnson in that he respected and observed the rules of golf. Jimmy Carter had no interest in golf, but the four presidents who followed him were all active players who did not fret over public acceptance of a chief executive on the links. The American public and especially the press were generally supportive of the golfing exploits of Ronald Reagan, George H. W. Bush, and George W. Bush, but commentators were far more critical of Bill Clinton's golf game. Reagan played only about a dozen rounds during his eight years in the White House, and his staff kept his scores secret. As president he much preferred to spend his leisure time riding horses or chopping wood. George H. W. Bush and his son were accomplished and enthusiastic golfers, partly no doubt because of generations of family tradition. George H. W. Bush's maternal grandfather, George Herbert Walker, was a former president of the USGA and also the founder of the Walker Cup competition between American and British amateur golfers. His father, Senator Prescott Bush, was also a past president of the USGA. Perhaps because of this lineage, George Bush and his son had much more respect for the rules of the game than many of their predecessors in the Oval Office. Early in his first term George W. Bush did not view golf as a political liability, but in the fall of 2003, a few months after American troops invaded Iraq, he quit the game. He explained: "I think playing golf during a war just sends the wrong signal."

In an interview with *Golf Digest* published in November 2000, Bill Clinton stated that he believed that the public and the press did not begrudge his playing golf because they knew he was a hard worker. But early in his first term a political advisor, Dick Morris, told him that polls suggested that the public preferred him to take his vacation in the mountains or in a national park rather than on a golf course. Clinton followed that advice and went camping at Yellowstone and Grand Teton National Parks, but he also found a way to play thirty-seven holes of golf in a single day. Later in his presidency Clinton did not hesitate to spend much of his vacation time playing golf. Most observers were not much troubled about his time on the links. But they were much more critical of his habit of reporting scores that counted conceded long "gimme" putts but did not include mulligans, practice strokes, and any shots over a double-bogey on any single hole. In truth, Clinton was actually a talented golfer whom Palmer called "the best ball-striker of any president I've known." But he had a hard time with the strict observance of the rules, as he did in his personal and political lives. In the end it is doubtful whether Clinton significantly advanced the popularity of golf in the United States during his presidency.

⊚ ⊚ ⊚

In the spring of 1971 Max Brown and his fellow editors of *Golf Digest* published a two-part series on the "Crisis in Club Golf" in which they asked the question: "Can American golf and country clubs withstand in their present form the economic and social pressures of the new decade?" As it turned out, the financial, legal, social, and environmental challenges facing private golf clubs would persist and intensify for decades beyond the troubling times of the 1970s, right up to the present. The magazine's investigative report began with the financial pressures facing clubs during the recession of the early 1970s: soaring property and other local taxes, new rules on income taxes on clubs, other local taxes, reduced spending by members, increased costs for services, and declining applications for memberships. Part II of *Golf Digest's* study examined legal and social trends that were potentially more threatening to private clubs than balancing their budgets. These included the critical issue of conflicting constitutional principles: the right of free association versus the egalitarian goals of a democracy. In short, did these organizations have a constitutional right to practice racial, religious, and gender discrimination in choosing their membership and in drawing up their bylaws? Of special concern was declining interest among younger people in joining clubs that excluded ethnic or racial minorities.

Financial pressures that forced the closing or relocation of hundreds of urban and suburban country clubs during the 1960s raised concerns over the loss of beneficial open space or greenbelts in metropolitan regions. But when state legislatures offered tax breaks to clubs to help them stay solvent and thus preserve precious open space, critics complained that the government was subsidizing private associations that practiced ethnic or racial discrimination. In October 1970 *Golf Magazine* warned about "America's Vanishing Green Belt," as commercial and residential land developers purchased courses and transformed the land into office buildings, shopping malls, apartments, and homes. That journal lamented: "Hundreds of golf courses offering green respite to the dreary concrete shroud of urban development are surrendering the land to asphalt, steel, and concrete. Taxes and the too-sweet deals of builders are smothering the fairways and greens that once made urban life more than endless stone." In an effort to prevent this outcome in Montgomery County, Maryland, that state's legislature offered special tax abatements to clubs to keep them from selling to developers. But that action drew the wrath of one of Ralph Nader's "raiders," who released a study demonstrating that the tax breaks provided yearly savings of $165,000 to such ultra-exclusive organizations as the Chevy Chase Club. The problem raised a quandary for state governments: should they try to preserve golf courses that provided open space for trees, grass, and wildlife, even at the price of propping up private clubs that excluded ethnic and racial minorities?

Most country clubs weathered the economic storms of the 1970s reasonably well, but another recession during the early 1990s compelled many of them to review their budgets and open their doors to more new members, including women and minorities. In addition, during the 1980s and 1990s the Shoal Creek and Augusta National incidents discussed in previous chapters plus numerous lawsuits forced them to make some changes in their admission policies and their rules pertaining to the rights of female members. This was especially true when courts made a distinction between the purely private and the quasi-public, mandating nondiscriminatory practices by country clubs that opened their grounds and clubhouses for public events or functions.

During the post–World War II era the vast majority of American country clubs continued the religious restrictions on membership they had practiced since their founding. Gentiles and Jews preferred to play golf and socialize with their own kind, although occasionally a wealthy Jew might attempt to join an exclusive association. In 1962 the Jewish Anti-Defamation League (ADL) conducted a study of more than eight hundred country clubs. Its survey found evidence that 72 percent applied religious restrictions, with Jewish clubs just as likely to discriminate as Gentile clubs. Although many Jewish clubs were the direct result of exclusion by Gentile associations, according to the ADL the Jewish organizations had become a major force for "the institutionalization of prejudice."

In the wake of the Shoal Creek episode, admission policies of country clubs came under greater scrutiny, especially concerning the exclusion of Jews and African Americans. In 1990 the Kansas City Country Club's denial of Henry Bloch's application was a major news story, mostly because of Tom Watson's resignation from the club in protest. Watson accused the club of rejecting Bloch (the chairman and co-founder of H&R Block) because he was Jewish. He explained: "It's something I can't personally live with because my family is Jewish." (Watson's wife and two children are Jewish; he is not.) In an op-ed piece in the *New York Times* on June 17, 1991, Watson suggested that he was more upset with his club's secrecy and refusal to admit its own discriminatory practices than with its denial of Bloch's application. Watson's resignation drew widespread support across the nation, and even spurred the Kansas City club to invite Bloch to re apply. Bloch did so and was accepted in 1991. Four years later Watson rejoined the club. During recent decades many formerly exclusive clubs were slightly more willing to admit Jewish or other minority members, but the large majority of Jews who aspired to country club life preferred to join associations founded to serve persons of their own faith.

Perhaps most noteworthy were a few country clubs that aspired to achieve a more diverse membership. In the 1960s the Old Westbury (New York) Golf and Country Club launched an experiment in interreligious cooperation when its board of directors (six Jews, five Gentiles, and four from mixed marriages) sought to recruit a balanced Jewish and Christian membership. The attempt foundered when Jewish applicants far outnumbered their Christian counterparts, and the members narrowly defeated a proposal to establish a quota system that favored Gentile candidates by a three-to-one margin. Far more successful was the Mill River Country Club of Upper Brookville, Long Island, New York. Founded in 1965, its bylaws stipulated that its membership be 50 percent Jewish and 50 percent Christian or other faiths. During its early years Mill River had some difficulty attracting Christian applicants, but by 1990 it had enrolled a diverse group of Jews, Gentiles, African Americans, Japanese, Indians, and others.

In the aftermath of the Shoal Creek episode many exclusive country clubs began admitting a few affluent African Americans, but there were only a few courses that were owned and managed by black golfers. Even in those cases, the facilities were open to the public, with whites included as members. Three examples are the Clearview Golf Course, near East Canton, Ohio; the Freeway Golf Course in Sicklerville, New Jersey; and the Bull Creek Golf and Country Club in Louisburg, North Carolina. The Clearview club was the brainchild and creation of William Powell, who returned to his home in Stark County, Ohio, after army service in World War II with a determination to renew the love of golf he had in his youth as a caddie and captain of his high school team. In his spare time he built the nine-hole Clearview course on farmland, opened it in 1948, and eventually expanded it to eighteen holes during the 1970s. He also raised a talented daughter, Renee Powell, who earned a place on the LPGA tour in 1967, competed for thirteen years, and ultimately succeeded her father as teaching professional at Clearview in 1995. In 1967 a group of black investors in Philadelphia formed the Greater Philadelphia Golf and Country Club, purchased a course in Sicklerville, New Jersey, renamed it the Freeway Golf Course, and opened it to the public in 1968. Although several members proposed making the club all-black, the managers declined that option for both practical and policy reasons. As President Jesse Davis stated in 1990: "We have always had mixed play. . . . We enjoy the diversity. I know, as most black golfers do, that you feel a certain chill at some other golf clubs. We bought Freeway to get away from that treatment, so why would we want to do the same to others?" Five African American families constructed the Bull Creek club in North Carolina, which opened nine holes for play in 1996; the back nine followed two years later.

As managers of country clubs grappled with financial concerns and charges of ethnic and racial discrimination, they also struggled to cope with vexing environmental issues that went far beyond questions of preserving urban green belts or open space. They and their counterparts at semiprivate and public courses faced blistering criticism of their use of pesticides, wasting of water, and destruction of natural habitats of wildlife. For example, a 1991 study prepared by the New York attorney general's office found that some Long Island golf courses applied more than twenty-five tons of pesticides annually on courses—more than six times the amount that farmers used per acre. Birds and fish were often victims of these chemicals or of golf course construction that bulldozed trees, plants, or wetlands.

In the mid-1990s officials of leading conservation and golf organizations joined in a collaborative effort to improve environmental practices on the nation's courses. A 1995 conference at Pebble Beach, California, planned a set of guidelines to protect wildlife habitats around courses, reduce reliance upon pesticides, minimize water usage, and recycle grass clippings. Representatives of the USGA and the National Fish and Wildlife Foundation launched a partnership through the Wildlife Links Program, and they met in 1997 to discuss ways to integrate wildlife conservation into golf courses. The USGA's Green Section undertook several initiatives to examine golf's environmental impact, and it joined with the Audubon Society of New York to formulate a cooperative effort called the Audubon Cooperative Sanctuary Program for Golf Courses. In addition, the Audubon International's Signature Program devised a certification process that works with golf course developers to integrate environmentally sound practices into the design and construction of courses. As it responded to critics and joined in these cooperative initiatives, the USGA also defended the sport by identifying specific environmental benefits of golf in general and turf grasses in particular. These included protecting valuable topsoil against erosion from water and wind, maintaining open space, restoring damaged areas such as mines and landfills, cooling surrounding landscapes, reducing pollution, decreasing noxious pests and allergy-related pollen, and enhancing human health through exercise. All in all, the American golf establishment has become more sensitive to environmental concerns and has cooperated with the "greening" of the sport, but there is still much room for improvement, especially concerning pesticides and water management in arid areas.

◎ ◎ ◎

In November 1984 *Golf Digest* began its ranking of "America's 75 Best Public Courses" by proclaiming: "The kingdom of golf, once the private duchy of the upper crust, declared itself a democratic state in 1962—the year that public courses in the United States outnumbered private courses for the first time." It added: "Since then, serious golfers have discovered to their delight that some of the nation's best courses are not private and never have been." The decade of the 1960s marked a critical transition in the growth of American golf mainly because of the dramatic increase in the number of players, from 3.9 million in 1958 to 11.2 million in 1970. More significantly, of the 3,500 new courses built to accommodate this flood of new participants, only about 600 were municipal links. The majority of the new courses were privately owned, daily-fee facilities open to the public. In 1967 the National Golf Foundation (NGF) counted 4,166 private courses, 3,960 semiprivate grounds, and 1,210 municipal links in the United States. Eight years later that organization reported 4,685 private links and 5,698 public layouts in the nation, including 1,747 that were municipal facilities. About 45 percent of golfers (about 5.2 million) patronized municipal links, competing for space and crowding each other on only 14 percent of the courses. Not surprisingly, those who could afford higher prices flocked to the daily-fee grounds. For the remainder of the twentieth century semiprivate courses would challenge and ultimately surpass both municipal courses and private country clubs as the main venue for the American golfing experience. A 1998 study prepared by the NGF reported proof of the long-term trend from private to public golf. Between 1986 and 1997 the proportion of American golfers who played more than half of their rounds on public courses increased from 76 percent to 79 percent. During that period their numbers rose by more than 39 percent, from about 15 million to almost 21 million. In 1985, 61 percent of the nation's thirteen thousand courses were open to the public; in 1998, 71 percent of the sixteen thousand links in the United States were accessible to all, and about 75 percent of the total rounds were played on those municipal or daily-fee grounds. By the end of 2001, the surge in high-end upscale semiprivate facilities threatened to create a glut of courses in certain markets, but in many cities there was still a shortage of inexpensive municipal grounds. In 2007 there were 9,105 daily-fee courses and 2,361 municipal links.

As middle- and working-class golfers of modest means populated both municipal and semiprivate facilities during this era, many became dissatisfied with the simple layouts and the poor condition of fairways and greens. They demanded more exciting designs and superior facilities, service, and maintenance; in many cases they were rewarded, although at higher prices. In reviewing the issues concerning construction of new public courses in 1967, Geoffrey S. Cornish and William G. Robinson reported that the current trend featured a course "exciting and interesting for nearly every type of golfer, of major tournament caliber, and on which play can be accelerated on crowded holidays." They concluded: "These new courses attract all types of golfers despite higher fees required to maintain superior playing conditions, and they are sources of deep pride to officials and communities owning them." Two years later architect William F. Mitchell declared: "The principle of get 'em on; get 'em around and get 'em off has guided public course plans since golf came to this country. It's high time public courses were designed with the idea that the public golfer likes and deserves to play the game the way it's supposed to be played." In March 1976 *Golf Digest* quoted Mickey Powell, who opened his public facility, the Golf Club of Indiana, near Indianapolis, in 1974: "The publinx golfer wants a country club atmosphere. Our golfers get an excellent, well-conditioned course . . . and they get service second to none." In May 1975, writing in *Golf Magazine*, golf architect Robert Trent Jones stressed the importance of municipal and semiprivate facilities, criticized most of the existing courses, and proposed innovative designs for public links. He lamented the "plethora of featureless, assembly-line golf courses with teeing areas disfigured by rubber mats and the like, fairways unrestricted by hazards except for inconsequential or ornamental bunkers, and unprotected greens with all the subtleties of a billiard table." As an alternative he proposed that "a public course should be a strategic golf course" that "offers more than one way to play a hole and leaves to the individual player the weight of that decision."

As town and parks officials and private operators of daily-fee facilities strove to upgrade their courses during the 1970s, they faced daunting challenges due to national, state, and especially local financial problems. The Middle East oil crisis coupled with a recession resulted in both inflation and higher unemployment. Counties and municipalities reacted to large budget deficits by slashing spending, especially for parks and recreational programs. As a result the construction of both municipal and daily-fee courses declined during that decade to 496 and about 1,200, respectively. But the impact of the hard times on public golf varied considerably between urban and suburban areas and among large metropolitan regions across the country. In Los Angeles and Chicago, city, county, and semiprivate links continued to thrive, while in New York City participation plummeted as course maintenance dramatically deteriorated.

In March 1976 *Golf Digest* remarked that while Los Angeles was "known for its lotus-land atmosphere of motion pictures, television shows and opulent private clubs," it also claimed "a more proletarian distinction as the public golf capital of the world." For proof it cited the more than 2.7 million rounds played during 1975 on the thirty-three courses administered by the parks and recreation departments of the City of Los Angeles and Los Angeles County. During the mid-1970s golfers in the Chicago metropolitan area could make an excellent case that their region ranked ahead of Los Angeles as the premier golf center in the nation. In a 2,500–square-mile stretch around Lake Michigan there were more than 135 municipal or daily-fee courses serving half a million golfers. *Golf Digest* critiqued the city and county links offerings as "pretty skimpy," with courses that were for the most part "flat, uninteresting and in mediocre-to-poor condition." But it rated the suburban municipal and semiprivate layouts far superior in appeal and challenges. Course maintenance and design generally rated from decent to the sensational, such as Joe Jemsek's Cog Hill No. 4 in southwestern Lemont. Chicago's public golfers were also especially active in two organizations that sponsored tournaments, provided players with a handicap scoring system, and generally promoted the interests of public links golfers.

While public golf remained in a relatively healthy state in the greater metropolitan New York City region during the late 1970s, the situation was far bleaker (and even sometimes frightening) within the five boroughs. While more than 130 public golf facilities served suburban residents of northern New Jersey, adjacent counties of New York State, and southwestern Connecticut, city dwellers had to contend with deteriorating conditions on thirteen municipal courses. Perhaps the only good news was that waiting times to tee off decreased markedly as patronage plummeted from 760,000 patrons in 1970–71 to 476,000 in 1977–78. Part of this dropoff was no doubt due to a mass exodus of golfers to suburban enclaves, but a good deal of it was because of poor maintenance caused by slashed spending due to New York City's bankruptcy, mismanagement, and just plain indifference.

In March 1981 *Golf Digest* called the four-hour wait on weekends on New York City links "a thing of the past." It described grim, poorly maintained clubhouses, broomsticks, bamboo poles and even tree branches used as flagsticks, listlessness of employees, and the lack of new equipment or repairs on the old machines. On March 28, 1982, the *New York Times* reported that when a golfer on the par-three, 140–yard fifth hole at Douglaston, Queens, struck his tee shot, "his eyes are cast upon a forbidden, dried-out gully replete with carcasses of shopping carts, automobile tires and other golf course anachronisms that makes his heart yearn for the tranquillity of a water trap." Other accounts of conditions on New York City's public links describe young people building campfires and drinking beer at night, stolen, stripped automobiles abandoned in bunkers, trash strewn on fairways, rampant rats, and graffiti everywhere. More scary and sensational were reports of armed robberies, golf cart thefts, and the occasional dead body left on the grounds.

Facing inflation, soaring labor costs, and increasing budget deficits, during the 1980s New York City, Philadelphia, Los Angeles County, and many other large communities chose the strategy of "privatization"—contracting out golf courses to management corporations. Faced with losses running about $2 million a year, in 1983 New York City leased six of its thirteen grounds to the American Golf Corporation and sublet three others to two former golf professionals. In 1986 the chief of the Revenue Division of New York City's Department of Parks and Recreation claimed that the city was "netting between $50,000 and $75,000 on the leased American Golf Courses, against a former loss of about $200,000 a course." That year the National Golf Foundation counted about 150 municipal courses in the United States that were privately managed, with only a modest increase in players' fees. American Golf, Kemper Sports Management, and other companies were able to reduce costs by hiring nonunion maintenance workers, by employing experts to supervise several facilities instead of just one, and by utilizing more efficient purchasing and decision-making procedures. But the trend toward privatization also drew some critics. Some golf club professionals who lost pro shop revenue and labor officials who lost jobs were understandably upset with the shift toward management companies. But in several cities officials thought their operations could do just as well financially without leasing their courses. The city of Los Angeles rejected the leasing option favored by Los Angeles County and instead concentrated on better hiring and management procedures. Yet over the next decade the nationwide trend was clearly in favor of outsourcing golf management. In 1995 a survey of

120 communities found that between 1987 and 1995 the percentage of local governments that contracted out management of their golf courses grew from 16 to 24 percent. That year the American Golf Corporation alone operated more than 163 public and 37 resort and country club courses in twenty-two states and England.

During the final decades of the twentieth century municipal and semi-private courses continued to be the primary venues for the democratization of American golf, whether they were operated by public officials, individual owners, or corporations. In the largest cities these links frequently featured long waits at the first tee and crowded fairways. There and elsewhere on suburban and rural grounds a wide spectrum of social classes and ethnic groups gathered to enjoy a pastime first popularized in the United States by Scottish and English immigrants. They could afford the green fees, as average annual income for workers rose from $8,679 in 1970 to $32,117 in 1990. As they played their way across the courses, men, women, and children shared a camaraderie that became one of the primary benefits of belonging to the golfing community.

During the 1990s the Mid-Atlantic region was a hotbed of public golf. In New York City on June 11, 1995, the *New York Times* reported a resurgence of play at the nation's first municipal course, Van Cortlandt Park in the north Bronx, which celebrated its centennial in 1995. Its patrons numbered Koreans, Hispanics, and African Americans, and its tournaments were "frequent and maniacal; outings sponsored by nearby Irish bars are outdone only by the police and firefighters get-togethers, which sometimes degenerate into games of bumper carts." Retired bankers, transit workers, newspaper deliverymen, and countless others packed the grounds despite the distractions caused by highways that cut through the course and occasional discoveries of corpses. In July 2001 *Golf Digest* reported that on a weekday morning in May a solitary "walk on" at Van Cortlandt Park paid twenty-five dollars, waited thirty-two minutes to tee off, and finished eighteen holes in three hours seventeen minutes. He could also look forward to $18 million in renovations that would make the course "Big Apple's gem."

In August 1998 *Washington Golf Monthly* highlighted five public courses in Washington, D.C.; Virginia Beach and Richmond, Virginia; Laurel, Maryland; and Philadelphia, "where American Express is about as welcome as a triple bogey." It labeled East Potomac Park's links "a green palace of golf populism, a 36–hole island of egalitarianism . . . the home of the five-hour round and the wide-open fairways, possibly the best first date golf course in America." That periodical noted that "for all the talk about exclusive country clubs and luxurious new upscale layouts charging $100 a round, venues like East Potomac remain the face of golf for a majority of the country's hackers." East Potomac's general manager underscored the point: "You're going to see everybody here from the guy who collects tin cans to pay his greens fees to Supreme Court justices . . . the Swedish ambassador was a regular customer. . . . We get the full spectrum." The Middletown Country Club, just north of Philadelphia, attracted "Middle America"—men who "simply love the game of golf and the friends they have made playing it." They were "carpenters, independent general contractors, middle-level salesmen, store managers, small businessmen."

The experience of public golfers was no different in the Midwest and Southwest, as is apparent in the cases of Chicago and Dallas. On June 3, 1985, the *Chicago Tribune*, citing statistics compiled by the National Golf Foundation, reported that golfers in the Chicago area played eleven million rounds a year on 228 courses. The facilities ranged from such fancy private clubs on the North Shore as Old Elm, Onwentsia, and Shoreacres, to the modest MacArthur municipal layout adjacent to the heavily industrialized Indianapolis Boulevard in East Chicago. There steelworkers, students, and senior citizens flocked to that "oasis in this blacktop jungle," paying one dollar on weekdays for two trips around the nine-hole course. As recounted earlier, in Dallas a cross-section of that city's golfers flocked to the Tenison Park public links.

As public golf facilities proliferated during the late 1990s, conflicts intensified between town and county parks departments and owners of daily-fee courses. The fundamental issue was the proper role of government versus the private sector in the American economy. In the specific case of golf, was it appropriate or fair that tax-exempt public agencies were building and operating (or leasing) golf courses that competed directly with links owned by individuals who paid real estate taxes that in part helped to subsidize municipal and county grounds? While the problem had been part of the world of public golf since at least the 1920s, it became more acute after 1960 and especially during the 1990s, when parks officials built courses for the more upscale public golfers who were willing to pay higher greens fees for less crowded and better-maintained links. As early as 1965 John Rocco, owner of the semiprivate Musconetcony Country Club in Hackettstown, New Jersey, complained when a new county course in nearby Flanders drew players away from his grounds. As a result he and four other local operators of daily-fee courses either lost money in 1964 or barely broke even. Rocco was particularly upset at recent tax increases that forced businesses to pay governments that subsidized his competition.

More than three decades later, in September 1998, *Washington Golf Monthly* highlighted the "public versus public" competition in suburban counties surrounding Baltimore and Washington, D.C. That journal began with the premise that "the government these days not only is a problem but a competitor—and an unfair one at that." It cited the economic theory that governments "should step in to provide the goods and services—traffic lights, welfare checks, standing armies—that the private sector can't or won't produce on its own." It asked: "So what are the G men doing fooling around in golf?" In reply, local officials conceded that there were many good semiprivate grounds available for those who did not join country clubs, but they argued that not all segments of the market were being served. The magazine noted that the term "municipal . . . conjures up low-end images: $18 for eighteen holes, long lines at the first tee, relaxed dress codes, industrial-functional clubhouse designs, less-than-manicured fairways and greens." But it explained that "the reality was quite different: big-name architects, reserved tee times, fancy amenities, state-of-the art irrigation and groundskeeping systems." The prices were in the range of forty to fifty dollars a round, just below the fees charged by "the new generation of upscale, daily-fee courses." Private course operators insisted that the new municipal courses were not satisfying any demand that the private sector could not meet. They also argued that they were providing more public services than their rivals, such as free practice time for local college and high school teams and no fees for participants in junior golf programs. One owner put the matter simply: "There's a lot of things government should do. I just think golf isn't one of them."

By the end of the twentieth century the world of public golf had changed dramatically from its modest beginnings at the municipal course in Van Cortlandt Park in the Bronx, New York City. In general the quality of courses had improved markedly, but social class still shaped the overall golfing experience for public links players. Those of modest means or limited geographical options often wound up on low-cost, government-operated grounds, where they often encountered long waits at the first tee and less than ideal conditions on fairways and greens. Those who could afford to pay more than fifty dollars a round demanded a country club type of experience from the owners of semiprivate facilities. In May 1996 *Golf Digest* noted the transformation in its ranking of the top seventy-five affordable and top

seventy-five upscale (green fee above fifty dollars) public links. That magazine reflected: "There was a time when you could spot a public golf course by
its parched fairways, broom-handle flagsticks and tangle of wobbly pull carts
hogging the path to the first tee. The classier ones had a stack of colorful,
ad-laden scorecards, a box of recycled pencils and a sign announcing that
shirts were required at all times." In contrast, that journal proclaimed that
"in today's brave new world . . . there are public courses whose facilities and
standards of service would put most private country clubs to shame." And
the patrons of both modest city and more expensive semiprivate facilities
expected them to be well-managed. One of them wrote an open letter to
the nation's daily-fee operators in 1996 in which he described himself as a
weekend player who could not afford to join a country club and whose job
did not require entertaining clients on courses. He had no problem with the
fee charged for eighteen holes, but he did complain about mandatory cart
rentals on weekends, slow play, unfair enforcement of club rules, inadequate
course maintenance, and mistreatment of customers. In the democracy of
public golf, he and others expected good value for their time on the links.

⊙ ⊙ ⊙

During the late 1990s American public golf courses attracted men
and women from a variety of social class, ethnic, and racial groups. The
game was clearly becoming more middle-class and multicultural. In the
mid-1980s one-third of the nation's golfers had an annual household income of less than $30,000; during the late 1990s the household income of
the average golfer was just under $60,000. Participation by Irish, Italians,
and Jews sustained a trend begun during the early decades of the century,
but joining them were increasing numbers of Hispanic Americans, Asian
Americans, Native Americans, and African Americans. A 2003 study by the
NGF estimated that, exclusive of Native Americans, there were at least 14
million Americans from minority groups that expressed some interest in
the sport, with about 5.5 million active participants out of a total of 36.7
million American golfers. In addition, Asian American involvement in golf
nearly equaled that of whites (13.7 percent to 14.5 percent), while African
American and Hispanic American players lagged behind (7 percent and
5.4 percent respectively.) A more detailed analysis by income suggested
that minority participation was directly correlated to household earnings,
although at lower levels than whites. At the upper end (above $100,000)
white and minority involvement rates ranged between 20 percent and 30
percent. But at incomes between $50,000 and $75,000 golfing rates for

whites were between 19 percent and 24 percent, while for minorities they were between 8 percent and 18 percent. An occupational breakdown of these figures supports these findings. Minorities that hold professional, managerial, or administrative positions are nearly as likely to play golf as their white counterparts, but blue-collar employees show much less interest in the game then comparable white workers.

As Hispanic Americans asserted themselves throughout American society after 1990, they became noticeably more visible on the nation's golf courses. The 2003 NGF report counted 1,678,000 Latino players (5.4 percent of all Latin Americans), up from earlier estimates of 750,000 in 1998 (out of a total of 27 million) and about 450,000 in 1991. On September 12th of that year the *Denver Post* featured the golfing exploits of Hispanics on the city's Willis Case Golf Course. Joe Duran, a regular at that facility, declared: "I don't care where you go in the state, there are more Hispanics playing golf all over. It used to be a rich man's game, but now anyone can play." He recalled in particular how watching Lee Trevino motivated him to take up the sport. The success of Trevino, Chi Chi Rodriguez, and Nancy Lopez certainly were major factors behind the growing numbers of Hispanic golfers from the 1960s through the 1980s. The *Denver Post* also cited the impact of Tiger Woods, the booming economy, an abundance of golf courses, and the advent of minority golf programs after the mid-1990s.

The participation by Asians in American golf goes back to the 1920s, with Japanese Americans leading the way through the founding of the Kagero Club in Sacramento, California, in 1925. Its members first used local municipal courses, found a home at the Haggin Oaks Municipal Golf Course, and played in the annual Northern California Japanese Golf Association tournament. The Kagero Club flourished until World War II, when members were incarcerated in Japanese American detention camps. But in at least one such facility some were able to sustain their love of golf. At the Tule Lake Relocation Center in northern California a few men laid out a rough nine-hole course with sand greens. They ordered clubs and balls through a Sears mail order catalogue and played under the watchful eye of security guards, who sometimes retrieved errant shots struck out of bounds beyond the fence. After the war the Kagero Club reconstituted itself and celebrated its fiftieth anniversary in 1975.

During the late twentieth century Japanese Americans increased their presence on golf courses in metropolitan regions, and especially in suburban counties outside New York City and San Francisco. Joining them on the fairways and greens were native-born Japanese businessmen or family members who were temporary residents or tourists in the United States. They patronized public grounds that featured lower green fees and much shorter waiting times than comparable facilities in Japan. As golf gained greater popularity in Japan during the 1980s and early 1990s, several Japanese corporations aggressively purchased resorts and courses in the American market, partly for investment opportunities but also to provide recreation and vacations for their executives and clients. By early 1991 Japanese buyers had acquired at least 160 courses in the United States, including nearly all the private golf clubs in Hawaii. These deals resulted in part from the astronomical cost of club memberships in Japan and the willingness of wealthy Japanese to travel for both business and pleasure. Perhaps the most celebrated and controversial acquisition by Japanese investors was the 1990 purchase of the famed and historic Pebble Beach links on the Monterey Peninsula in northern California. But later in the decade the buyers of Pebble Beach and several other resort courses encountered heavy financial setbacks and sold their properties back to American companies. In 2000 Pebble Beach returned to American ownership when its Japanese owners sold it to a group headed by Peter Ueberroth, Dick Ferris, Clint Eastwood, and Arnold Palmer.

Koreans also joined in the rage for golf. In the neighborhoods of Flushing, Bayside, and Douglaston, Queens, New York City, Korean immigrants were regulars at both municipal courses and especially at such driving ranges as the Alley Pond Golf Center. According to a June 20, 2005, article in the *New York Times*, that facility "dispenses the American dream by the bucketful." Koreans were attracted to the game because of its affordability compared to astronomical prices charged in their homeland. But some also liked golf because it gave them an opportunity to display their newly acquired affluence in their adopted country. According to Johnny Mun, a Korean immigrant from Flushing, most Koreans took up golf "as a status thing, to show off," citing the spending of thousands of dollars on lessons and clubs. David Long, a computer consultant who is part Korean, believed that golf provided Korean American immigrants with a challenge to succeed at a game that required inner discipline and a meditative, repetitive approach. Nationwide the 2003 NGF study counted 1,520,000 Asian American golfers, a majority of them of Japanese or Korean ancestry. Significantly, the golf participation rate of Asian Americans compared to their total population in the United States nearly equaled that of whites (13.7 percent to 14.5 percent).

Over the past few decades Native American Indians have asserted themselves on the American golfing landscape primarily through their ownership and operation of courses at resorts that also feature hotels and casinos. While Indians had long experienced contentious disputes with private clubs over access to ancestral lands (most notably at the Shinnecock Hills Golf Club on eastern Long Island), beginning in the 1970s a few tribes began to profit from the growing golf mania by planning resort complexes that included first-class links. Wendell Chino, president of the Mescalero Apache Nation in southeastern New Mexico, pioneered the concept in the 1960s. In 1975 he opened the Inn of the Mountain Gods and its course, which was seven thousand feet above sea level, the first one owned by a tribe in the United States. By 2006 there were more than fifty tribal-owned courses in seventeen states, nearly all of them situated near casinos. Furthermore, golf architecture critics praised many of them for their impressive landscape layouts, made possible in part because their designers were not constrained by bordering real estate housing developments. New Mexico was the site of many of these new tribal facilities, all but one located at high elevations between Albuquerque and Santa Fe. Although some criticized these tribal courses for their extreme demands on the region's scarce water supply, most Indians welcomed the influx of tourist revenues that provided jobs, income, and social services for their people. The new resorts also introduced golf to many Indians who became enthusiastic players.

While the western resorts helped to popularize golf among Native Americans, far more important was the impact of the game's first genuine Indian star, Notah Begay III. Born September 14, 1972, in Albuquerque, New Mexico, he is half Navaho and half Pueblo. The son of a Bureau of Indian Affairs employee, he was a state champion as a junior golfer, a three-time All-American at Stanford and member of its national collegiate championship squad, and a teammate of Tiger Woods. After joining the PGA Tour in 1999 (as its first "full-blooded" Indian ever) he won two tournaments in his rookie year, earning more than $1.2 million and qualifying for the 2000 Masters. A hero to the Indian community, he promoted golf among Native American youth through motivational talks and instructional sessions for tribal youngsters at clinics and camps. Begay also represented the Native American Sports Council, which received nearly $250,000 from the USGA and about $500,000 worth of equipment from Nike to support golf among Indian youth.

Of all the minority groups in the United States, none had a longer period of participation or made a greater contribution to American golf than African Americans, despite the relatively small number of players prior to 1980. But the level of interest in golf among the black masses grew dramatically during the late 1980s and accelerated during the 1990s and early years of the twenty-first century. Demographic studies by the NGF found that the number of active black golfers in the nation (age five and above) grew from 360,000 in 1986 to 649,000 in 1990 to 882,000 in 1999 to 2,330,000 in 2003 (7 percent of the total black population). Although during the past twenty years many African Americans remained indifferent to the sport, broader sociological forces (especially the expansion of the black middle class in suburbia), inner-city and youth golf development programs, and new opportunities in high schools and colleges all helped boost golf in black communities. Of course, since the mid-1990s perhaps the single most influential factor has been the enormous success and popularity of Tiger Woods, who has generated great enthusiasm for golf among minority youth and adults alike.

In 1995, one year before Woods turned professional, the USGA and *Golf Digest* co-sponsored a marketing research study that surveyed black interest in golf and pointed toward possible strategies for generating higher rates of participation (and thus more spending) among African Americans. The report found that many black Americans had little or no interest in golf because they viewed it as boring, lacking action, and too time-consuming. Other reasons cited included no knowledge of the game, racist associations, expense, and lack of courses near their homes. Significantly, the research also suggested that golf instruction in schools and clinics and endorsements by African American celebrities (such as basketball superstar Michael Jordan) and black professional golfers were vital in converting black nongolfers into enthusiastic players. Quite prophetically, the study concluded that with proper educational programs and media exposure that featured a star performer (like Woods) the black golf market contained great potential for large-scale growth.

A major factor in boosting black golf in the United States over the past few decades has been the steady rise of the African American middle and upper-middle classes, both in urban centers and especially in suburbs outside Washington, D.C., New York City, Atlanta, and Los Angeles. In Boston a group of blacks founded the Franklin Park Golfers Association to resurrect the links, which by 1983 had featured stray dogs, abandoned refrigerators and cars, but only four playable holes. They obtained a contract from the Parks Department to manage the course, received state funding to improve the grounds, and reopened a fully renovated eighteen-hole facility in August 1989. Archie Williams, a businessman, community activist, and avid golfer, described the project: "Diversity is what this country was founded on. . . .

What we have here is everyone playing together. Our goal was to make it a multiracial, multigender golf course. We hear repeatedly from people outside the community who enjoy coming here and playing. It's what the whole city should be like."

A prime example of the suburban trend may be found in Prince George's County outside Washington, D.C. On August 17, 2000, a *Washington Post* feature article noted that in Prince George's County black residents had sufficient disposable income to play the game and use it to enhance their professional or business careers. Memberships at many of that county's public and private courses and clubs were at least 50 percent African American, with several of the most exclusive organizations admitting a few black members. The *Post* interviewed William Ritchie, a fifty-three-year-old resident, who recalled that during his youth he had no interest in the game but took it up at the age of thirty-nine with his father as instructor. He explained: "Golf was definitely not considered a manly game when I was growing up. We saw our sports figures, our role models, in baseball, football and basketball, and those sports were readily available to us. . . . We knew little about golf." But in his later years, with enough money and access to good courses, Ritchie could enjoy the sport. Another NGF report found that the demographics of black golfers matched those of their white middle-class counterparts—they were typically older than forty and had household incomes above $65,000.

As more affluent black Americans embraced golf during this period, leading professionals and golf organizations tried to kindle more interest in the sport among inner-city minority youth. Lee Elder, Calvin Peete, Tiger Woods, and other black players and supporters contributed generously to this cause, donating their time and financial support to a variety of foundations. In 1983 Bill Dickey launched the National Minority Junior Golf Scholarship Association to provide financial assistance to minority students to obtain a quality education while they played golf. During the fall of 1992 the USGA co-sponsored a Minority Golf Symposium, which gave birth to the National Minority Golf Foundation. In 1997 the World Golf Foundation started the First Tee program to provide learning facilities and educational programs that promote character development and life-enhancing values through golf. Three years later it appointed Joe Louis Barrow, Jr. (son of the famed boxer) as its director. The PGA Tour has also sponsored summer internships for minority students.

While Woods was still a youngster, early efforts to promote golf among minority youth began to pay off, as a few African Americans competed on teams at historically black colleges. Of 183 Division I college golf teams in

1986, only three were at predominantly African American schools. But the following year some progress was achieved when the National Minority College Golf Scholarship Fund was chartered to support golf programs at those institutions. It also financed the annual National Minority College Golf Championship Tournament. First held in Cleveland, Ohio, in 1998, the event moved to the PGA Golf Club in Port St. Lucie, Florida. During this period Jackson State University of Mississippi became the powerhouse of national black collegiate golf, as coach Eddie Payton recruited talented white and black golfers. In 1995 his Jackson State squad was ranked in the top twenty-five among all NCAA golf teams, with Tim O'Neal, an African American from Savannah, Georgia, as its star. But black golfers remained scarce at the white NCAA schools; in 1990 there were only two of them in Division I programs. Despite the phenomenal record of Woods, over the past decade there have been only a few black collegiate golfers at predominantly white schools.

◎ ◎ ◎

Another striking indicator of the democratization of American golf in the latter decades of the twentieth century was the growing number of disabled participants—especially blind and amputee players. The two national organizations that serve these populations are the United States Blind Golfers Association (USBGA), founded in 1953, and the National Amputee Golf Association (NAGA), launched in 1954. In addition, the USGA addressed the special needs of disabled golfers by approving rules modifications that allowed them "to play equitably with an able-bodied individual or a golfer with another type of disability." In 2006 it published a twenty-page brochure that listed codes for five classes of persons: blind golfers, amputee golfers, golfers requiring canes or crutches, golfers requiring wheelchairs, and mentally handicapped golfers.

Charley Boswell dominated the USBGA national championships during the 1940s and 1950s (winning sixteen titles), but during the late 1990s Pat Browne, Jr. eclipsed his record with twenty-two victories (including an amazing twenty consecutive crowns). In a feature story in the July 17, 1954, *Saturday Evening Post* Boswell explained why golf was "an ideal game for the blind." "The swing is mechanical," he stated, and unlike sports in which a moving object was an integral part of the game, a golf ball "just lies there until you hit it. . . . We can hit a stationary object even though we can't see it." With the assistance of a guide, he and other skilled blind golfers consistently scored in the 90s or low 100s for eighteen holes. Browne was a former varsity golfer for Tulane University and an avid recreational player before an automobile accident in 1966 deprived him of his sight just prior to his thirty-third birthday. With the encouragement of friends and family (and inspired as he listened to them read him Boswell's autobiography *Now I See*) Browne dedicated himself to the sport. His string of championships (beginning in 1978) earned him the 1988 Ben Hogan Award from the Golf Writers Association of America for his achievements in golf despite a physical handicap. Browne also holds the record for the lowest score recorded in a USBGA tournament—a 74 at the Mission Hills Country Club in California.

While a few one-armed and one-legged golfers performed exhibitions during the 1930s, soldiers who sustained injuries in World War II founded the first national organization of amputee players. The driving force behind its creation was Dale Bourisseau, who lost half of his right leg after stepping on a land mine in Italy in 1943. After the war he recruited eleven other amputees to compete in a tournament in 1947. The small band expanded and in 1954 incorporated itself as the NAGA. Bourisseau also worked with Possibilities Unlimited to promote golf among disabled persons. In 1989 NAGA created its First Swing program, which introduced golf as a means of physical, occupational, and recreational therapy at hospitals and rehabilitation centers. In 1958 Bourisseau received the Ben Hogan Award given by the Metropolitan Golf Writers Association. By the early 2000s NAGA had more than four thousand members in the United States, plus two hundred foreign players from seventeen countries. Several of its players were highly proficient. Among the contestants at its fiftieth anniversary tournament in 1997, twenty-six regularly scored in the 70s for a round, with another forty-four shooting in the 80s. While the officers and members of NAGA enjoyed the competition of tournaments, many of them also visited hospitals and rehabilitation centers, using the golf club as a tool in therapy. In the words of its executive director Jim Coombes: "We use it to get people to realize they need to be active, to move. We work with not just amputees, but people with multiple sclerosis, muscular dystrophy, cystic fibrosis, stroke victims. Even if they just get to the driving range, it gets them off the couch, outdoors, engaged."

The rights of one prominent disabled golfer became headline news throughout the nation in the late 1990s when the PGA Tour denied Casey Martin the use of a golf cart during its tournaments. A member of Stanford University's NCAA championship team in 1994 and later a teammate of Tiger Woods, Martin suffered from Klippel Trenaunay Weber Syndrome, which caused the muscle and bone in the lower part of his right leg to atrophy. In 1997 he filed a lawsuit against the PGA Tour, grounding his case on the Americans With Disabilities Act, which requires operators of public accommodations to make "reasonable modifications" for disabled persons unless the changes would "fundamentally alter the nature" of the activity. The key issues in Martin's case were whether walking was in fact an integral part of golf and whether the PGA Tour's rule that required competitors to walk the course was discriminatory. Supporters of Martin pointed to the PGA Tour's policy of permitting carts during the first two rounds of its qualifying events and on all tournaments on the Senior PGA Tour. In defending its policy the PGA Tour argued that walking had been an essential element in golf for centuries, and that using carts gave riders an unfair advantage over opponents who were required to walk the course, especially those who might be afflicted with temporary injuries. Opponents of Martin sympathized with his plight, but still backed the PGA Tour. As pro golfer Curtis Strange reasoned: "To perform at the highest level of an athletic competition you must be physically fit and able to perform under all types of conditions. An exception to the Tour's walking only rule would change the nature of the game and under certain circumstances would give Martin an unfair advantage over the rest of the field." Others worried that if Martin won his case, others with lesser ailments would also demand the right to use a cart. By winning his lawsuit at the lower levels of the federal court system Martin was able to use a cart during one year on the PGA Tour and two years on minor pro circuits.

Four years elapsed before Martin's case against the PGA Tour reached the United States Supreme Court. On May 29, 2001, the nation's highest tribunal voted 7-2 in Martin's favor (*PGA Tour v. Martin*), rejecting the organization's claim that allowing Martin to ride in a cart during its tournaments would fundamentally alter the nature of championship golf. In his majority opinion Justice John Paul Stevens labeled the PGA's walking rule "at best peripheral" and "not an indispensable feature" of golf at any level. But the court also declared that its ruling applied only to those persons for whom walking was "beyond their capacity" and not simply uncomfortable or difficult. The Supreme Court's decision generated much speculation over its consequences, especially concerning what constituted a disability and who might decide which players qualified for the exemption from the rule that required walking during a tournament. As for Martin, with the use of a cart he continued to pursue his dream, but with little success. In 2005 he missed the cut in eight of nine events on the minor league Nationwide

Tour, earning only $1,934. The following year he accepted a position as the men's golf coach at the University of Oregon.

Casey Martin's story was certainly unusual, but it was also just one of millions of golf sagas experienced by masses of Americans who were passionate about their favorite pastime. Seeking the perfect shot, the personal best round, the championship trophy, they drove countless balls off tees and out of the rough, woods, and sand traps, onto the greens, enduring endless frustration. Presidential hackers, proficient professionals, weekday or weekend enthusiasts, they persevered. A great democratic wave of golf lovers swept up members of exclusive upscale private country clubs, middle- and working-class patrons of public grounds, immigrants and African Americans, men, women, children, and the able-bodied, blind, and disabled. Just over a century after the Scottish game invaded America, it had conquered the land.

SELECTED BIBLIOGRAPHY

Newspapers:

Atlanta Daily World; Baltimore Afro-American; Boston Globe; Chicago Defender; Chicago Tribune; Christian Science Monitor; Denver Post; Houston Chronicle; Jewish Daily Forward; Knight Ridder Tribune Business News; Knoxville Journal; Los Angeles Times; Montclair (N.J.) Times; New York Times; Orange Country Business Journal; San Francisco Chronicle; St. Louis Post-Dispatch; Times-Picayune (New Orleans); Wall Street Journal; Washington Post; Wilmington News Journal.

Periodicals:

Alternatives Journal; American City; American Golfer; American Hebrew; American History Illustrated; American Mercury; American Monthly Review of Reviews; Architects' and Build-ers' Magazine; Atlantic Monthly; Business Week; Century Illustrated Monthly Magazine; Cosmopolitan; Collier's; Country Life in America; Defense Counsel Journal; E Magazine; Everybody's Magazine; Fairway Magazine; Geographical Review; Golf; Golf Digest; Golf Illustrated; Golf Journal; Golf Magazine; Golf World; Golfdom; Golfing; Harper's Magazine; Harper's Weekly; The Independent; International Journal of the History of Sport; Inter-national Wildlife; Journal of Property Management; Journal of Sport History; Journal of Urban History; Literary Digest; Munsey's Magazine; The Nation; New England Quarterly; New Republic; New Yorker; Outing; Outlook; Parks and Recreation; Planning; Playground; Recreation; St. Nicholas; Saturday Evening Post; Spirit of the Times; Sport History Review; Sports Illustrated; Time; USGA Journal and Turf Management; Vermont History; Wash-ington Golf Monthly; World's Work.

General histories of American golf:

Charles B. Macdonald, *Scotland's Gift, Golf: Reminiscences* (New York, 1928); H. B. Martin, *Fifty Years of American Golf* (New York, 1936); Herbert Warren Wind, *The Story of American Golf* (New York, 1956).

Origins and early appeal of golf:

"America's Pioneer Golf Course at White Sulphur Springs," *New York Times*, June 28, 1914, X-2; David Barrett, "How Old Are We?" *Golf* 28 (May 1986): 47–48; William Garrot Brown, "Golf," *Atlantic Monthly* 89 (June 1902): 725–35; Andrew Carnegie, "Dr. Golf," *Independent* 70 (June 1, 1911): 1184–92; Price Collier, "The Rise of Golf in America," *The American Monthly Review of Reviews* 22 (October 1900): 459–64; Hawthorne Daniel, "Golf and Good Health," *World's Work* 40 (August 1920): 393–401; Paula DiPerna and Vikki Keller, *Oakhurst: The Birth and Rebirth of America's First Golf Course* (New York, 2002); Peter Dobereiner, "A Rebuttal: How Golf Really Began," *Golf Digest* 43 (February 1992): 52; Kathleen Doyle, "In John Reid's Cow Pasture," *American History Illustrated* 23 (Summer 1988): 34–45; Ross Goodner, "In Search of the Oldest Club," *Golf Digest* 38 (August 1987): 62–69; Arnold Haultain, "Golf," *Golf* 9 (November 1901): 349–54; Gustav Kobbé, "A Country Gone to Golf," *Harper's Weekly* 45 (June 29, 1901): 653; Charles B. Macdonald, "Golf: The Ethical and Physical Aspects of the Game," *Golf* 2 (January 1901): 20–23; Charles Price, "How Golf Began," *Golf Digest* 42 (December 1991): 126–28.

Early golf course design and location:

J. A. T. Bramston, "Some Reflections Upon American Golf-Courses," *Golf* 13 (November 1903): 318–20, *Golf*, 14 (January 1904): 16–19; William P. Comstock, "The Country Club in America—III," *Architects' and Builders' Magazine* 37 (August 1905): 506; Geoffrey S. Cornish and Ronald E. Whitten, *The Architects of Golf* (New York, 1993); Robert Hunter, *The Links* (New York, 1926); Richard J. Moss, "Constructing Eden: The Early Days of Pinehurst, North Carolina," *New England Quarterly* 72 (September 1999): 388–414; R. Stuart Wallace, "The Summer Ritual of Leisure and Recreation: White Mountain Tourism at the Turn of the Century," *Historical New Hampshire* 50 (Spring/Summer 1995): 119–20; H. J. Whigham, *How to Play Golf* (Chicago and New York, 1898).

Americanization of equipment:

J. A. T. Bramston, "American and British Golf, Some Points of Difference," *Golf* 14 (January 1904): 16–19; Leighton Calkins, "A Crisis in Golf," *Harper's Weekly* 55 (January 14, 1911): 13; Horace Hutchinson, "American Balls and British Golfers," *Outing* 43 (October 1903): 35; J. G. McPherson, "The Rubber-Cored Ball," *Golf* 11 (November 1902): 312; Wray Vamplew, "Sporting Innovation: The American Invasion of the British Turf and Links, 1895–1905," *Sport History Review* 35 (November 2004): 122–37.

Early country clubs:

Frank S. Arnett, "American Country Clubs," *Munsey's Magazine* 27:4 (1902): 484; H. C. Chatfield-Taylor, "Country-Club Life in Chicago," *Harper's Weekly* 40 (August 1,

1896): 761–62; Frederic H. Curtiss and John Heard, *The Country Club, 1882–1932* (Brookline, Mass., 1932); Charles Phelps Cushing, "Modern Tendencies of the Country Club," *American Golfer* 24 (February 12, 1921): 12–13; Robert Dunn, "The Country Club: A National Expression," *Outing* 47 (November 1905): 165; Edward Lyle Fox, "Country Clubs for Everyone," *Outing* 61 (October 1912): 108–18; "Golf and the Business Man," *Golf Illustrated* 15 (May 1921): 11; John Steele Gordon, "The Country Club," *American Heritage* 41 (September/October 1990): 75–84; Louis G. Kibbe, "The Golf Course as a Community Builder," *Golf Illustrated* 19 (April 1923): 32–33; Gustav Kobbé, "The Country Club and its Influence upon American Social Life," *The Outlook* 68 (June 1, 1901): 253–56; James M. Mayo, *The American Country Club: Its Origin and Development* (New Brunswick, N.J., 1998); C. O. Morris, "Country Clubs for Everybody," *Country Life in America* 16 (July 1909): 295; Richard Moss, "Sport and Social Status: Golf and the Making of the Country Club in the United States, 1882–1920," *International Journal of the History of Sport* 10 (April 1993): 93–100; Richard Moss, *Golf and the American Country Club* (Urbana, Ill., 2001); Grantland Rice, "Golf and the Little Towns," *American Golfer* 28 (September 5, 1928): 7; Caspar Whitney, "Evolution of the Country Club," *Harper's Magazine* 90 (December 1894): 16–33.

Jewish country clubs:

Michael H. Ebner, *Creating Chicago's North Shore: A Suburban History* (Chicago, 1988), 221–25; Peter Levine, "'Our Crowd' at Play: The Elite Jewish Country Club in the 1920s," in Steven A. Riess, *Sports and the American Jew* (Syracuse, N.Y., 1998), 160–184; Deborah Weiner, "A Club of Their Own: Suburban and Woodholme Through the Years," *Generations* (Jewish Museum of Maryland, 2004): 5–8; *Woodmont Country Club: A History* (Rockville, Md., 1988).

Country clubs and the Depression:

Innis Brown, "Saving Strokes on the Club's Financial Score," *American Golfer* 35 (March 1932): 47; "The Country Club Comes Back," *Sports Illustrated and the American Golfer* 3 (December 1937): 42–43; Joe Graffis, "New Ideas, Work, and Enthusiasm Outsmart Depression at Clubs," *Golfdom* (March 1933): 11; George T Hammond, "We Still Have Golf Clubs," *American Golfer* 36 (July 1933): 14, 40; Kenneth Payson Kempton, "Golf Is a Poor Man's Game," *American Mercury* 28 (February 1933): 158–65; Gregory Mason, "Golf Is Happily Disappearing," *American Mercury* 32 (August 1934): 485–88; "Saving Millions for Golfers," *American Golfer* 35 (July 1932): 27.

Country clubs since 1970: Environmental issues.

Peter Bronski, "Enforcing Environmentalism," *Planning* 78 (August/September 2005): 24–27; "Golf: America's Vanishing Green Belt," *Golf* 12 (October 1970): 35–41; Donna Kuttnahas, "Counties Begin Maintaining Greens the Organic Way," *New York Times*, July 25, 1999, LI-13; Carol Leonetti, "Green Golf," *E Magazine* 6 (May/June 1995):

22–25; Deborah Odhiambo, "Golf Claims Green Credentials," *Alternatives Journal* 22 (January 1996): 3; "Pesticides: Will the Regulations On Them Destroy Our Golf Courses?" *Golf Magazine* 14 (April 1972): 74–77, 92; Marty Parkes, "Golf Courses Benefit the Environment," *Parks and Recreation* 31 (April 1996): 82–91; "The Vanishing Urban Course," *Golfdom* 44 (September 1970): 36–39.

Country clubs since 1970: Social issues.

J. William Barry, "Clubs on the Brink," *Golf Magazine* 24 (November 1982): 42–45, 68 (December 1982): 46–47, 85–87; Elsa Brenner, "Bias Still a Concern at Private Golf Clubs," *New York Times*, May 18, 1997, WC 1, 10; Max Brown, "Crisis in Club Golf," *Golf Digest* 22 (March 1971): 28–33 (April 1971): 50–53, 88–89; "The Coming Crisis in Club Golf," *Golf Digest* 39 (April 1988): 33–34, 152–62; Marcia Chambers, "A Revolution in Private Clubs," *Golf Digest* 41 (May 1990): 123–36; "Knocking on the Clubhouse Door," *Golf Digest* 41 (June 1990); "Club Doors Not Tightly Shut Anymore," *Golf Digest* 42 (June 1991): 28–31; "Five Years After 'Shoal Creek,'" *Golf Digest* 46 (October 1995): 44–45, 178–96; "The Changing Face of Private Clubs," *Golf Digest* 51 (August 2000): 92–102; Judith Gaines, "Country Clubs Still Draw Despite Negative Image," *Boston Globe*, August 8, 1993, 1; Richard Miller, "The 50 Snobbiest Clubs in America," *Golf Magazine* 27 (June 1985): 58–62; Geoff Russell, "Club Doors Not Tightly Shut Anymore," *Golf Digest* 42 (June 1991): 28–31; Mark Singer, "The Haves and the Haves," *The New Yorker*, August 11, 2003, 56–61; "This Time You're Wrong, Ralph Nader!" *Golf* 13 (May 1971): 56–60; "What's Behind Nader's Attack on Golf?" *Golfdom* 45 (April 1971): 53–56; Tom Watson, "The American Way of Golf," *New York Times*, June 17, 1991, A-15.

Amateur and professional champions:

Al Barkow, *Gettin' to the Dance Floor* (New York 1986), 15–23; "Lee [Trevino], the People's Pro," *Golf* 13 (September 1971): 24–25, 74–75; Gary Cartwright, "The Secret Life of Juan Rodriguez," *Golf Digest* 15 (August 1964): 27–30, 76–78; Ray Cave, "Sportsman of the Year: Arnold Palmer," *Sports Illustrated* 14 (January 9, 1961); 23–31, 131–33; Tom Cunneff, "State of the Game: The Tours," *Golf Magazine* 41 (November 1999): 108–13, 181; Jolee Edmondson, "Poor Mex, Rich Mex," *Golf Magazine* 20 (February 1978): 72–75, 84–86; "There's Only One Chi Chi," *Golf Magazine* 22 (May 1980): 57, 122–25; Mark Frost, *The Greatest Game Ever Played: Harry Vardon, Francis Ouimet, and the Birth of Modern Golf* (New York, 2002); *The Match: The Day the Game of Golf Changed Forever* (New York, 2007); Shav Glick, "Out of the Sticks," *Golf Magazine* 26 (July 1984): 72–75; "Golf's Newest Star, Lee Still Has Doubts About His Future," *Golf Digest* 19 (February 1968): 28–29, 96–97; Ellen Goodman, "Challenging the Categories," *Boston Globe*, April 13, 1995, 19; Red Hoffman, "Jerry Travers: The Forgotten Champion," *Golf Journal* (August 1985): 32–36; Bob Labbance, *The Old Man: The Biography of Walter J. Travis* (Chelsea, Mich., 2000), 40–41; Henry Leach,

"The U.S. Open Championship," *American Golfer* 10 (October 1913): 573–89; "Mr. Jerome D. Travers," *American Golfer* 15 (March 1916): 313–14; Stephen R. Lowe, *Sir Walter and Mr. Jones: Walter Hagen, Bobby Jones, and the Rise of American Golf* (Chelsea, Mich., 2000); Charles B. Macdonald, "The Spirit of the USGA," *Golf Illustrated* 61 (January 1917): 9–10; Pete McDaniel, "The PGA's Tour Jackpot," *Golf Digest* 50 (February 1999): 33–34; Cameron Morfit, "You Are Tiger Woods," *Golf Magazine* 48 (April 2006): 143–44; Mark Mulvoy, "The Revolt of the Touring Pros," *Sports Illustrated* 29 (September 2, 1968): 20–21; Jack Nicklaus with Ken Bowden, *My Story* (New York, 1997); "Rebuttal to a Searing Attack," *Sports Illustrated* 29 (September 16, 1968): 30–31; Ian O'Connor, *Arnie & Jack: Palmer, Nicklaus, and Golf's Greatest Rivalry* (Boston, 2008); Arnold Palmer with James Dodson, *A Golfer's Life* (New York, 1999); Grantland Rice, "The Most Consistent Golfer," *American Golfer* 27 (June 14, 1924): 19; Curt Sampson, *Hogan* (New York, 1996); Gene Sarazen with Herbert Warren Wind, *Thirty Years of Championship Golf* (New York, 1950); Nick Seitz, "Lee Trevino's Show Must Go On," *Golf Digest* 22 (March 1971): 25–27; Gary Smith, "The Chosen One," *Sports Illustrated* 85 (December 23, 1996): 28–44; Howard Sounes, *The Wicked Game: Arnold Palmer, Jack Nicklaus, Tiger Woods, and the Business of Modern Golf* (New York, 2004); Jerome Travers, *Travers' Golf Book* (New York, 1913); Jerome D. Travers and James R. Crowell, *The Fifth Estate: Thirty Years of Golf* (New York, 1926); Walter J. Travis, "Twenty Years of Golf: An Autobiography," *American Golfer* 23 (April 3, June 20, August 7, 14, 1920); Lee Trevino, "I Learned to Eat Bologna and Crackers at an Early Age," *Golf Magazine* 16 (September 1974): 47, 73–74; Herbert Warren Wind, "Gasps for a Fabulous Finish," *Sports Illustrated* 12 (April 18, 1960): 12–15; "Destiny's New Favorite" (June 27, 1960): 24–25, 65; "Can Golf's Greatest Traditions Survive the 70's?" *Golf Digest* 23 (March 1972): 38.

Walker and Ryder Cups:

Colin M. Jarman, *The Ryder Cup: The Definitive History of Playing Golf for Pride and Country* (Chicago, 1999); Gordon G. Simmonds, *The Walker Cup, 1922 to 1999: Golf's Finest Contest* (Worcestershire, England, 2000); Michael Williams, *The Official History of the Ryder Cup, 1927–1989* (London, 1989)

African Americans:

Marvin P. Dawkins and Graham C. Kinloch, *African American Golfers During the Jim Crow Era* (Westport, Conn., 2000); M. Mikell Johnson, *The African American Woman Golfer* (Westport, Conn., 2008); Pete McDaniel, *Uneven Lies: The Heroic Story of African-Americans in Golf* (Greenwich, Conn., 2000); Courtney Milloy, "For Black Women, Golf Wasn't Easy," *Washington Post*, April 26, 1987, B-3; Monte Reel, "A Golf Mecca in Need of Green," [Langston Course] *Washington Post*, June 26, 2003, T-10; Charles Sifford and James Gallo, *Just Let Me Play* (Latham, N.Y., 1992); Calvin Sinnette, *Forbidden Fairways: African Americans and the Game of Golf* (Chelsea, Mich., 1998);

Leonard Shapiro, "For Years, Black Golfers' Best Club Was Their Own," *Washington Post*, May 28, 1997, A-1; Robert Sommers, "John Shippen: A Golfing Pioneer," *The Golf Journal* (August 1968): 18–19; "Taking Root," *Golf Magazine* 42 (August 2000): 102–104; Nicholas Veronis, "A Black on the Greens," [John Shippen] *Sunday Star-Ledger* (Newark, N.J.), June 16, 1991, 1–3.

Desegregation of municipal courses:

Dawson v. Mayor and City Council of Baltimore City, March 14, 1955, U.S. Court of Appeals for the Fourth Circuit, 220 F.2d 386, 1955 App. LEXIS 4923; affirmed, November 7, 1955, U.S. Supreme Court, 350 U.S. 877; *Fayson v. Beard*, September 7, 1955, United States District Court for the Eastern District of Texas, Beaumont Division, 134 F. Supp. 379; 1955 U.S. Dist. LEXIS 3869; *Hampton v. City of Jacksonville*, May 17, 1962, U.S. Court of Appeals Fifth Circuit, 304 F.2d 320; 1962 U.S. App. LEXIS 5074; *Hayes v. Crutcher*, November 21, 1952, U.S. District Court for the Middle District of Tennessee, 108 F. Supp. 582, 1952 U.S. Dist. LEXIS 2323; on renewed motion, January 16, 1956, 137 F. Supp. 853, 1956 U.S. Dist. LEXIS 3944; *Holmes v. City of Atlanta*, July 8, 1954, U.S. District Court for the Northern District of Georgia, 124 F. Supp. 290, 1954 U.S. Dist. LEXIS 2861; affirmed, June 17, 1955, U.S. Court of Appeals for the Fifth Circuit, 223 F.2d. 93, 1955 U.S. App. LEXIS 3924; vacated, November 7, 1955, U.S. Supreme Court, 350 U.S. 879; George B. Kirsch, "Municipal Golf and Civil Rights in the United States: 1910–1965," *Journal of African American History* 92 (Summer 2007): 371–91; Kevin M. Kruse, "The Politics of Race and Public Space: Desegregation, Privatization, and the Tax Revolt in Atlanta," *Journal of Urban History* 31 (July 2005): 613–615; William A. Nunnelley, *Bull Connor* (Tuscaloosa, Ala., 1991), 112–17; *Simkins v. City of Greensboro*, March 20, 1957, U.S. District Court for the Middle District of North Carolina, 149 F. Supp. 562, 1957 U.S. Dist. LEXIS 3900; affirmed, June 28, 1957, U.S. Court of Appeals for the Fourth Circuit 246 F. 2d 425, 1957 U.S. LEXIS 4657; *Watson v. City of Memphis*, May 27, 1963, U.S. Supreme Court 373 U.S. 526, U.S. Lexis 261.

Desegregation of professional golf:

Robert Joseph Allen, "The Odyssey of Ted Rhodes," *Golf* 3 (February 1961): 18–19, 46–53; "Bill Spiller," in Al Barkow, *Gettin' to the Dance Floor* (New York, 1986), 225–28; Jaime Diaz, "Shoal Creek Reflections," *Sports Illustrated* 83 (August 14, 1995): G-6–13; Rick Lipsey, "Ted Rhodes," *Golf* 34 (November 1992): 108–109; Frank Littler, "The Problem World of Negro Golf," *Golf* 10 (October 1968): 34–37, 67–72; Dwayne Netland, "Lee Elder's Long Road to Augusta," *Golf Digest* 26 (April 1975): 60–64; Mike Purkey, "Shoal Creek," *Golf* 33 (August 1991): 80–82, 122; Nick Seitz, "Lee Elder Plays It Cool," *Golf Digest* 19 (December 1968): 28–30, 55–57.

Women golfers (general):

Todd W. Crosset, *Outsiders in the Clubhouse: The World of Women's Professional Golf* (Albany, N.Y., 1995); Rhonda Glenn, *The Illustrated History of Women's Golf* (Dallas, Tex., 1991); David L. Hudson, *Women in Golf: The Players, Their History, and the Future of the Sport* (Westport, Conn., 2008); Liz Kahn, *The LPGA: The Unauthorized Version* (Menlo Park, Calif., 1996); Robert S. Macdonald and Herbert Warren Wind, eds., *The Great Women Golfers* (New York, 1994); Roger Vaughan, *Golf: The Woman's Game* (New York, 2000).

Women and early golf:

John Ashley, "Men vs. Women Golfers," *Outing* 60 (May 1912): 196; Glenna Collett, *Ladies in the Rough* (New York, 1928); "A Conversation with Glenna Collett Vare," *Golf* (March 1989): 40–43; Mrs. Reginald De Koven, "The New Woman and Golf Playing," *Cosmopolitan* 21 (August 1896): 352, 358; Isabella Halsted, *The Aunts* (Manchester, Mass., 1992); Nancy Jupp, "Miss Margaret Curtis Gracious Yet Dynamic, *USGA Journal and Turf Management* 11 (April 1958): 5–7; Joe Looney, "The Curtis Sisters of Boston," *USGA Golf Journal* 8 (April 1965): 16–17; David Outerbridge, *Champion in a Man's World* (Chelsea, Mich., 1998); Dennis Pottenger, "The Midas Touch," *Golf Journal* 50 (June 1997): 42–45; Janet Seagle, "Atlanta's Stirling Glory," *Golf Journal* 29 (June 1976): 20–21; Theodora Sohst, "The Lady on the Links," *Country Life in America* 38 (June 1920): 56; Alexa W. Stirling, "A Plea for the Woman Expert," *Golf Illustrated* 7 (June 1917): 23–24; Ruth Underhill, "Golf: The Women," in *The Book of Sport*, ed. William Patten (New York, 1901), 39–40; W. G. Van Tassel Sutphen, "The Golfing Woman," *Outlook* (June 1899): 254; Ned Vare, "Glenna, She Was, Simply, The Queen," *The 1988 U.S. Women's Open*, official magazine, Baltimore Country Club, July 18–24, 1988, 126–28.

Women in professional golf:

Dave Anderson, "Remembering the Babe," *Golf Digest* 32 (September 1981): 57; Peter Andrews, "Baseball, Motherhood, Apple Pie—and Nancy Lopez," *Golf Digest* 35 (August 1984): 54–57; "Patty Berg," in Al Barkow, *Gettin' to the Dance Floor* (New York, 1986), 157–64; "Interview: Patty Berg," *Golf* 31 (February 1989): 129–31; Susan Cayleff, *Babe: The Life and Legend of Babe Didrikson Zaharias* (Urbana, Ill., 1995); Jolee Edmondson, "The Masterpiece That Is Lopez," *Golf Magazine* 21 (September 1979): 57, 79–83; John Feinstein, "Year of the Woman," *Golf Magazine* 45 (September 2003): 28–33; John Garrity and Amy Nutt, "No More Disguises," *Sports Illustrated* 84 (March 18, 1996): 70–75; "Rhonda Glenn, "Playing Through Racial Barriers," *Sports Illustrated* 74 (May 20, 1991): 4–8; Steve Goldstein, "Sex Vs. Sock," *Golf Magazine* 23 (June 1981): 64–67, 91; William Oscar Johnson and Nancy P. Williamson, "Babe:

Conflict and Glory," *Golf Magazine* 19 (September 1977): 59; Ron Kaspriske, "Korea in the News," *Golf Digest* 54 (April 2003): 65; Peter Kessler, "Jan Stephenson," *Golf Magazine* 45 (November 2003): 120–27; Lee Mueller, "Laura," *Golf Magazine* 15 (October 1973): 43–47, 81–83; Dwayne Netland, "Nancy Lopez: Almost Too Good To Be True," *Golf Digest* 29 (June 1978): 70–73; "The Women's Tour Finally Hits the Jackpot," (November 1978): 63–67; "Lopez Fighting a New Opponent: Jealousy," *Golf Digest* 30 (August 1979): 56–61; David Owen, "Title IX Babies," *The New Yorker*, May 15, 2006, 44–49; Mike Purkey, "Just One of the Boys," *Golf Magazine* 45 (May 2003): 32–33; Clell Thorpe, "Miss Didrikson Still Hits 'Em,'" *American Golfer* 38 (May 1935): 36; Don Wade, "The Impact of Title IX on College Golf," *Golf Digest* 31 (April 1980): 131–36; Babe Didrikson Zaharias as told to Harry Paxton, *This Life I've Led* (New York, 1955).

Women and equality:

Phyllis Batelle, "In Defense of Women Golfers," *Golf* 7 (January 1965): 60, 91–92; Martha Burk, *Cult of Power: Sex Discrimination in Corporate America and What Can Be Done About It* (New York, 2005), 85–87; Marcia Chambers, "Digging Deeper at Augusta," *Golf Digest* 53 (November 2002): 69–71; *The Unplayable Lie: The Untold Story of Women and Discrimination in American Golf* (New York, 1995); "What's A Family," *Golf Digest* 54 (March 2003): 66–68; Lester David, "Ten Ways to Keep a Golf Widow Happy," *Golf* 5 (July 1963): 26–28, 52–55; Oscar Fraley, "I Say, Ban Women Golfers!" *Golf* 6 (October 1964): 59–64; Roland Hill, "Lucky With the Ladies," *Golfing* 20 (July 1956): 11; Lynette Holloway, Marcia Chambers, "The Battle for Tee-Time Equity," *Golf Digest* 46 (June 1995): 33–35; Andria Lewis, "Martha Burk Takes A Swing," *The Progressive* 67 (June 2003): 32; Peter McCleery, "Minnesota Bill Challenges Club Policies on Women," *Golf Digest* (May 1986): 34–35; Charles McGrath, "Augusta's Battle of the Sexes," *Golf Digest* 53 (September 2002): 87–88; Marven Moss, "No Women Allowed!" *Golf Magazine* 21 (December 1979): 67–67–69, 88; Dwayne Netland, "Examining Women's Tee Times," *Golf Digest* 40 (September 1989): 25–26; Gene O'Brien, "Women Players: They Need Understanding," *Golfdom* 36 (March 1962): 80–82; David Owen, "The Case For All-Male Golf Clubs," *Golf Digest* 54 (March 2003): 112–20; Don A. Rossi, "The Ladies Are Coming," *Golf Digest* 22 (March 1971): 7; Blackie Sherrod, "Preston Trail: Last Bastion of Male Chauvinism," *Golf Digest* 24 (May 1973): 60–65.

Presidential golf:

Shepherd Campbell and Peter Landau, *Presidential Lies: The Illustrated History of White House Golf* (New York, 1996); Don Van Natta, Jr., *First Off the Tee: Presidential Hackers, Duffers, and Cheaters from Taft to Bush* (New York, 2003); see also "Bill Clinton," interview in *Golf Digest* 51 (November 2000): 94; James Dodson, "Nixon Was One of Us," *Golf Magazine* 36 (October 1994): 20–22; James F. Drey, "The President's Golf,"

The Independent, September 1, 1910, 473; John Fitzpatrick, "Ike Likes Golf . . . and it Booms!" *Golf Digest* 4 (July 1953): 33; Max Frankel, "Johnson Takes a Whole Day Off," *New York Times*, March 4, 1968, 7; Cary Travers Grayson, *Woodrow Wilson: An Intimate Memoir* (New York, 1960), 46, 47; James Reston, "Washington: Golf, Whisky and Mr. Johnson," *New York Times*, September 29, 1967, 46; John M. Ross, "'Plain Talk on Weekdays, Golf on Sunday,'" *Golf* 16 (December 1974): 27–31, 84–88; Nick Seitz, "Gauging Clinton's Impact on Golf," *Golf Digest* 51 (May 2000): 72; Edmund W. Starling, *Starling of the White House* (New York, 1946), 46, 66, 91; Dick Taylor, "Kennedy's Game—Long Drives, Low Scores," *Golf Digest* 12 (March 1961): 30–32; A. E. Thomas, "Golfing with the President," *Everybody's Magazine* 23 (July 1910): 24; Walter J. Travis, "Golfing with President Taft," *Century Illustrated Monthly Magazine* 80 (September 1910): 651–52; Don Van Natta, Jr., "Taking Second Chances: Par for Clinton's Course," *New York Times*, August 29, 1999, Section 4, Week in Review, 1, 4.

Golf and war:

Ed Dudley, "Golf in Wartime," *Golfdom* 17 (April 1943): 24; Herb Graffis, "What Will War Do to Golf?" *Golfdom* 14 (October): 15; "Golf Due to Grow in '41," *Golfdom* 15 (January 1941): 9–10; "War: Golf Sets Itself to Serve," *Golfdom* 16 (January 1942): 12; "How to Fit Your Club to the War Effort," *Golfdom* 17 (January 1943): 8–11; "Golf in War? Here's Why," *Golfdom* 17 (March 1943): 20; "Golf Booms Among Men in Uniform," *Golfdom* 17 (May 1943): 9–11; "Clubs in Record Activity as War Strain Continues," *Golfdom* 17 (September 1943): 7–10, 33; "V-Garden Crop Amazes as War Effort Success," *Golfdom* 17 (September 1943): 11–13; Henry Leach, "Foreign Notes," *American Golfer* 11 (October 1914): 1150, 1152; Judith Lee, "Golf Helps Army Rebuild War-torn Veterans," *Golfdom* 18 (May 1944): 11–13.

Municipal and daily-fee golf:

"Are City Golfers Free and Equal?" *Colliers* 72 (July 7, 1923): 9–10; Tom Bendelow, "Municipal Golf," *The American City* 15 (July 1916): 1–8; Lee Blauner, "Should You Go Public or Private?" *Golfdom* 42 (May 1968): 41–42, 90; A. D. Britton, "Public Links for Public Works," *American Golfer* 38 (July 1935): 10, 45; Joseph H. Burbeck, "The 'Peepul's Club,'" *Golfdom* 10 (May 1936): 19–21; Walter Camp, "The Craze for Costliness in Golf," *World's Work* 48 (July 1924): 313–17; Robert Carney, "Take My Golf Course, Please," *Golf Digest* 37 (March 1986): 39–41; Leslie S. Claytor, "Evolution of the American Municipal Golf Course: 1895–1940" (Masters thesis, Landscape Architecture, University of California, Berkeley, 1992); Geoffrey S. Cornish and William G. Robinson, "The Country Club Look for Public Golf Courses," *Parks and Recreation*, New Series, 2 (May 1967): 29, 48–49; Lincoln C. Cummings, "The Movement for Public Golf Links," *The American Golfer* 9 (April 1913): 487–88; Larry Dennis, "The Changing Face of Public Course Golf," *Golf Digest* 27 (March 1976): 48–50; "The Disgrace of Gotham's Public Courses," *Golf Illustrated* 40 (January

1934): 13; R. Bruce Dold, "For Richer, For Poorer, Golf Season Tees Off," *Chicago Tribune*, June 3, 1985, Chicagoland section, 1; John W. Duncan, "Golf in Public Parks," *American City* 25 (November 1921): 376; Harry C. Eckhoff, "Growth of Municipal Golf is Phenomena of the '60s," *Golfdom* 37 (April 1963): 96–105; *Golf Digest* 20 (September 1969); 36–40; William Barry Furlong, "Champagne Golf for the Beer Budget," *Golf Digest* 20 (September 1969): 36–40; "Golf: Now Everyone's Playing," *Business Week*, June 25, 1955, 88, 90; Jim Gorant, "Private Club vs. Daily Fee," *Golf Magazine* 44 (December 2002): 156; Harvey Haight, "A Public Course Player Speaks Out," *Golf Digest* 47 (May 1996): 110–16; Stephen Hardy, *How Boston Played: Sport, Recreation, and Community, 1865–1915* (Boston, 1982), ch. 4; Paul Hughes, "American Golf Scores on OC, National Scene," *Orange County Business Journal* 18 (September 11, 1995): 20; Robert H. Humphreys, "Emergency Employment on Golf Courses," *American City* 46 (May 1932): 70; R. Walter Jarvis, "Municipal Golf in Indianapolis," *Playground* 19 (August 1925): 281; Sylvanus Pierson Jermain, "The Emphatic Need of Public Golf," *Golf Illustrated* 17 (May 1922): 32; Rand Jerris, "A New Deal," Official Program of the 2002 U.S. Open Championship, United States Golf Association, 2002, 70, 72; Robert Trent Jones, "A Public Course Doesn't Have to Be Dull," *Golf Magazine* 17 (May 1975): 54–56; George B. Kirsch, "Municipal Golf Courses in the United States: 1895 to 1930," *Journal of Sport History* 32 (Spring 2005): 23–44; Eugene Levy, "'The Links are for the People': The Movement for Municipally-Owned Golf Courses in Early Twentieth Century America," paper delivered at the California American Studies conference, May 3, 1997, 5–11; Harry Brownlow Martin, "Old Days at Van Cortlandt," *American Golfer* 37 (May 1934): 46; Ralph Monti, "The Special Hazards of New York's Golf Courses," *New York Times*, March 28, 1982; *Municipal Golf Courses: A Report Compiled by the Chamber of Commerce of the United States* (1930), 26–28; "Municipal Golf in Indianapolis," *American Golfer* 23 (September 4, 1920): 17; Muny Competition Hurts If Golfers Aren't Plentiful," *Golfdom* 39 (June 1965): 48–50; National Golf Foundation, "The Growth of U.S. Golf," May 1990, and "Trends in the Golf Industry, 1986–1997" (1998): 10, 31; Dwayne Netland, "Public Golf Differs in the Big Cities," *Golf Digest* 27 (March 1976): 56–60; "Putting Golf into the New Deal," *American Golfer* 36 (November 1933): 15, 44; Rebecca Rankin, "Municipal Golf in a Hundred Cities," *American City* 30 (June 1924): 597–602; Grantland Rice, "100 Per Cent Golf Bug," *American Golfer* 23 (June 12, 1920): 10; Steven A. Riess, *City Games: The Evolution of American Urban Society and the Rise of Sports* (Urbana, Ill., 1989), 41–46, 128–32; Arthur Ruhl, "What Golf Means to a Big City," *Outing* 42 (June 1903): 292, 295; David R. Sands, "Public vs. Public," *Washington Golf Monthly* (September 1998): 95–97; Donald R. Sands and Dave Paton, "The Public Player," *Washington Golf Monthly* (August 1998): 83–94; Bart J. Scanlon, "Variety Makes IBM Club Hum," *Golfdom* 15 (April 1941): 23–25; Parker Smith, "A Word to the Downtrodden Public Golfer: Organize!" *Golf* 13 (November 1971): 38, 62; Stan Sousa, "Public Golf Courses—With a Difference," *Parks and Recreation*, New Series 4 (May 1969): 49; Jesse F. Steiner, *Americans at Play* (New York, 1933), 71–76; Marty Tregnan, "Griffith Park, Birthplace of Municipal Golf in the City of Los Angeles!" *Griffith Park Quarterly* 3 (May/June 1982): 7–18; Benjamin L. Van Schaik, "The Courses at Bethpage," *Golf Illustrated* 41 (April 1934): 30–31; "A Tale of Two Cities," *Golf Digest* 32 (March 1981): 66; Kent Hansen Wadsworth, "Strike it Niche!: Municipal Golf Courses," *Journal of Property Management* 61 (May/June 1996): 18; H. S. Wagner, "Municipal Golf—Its Influence on Park Recreation Affairs," *Playground* 21 (May 1927): 94–98; Sam Walker, "America's Melting Pot Moves to the Public Links," *Christian Science Monitor* June 19, 1997, 1; Theodore Wirth, "Let's Work for More Public Golf Courses," *Parks and Recreation* 7 (March/April 1924): 388–95; "How to Build Your Municipal Golf Course," *American Golfer* 28 (April 4, 1925): 21, 42.

Industrial golf:

"'Blue-shirt' Golf," *Golf Digest* 9 (September 1958): 35–36; John M. Brennan, "Industry's Courses Become Valuable Golf Service," 27 (August 1953): 34, 36–37, 59; Gwilym S. Brown, "Where Is the Golf Course of the Workers?" *Sports Illustrated* 19 (August 26, 1963): 42; John Budd, "Industrial Golf Destined to Grow Gigantic," 21 (July 1947): 26 27, 30; "Golf Goes Industrial," *Recreation* 43 (August 1949): 260–61; Joseph W. Dragonetti, "DuPont Club, Courses, Prize Exhibit of Employee's Golf," *Golfdom* 25 (February 1951): 38, 40; "Golf as a Fringe Benefit," *Golf* 12 (June 1970): 78–81; "Golf at DuPont," 36 (April 1962): 42, 44, 118, 120, 122, 124; "Golf Course Feature of New IBM Recreation Center," *Golfdom* 18 (September 1944): 32, 34; George Hammond, "Pursuing Par in Overalls," *American Golfer* 36 (August 1933): 29, 40; 41; "Should Your Company Have a Golf Course?" *Golf Digest* 25 (March 1974): 68–69; Bob E. Thomas, "How to Organize a Golf League for Your Company," *Golf Digest* 25 (March 1974): 68–69.

Growth of golf:

Robert L. A. Adams and John F. Rooney, Jr., "Evolution of American Golf Facilities," *Geographical Review* 75 (October 1985): 419–38; Harvey Berman, "Golf and Business DO Mix," *Golf Digest* 7 (May 1956): 37–41; Charles Curtis, "Chief Cook at the Clambake," *Golfing* 23 (June 1959): 11–12, 34–35; Arthur Daley, "3,265,000 Reasons for Playing Golf," *New York Times*, May 31, 1953, Sunday Magazine, 16; John Fitzpatrick, "Road to Par with Bing and Bob," *Golf Digest* 4 (June 1953): 27–30; Thomas L. Friedman, "The New National Pastime," *Golf Digest* 56 (August 2005): 81–83; Roger Ganem, "A Bright Future," *Golfdom* 42 (March 1968): 62, 64, 96; Ross Goodner, "Golf's Power Brokers," *Golf* 11 (May 1969): 47–49, 82–84; Will Grimsley, "Golf Must Heed the Danger Signals," *Golf* 10 (February 1968): 29–30, 72–76; Roy Holland, "It's Cheaper to Play Golf Today!" *Golf Digest* 12 (April 1961): 40–47; Dick Kemp, "Golf Is a *Must* in Webb's Retirement Cities," *Golfdom* 36 (June 1962): 21–24, 112–15; Ray Olsen, "New 18-Hole Golf Course—Free," *American City* 73 (August 1958): 104–105; Charles Price, "Why Golf Really Grew," *Golf Digest* 40 (April 1989):

45–48; Walter Roessing, "Bob Hope's Wacky World of Golf," *Golfing* 28 (May 1964): 11–12, 33–34; Len Shapiro, "State of the Game: Access," *Golf Magazine* 41 (June 1999): 130–32, 209–14; Ron Whitten, "If You Build It, Will They Still Come?" *Golf Digest* 52 (December 2001): 54.

Golf carts:

"Automation and the Caddies," *Golfing* 19 (April 1955): 5–6; "Golf Cars: 1960 Report," *Golf Digest* 11 (March 1960): 51–56; "The Golf Car Boom," *Golf Digest* 6 (August 1955): 21–25; "Golf Takes to Wheels," *Golf Digest* 5 (August 1954): 33–34; William J. Freund, "Rules for Golf Car Use Call for Study and Foresight," *Golfdom* (October 1954): 73; "Metropolitan, Chicago Associations Report on Golf Car Surveys," *Golfdom* 34 (April 1960): 31–33, 119–20; Tom Siler, "Golf a la Car," *Golf* 4 (February 1962): 102–108; Tom Walsh, "I Changed My Mind about Golf Cars," *Golfdom* (February 1957): 44, 72.

Television and golf:

Stanley Anderson, "Golf's Radio and TV Shows Need Fresh Showmanship," *Golfdom* (April 1951): 31–32; Dick Aultman, "Fall TV Preview," *Golf Digest* 10 (November 1959): 18–19, 22–23; Al Barkow, "The Shot That Turned on the Tube," *Golf Magazine* 20 (August 1978): 64–65, 83–85; "Cosell on Golf," *Golf Magazine* 21 (August 1979): 63, 68; Oscar Fraley, "The New Matinee Idols," *Golf* 8 (March, 1966): 28, 62–66; Donald Freeman, "Backstage with All-Star Golf," *Golf* 2 (January 1960): 10–13, 54–55; Barry Gottehrer, "The Widening World of TV Golf," *Golf* 5 (April 1963): 58–62, 73; Jack Murphy, "It's the Bing-Bob-Dean-Glen-Andy Show," *Golf Digest* 25 (January 1974): 46–48, 65; Mike Purkey, "The Shot Seen By a Million," *Golf Magazine* 39 (March 1997): 134; "The 'Tour' Goes on TV," *Golf Digest* 8 (November 1957): 42–44; "TV and Golf Going Steady," *Golf Digest* 9 (November 1958): 37–38; Herbert Warren Wind, "Can Golf's Great Traditions Survive the 70's?" *Golf Digest* 23 (March 1972): 34–35, 38.

Ethnicity, race, and golf:

Kristin Downey, "Teed Off Over Sales of Golf Courses; Japanese Buyers Have Some in U.S. Worried," *Washington Post*, February 9, 1991, E-1; Carlos Illescas, "Hispanics Hitting the Fairways in Droves: More Minority Golfers Inspire Others to Play," *Denver Post*, September 12, 1998, A-23; Bob Fukushima, "The Kagero Story," Kagero Golf Club Fiftieth Anniversary, files of the United States Golf Association; Corey Kilgannon, "Korean Word for Golf? There's a Place in Queens You're Sure to Hear It," *New York Times*, June 20, 2005, B-4; Colman McCarthy, "Golfer Begay Hopes to Set an Example," *Washington Post*, May 28, 1999, D-13; Peter McCleery, "Research Paves Way for Marketing to Blacks," *Golf Digest* 46 (February 1995): 46–47; National Golf Foundation, "Minority Golf Participation in the U.S." (National Golf Foundation, 2003), 1–5; Yumiko Ono, "American Golfers Who Are Teed Off at Japanese Acquisitions Can Relax," *Wall Street Journal*, June 17, 1991, A-5; Gene Rondinaro, "Golf Courses Luring Japanese," *New York Times*, May 2, 1982, A-8; Mark Seal, "The Sale of the Century," *Golf Digest* 51 (June 2000): 180–92; Bruce Selcraig, "Teeing Off In Indian Country," *New York Times*, March 17, 2006, F-1; Topsy Siderowf, "Spreading the Gospel of Golf," *Golf Digest* 52 (September 2001): 32; Scott Stossel, "The Golfing of America," *New Republic* 219 (August 3, 1998): 18–21; Pat Sullivan, "New Pebble Beach Owners Fitting In," *San Francisco Chronicle*, March 7, 1992, D-5; *Houston Chronicle*, April 16, 2000, 17; Avis Thomas-Lester, "Blacks Break Into The Swing of Golf: More African Americans Take Up Once-Restrictive Sport," *Washington Post*, August 17, 2000, J-9.

Blind and disabled golfers:

Andy Anderson, "Houston Puts Golf at Veterans' Hospital," *Golfdom* 19 (July 1945): 30, 40; Charley Boswell with Curt Anders, *Now I See* (New York, 1969); Thomas Boswell, "The Rules Are Still the Rules," *Washington Post*, January 14, 1998, D-1; Marcia Chambers, "The Martin Decision," *Golf Digest* 52 (August 2001): 60; Ed Harbert, "A Tourney for Wounded Vets," *Golfdom* 19 (June 1945): 20–21; Ray Haywood, "Golf Is 'Play-Therapy' For the War-Blinded," *Golfdom* 19 (April 1945): 22–24; Dan Morse, "Seeing Is Believing," *Sports Illustrated* 70 (May 22, 1989): 8–11; Tom Siler, "Those Amazing Blind Golfers," *Saturday Evening Post* 227 (July 17, 1954); 32–33, 75–76.

INDEX

GEORGE B. KIRSCH is Professor of History at Manhattan College. He is the author of *Baseball and Cricket: The Creation of American Team Sports, 1838–72* and *Baseball in Blue and Gray: The National Pastime during the Civil War;* editor of volumes 3 and 4 of *Sports in North America: A Documentary History;* and coeditor of the *Encyclopedia of Ethnicity and Sports in the United States.*

ILLINOIS HISTORY OF SPORTS

The Olympics: A History of the Modern Games (2d ed.)
   Allen Guttmann
Baseball: A History of America's Game (2d ed.)   *Benjamin G. Rader*
The World's Game: A History of Soccer   *Bill Murray*
Golf in America   *George B. Kirsch*

The University of Illinois Press
is a founding member of the
Association of American University Presses.

———————————————————

Composed in 10.25/13.5 Janson Text LT Std
with Copperplate Gothic Std display
at the University of Illinois Press
Designed by Dennis Roberts
Manufactured by Sheridan Books, Inc.

University of Illinois Press
1325 South Oak Street
Champaign, IL 61820-6903
www.press.uillinois.edu